T4-AEA-696

CONCORDIA UNIVERSITY
3 4211 00112 8332

THE MOTOR DOMAIN AND ITS CORRELATES IN EDUCATIONALLY HANDICAPPED CHILDREN

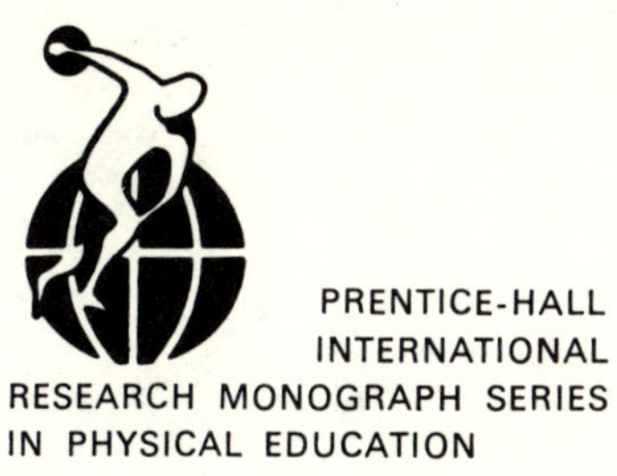

PRENTICE-HALL
INTERNATIONAL
RESEARCH MONOGRAPH SERIES
IN PHYSICAL EDUCATION

OTHER TITLES IN THE SERIES:

Muscular Strength and Endurance in Man, H. Harrison Clarke
Evaluation and Regulation of Body Build and Composition
Albert R. Behnke, Jr., and Jack H. Wilmore
Physical Activity and Health: An Epidemiologic Study of an Entire Community
Henry J. Montoye
Physical and Motor Tests in the Medford Boys' Growth Study
H. Harrison Clarke
The Harvard Fatigue Laboratory: Its History and Contributions
Steven M. Horvath and Elizabeth C. Horvath

The Motor Domain and its Correlates in Educationally Handicapped Children

G. LAWRENCE RARICK

University of California, Berkeley, California

D. ALAN DOBBINS

University of Texas, Austin, Texas

GEOFFREY D. BROADHEAD

Moray House College of Education, Edinburgh, Scotland

Prentice-Hall, Inc.

Englewood Cliffs, New Jersey

Library of Congress Cataloging in Publication Data

Rarick, George Lawrence, 1911–
The motor domain and its correlates in educationally handicapped children.

(Prentice-Hall international research monograph series in physical education)
Bibliography: p.
Includes index.
1. Physical education for mentally handicapped children. 2. Mentally handicapped children—Education. 3. Motor ability—Testing. I. Dobbins, D. Alan, 1942– joint author. II. Broadhead, Geoffrey D., 1937– joint author. III. Title. [DNLM: 1. Mental retardation. 2. Motor activity—In infancy and childhood. WS107 R221m]
GV445.R37 371.9'28 75-33290
ISBN 0-13-604116-7

Printed in the United States of America

10 9 8 7 6 5 4 3 2 1

PRENTICE-HALL INTERNATIONAL, INC., *London*
PRENTICE-HALL OF AUSTRALIA PTY. LIMITED, *Sydney*
PRENTICE-HALL OF CANADA, LTD., *Toronto*
PRENTICE-HALL OF INDIA PRIVATE LIMITED, *New Delhi*
PRENTICE-HALL OF JAPAN, INC., *Tokyo*
PRENTICE-HALL OF SOUTHEAST ASIA PTE. LTD., *Singapore*

Contents

Preface

This monograph is an account of two related investigations of the motor domain and its correlates in educationally handicapped children. Part I describes an investigation primarily concerned with the identification of the basic components of the motor behavior of educable mentally retarded children through the use of factor analytic techniques. The rationale for this approach rests on the premise that man's motor capabilities are in part made up of a number of general abilities, many of which provide the foundation upon which specific motor traits are built. That there are well defined basic components of motor performance in man has been repeatedly demonstrated with normal children and young adults, less frequently with the mentally retarded.

The unique features of the investigation reported in Part I include not only sizeable samples of educable mentally retarded and normal children upon whom a broad array of physical growth and motor performance measures were obtained, but also the methodologies employed in examining age, sex, and disability differences in the physical growth and motor performance of these children. The several factor analytic methods employed and extensions of these procedures made it possible to identify with considerable accuracy the factor structures of motor performance of both the normal and the educable mentally retarded children by age and sex. An extension of factor analysis provided the means of determining similarities and differences in the factor structures of the several groups of children. The results of the several factor analyses also gave the necessary information for employing person-clustering techniques and for the use of discriminant analysis in identifying the specific variables having the greatest discriminatory power when making comparisons of the motor performance of different samples of children. Thus, the quantity of data available and the extensive analyses employed have, we believe, made a significant advancement in our understanding of the many dimensions of the motor behavior of educable mentally retarded children.

Part II is a report of an experiment designed to determine the effects of individualized versus group oriented physical education programs upon selected parameters of the development of educable mentally retarded and minimally brain injured children.

The study was unique not only in terms of the number of children involved, but also in respect to the parameters of development assessed and in terms of the controls employed. The design of the study called for assessment of changes in measures of motor, intellectual, social and emotional development of EMR and MBI children exposed to 20 weeks of daily instruction in physical education in contrast to control groups of subjects. Thus, by applying appropriate pre-tests and post-tests, the effects of the special programs on the motor, social, intellectual, and emotional behavior of the retarded and brain injured children could be ascertained.

The study was also unique in the sense that it demonstrated what can be done to enhance the development of these children through the use of appropriate physical activities when taught by the special education teacher with appropriate supervision and in-service training. It also brought into clear focus the differential effects of individualized and group oriented programs of physical education instruction upon brain injured and educable mentally retarded children as a function of age and sex.

The time and effort of many people too numerous to mention by name were needed in the conduct of these two investigations. A special word of appreciation goes to the participating boys and girls in the San Francisco Bay Area and to those in the Pasadena, Galena Park, and Deer Park School Districts of Harris County, Texas. A necessary ingredient in the conduct of field studies of the type reported here is the cooperation of parents, teachers, supervisors, and school administrators. This we gratefully acknowledge, for throughout the course of both investigations the support provided in both localities was in every sense positive.

The investigation reported in Part I was supported by the Bureau of Education for the Handicapped, U.S. Office of Education, Department of Health, Education and Welfare, Grant No. OEG-0-70-2568(610) and the research summarized in Part II was funded jointly by the Joseph P. Kennedy,

Jr. Foundation and the Bureau of Education for the Handicapped, U.S. Office of Education, Department of Health, Education and Welfare, Grant No. OEG-0-8-071097-1760.

G.L.R.
D.A.D.
G.D.B.

Part I / BASIC COMPONENTS IN THE MOTOR PERFORMANCE OF EDUCABLE MENTALLY RETARDED CHILDREN

Chapter 1 / Background and Purpose of the Investigation

Background of the Investigation

Motor Proficiency of the Mentally Retarded

There is general agreement that mentally retarded children lag well behind children of normal intelligence in the development of both fine and gross motor skills. Evidence to this effect may be found in the records of clinicians who have devoted years of work to the mentally retarded and by published research reports on the motor performance of these children (Malpass, 1959; Francis and Rarick, 1959; Rarick et al., 1970). There would seem to be little doubt that the retarded motor development of these children is associated with their limited intellectual development, for the greater the mental deficiency the greater is the retardation in the acquisition of motor skills (Tredgold et al., 1956). This observation is supported by the research of Widdop (1967) which showed that there are statistically significant differences in motor proficiency between children in the I.Q. range of 60–70 as compared to those in the I.Q. range of 50–60. While independent investigators (Rabin, 1957; Rarick et al., 1970; Sloan, 1951) have reported relatively low correlations between tests of motor performance and measured intelligence, the correlations are consistently positive.

Although it is evident that the marginal intellectual capabilities of the mentally retarded have a limiting effect on their performance and learning of motor skills, the ways in which the neuromuscular mechanism and the motor learning processes function in these children are not yet fully understood. Clearly, the retarded child's difficulties in the execution of relatively simple movement patterns adversely affect the rate of acquisition of new and complex movement patterns.

The motor inadequacies of the mentally retarded may in part be a reflection of their poor general health and faulty physical development. Almost without exception, research findings have shown that mentally retarded children, on the average, are well behind intellectually normal children in physical growth (Kugel and Mohr, 1963). Furthermore, the evidence is clear that the greater the degree of mental retardation, the more pronounced is the lag in physical development. The work of Roberts and Clayton (1969) showed that the physical growth of undifferentiated mentally retarded children was markedly inferior to that of normal children, the proportion of moderately retarded below the 3rd percentile being approximately 5-1/2 times the expected number, whereas in the profoundly retarded the figure was 11 times that expected. In summarizing their findings, the investigators proposed that these children fail to grow normally because of some undefined neurophysiological reasons, the faulty mechanism conceivably being the same as that responsible for the mental retardation. One should, however, note the work of Pozsonji and Lobb (1967) and Dutton (1959), who found classes of mentally defective children with no stunting of linear growth. While the consensus of research points to a strong association between mental retardation and growth failure, particularly where the retardation is caused by chromosomal aberration or multiple congenital anomalies (Pryor and Thelander, 1967), evidence of a common causal relationship between the two has yet to be established.

That the general retardation in motor development observed in retarded children is not solely a function of mental deficiency is widely recognized. While the research is in general agreement that skill learning is slower in the retarded than in intellectually normal children (Holman, 1933; Clarke, 1962; Gordon, 1962; Kirby, 1969), the retarded children can achieve reasonable levels of motor proficiency provided the learning situations are adapted to their needs. Unfortunately, society has not provided these children with the same opportunities that are afforded to normal children for the acquisition of motor skills.

Basic Components in Motor Performance

It is evident from the foregoing remarks that research up to the present time has provided considerable information on the physical growth and the motor characteristics of the retarded. It is equally clear that, for the most part, this research has not been directly concerned with the underlying causes of the motor deficit in these children. Nor has it, with few exceptions, been oriented to identifying those fundamental behavioral components upon which the broad spectrum of motor abilities is based. It is to the latter that this investigation has addressed itself. This topic would seem to be particularly important since there is considerable evidence to indicate that there are certain basic abilities which man calls upon in the execution of the broad range of motor skills that he is required to perform. In the execution of most gross motor activities, such basic components as strength, speed of movement, agility, balance, flexibility, and endurance are required in varying degrees, depending upon the nature of the task. The extent to which a task is dominated by factors specific to that skill or by general abilities is dependent upon the complexity of the task. The simpler and less involved the skill, the more likely it is to be dominated by a general ability, whereas highly complex skills are more likely to require a combination of many specific skills in combination with several general abilities. Sufficient research has been done on mature subjects to indicate that underlying the execution of a wide variety of gross motor skills are certain general abilities which are common in varying degrees to these skills (Cumbee, 1954; Larson, 1941; Fleishman and Hempel, 1954; Fleishman, 1964; Rarick, 1937).

The concept that human abilities are made up of both general and specific traits is not new. The importance of verbal, numerical, and special abilities in achievement in academic pursuits is widely recognized. Such abilities are held to be fundamental in the child's formal education. The basic motor components alluded to above are believed to be qualities that begin to develop early in life and form the foundation upon which the more complex skills are built. For example, the balance mechanism begins to function when the child first sits up, becomes more effective when he learns to stand, and is called upon still further when the walking patterns are established. With advancing age, the child calls upon this mechanism and others in the execution of many new and different tasks which, when repeated, result in overlearning and constitute a general behavioral capability available upon call.

It is generally held that balance and other basic abilities are so thoroughly overlearned that they remain remarkably stable throughout life. For example, muscular strength, once firmly developed, tends to be retained at approximately the level at which it was developed even after long periods of relative inactivity. Fundamental to efficient learning of most gross motor skills is the presence of the basic components upon which each skill is built. This assumption is reasonably well supported by both experience and research. For example, without sufficient leg and back strength to support the body weight, walking cannot take place. The question then remains, what are the basic factors which are of major importance in the motor domain of educable mentally retarded children?

Numerous investigations have provided rather comprehensive information about the factor structure of motor abilities in man. In investigations on adults, strength has consistently emerged as a factor of importance in gross motor performance. However, the evidence (Clarke and Henry, 1961) now indicates that the force a muscle can exert in a strong, rapid movement is not necessarily reflected by the force it can exert isometrically (force against a fixed resistance). For example, Henry et al. (1962) support the point of view that static muscular strength plays a very limited role in many motor tasks. The muscular force required in rapid, powerful movements, which others have termed pure speed or explosive release of energy, is held by Henry to be strength in action, a quality not adequately measured by the dynamometer. Several investigators have provided evidence that what was originally held to be a general strength factor is, in fact, made up of three factors which are relatively independent, namely, (1) static strength (isometric muscular force), (2) muscular endurance (force repeated relatively slowly through the range of motion, as in chinning and dipping), and (3) explosive muscular force or strength in action (force exerted in a powerful, rapidly executed movement, such as jumping or hurling a heavy object).

Independent investigations (Coleman, 1937; Larson, 1941; Fleishman, 1964; Rarick, 1937; Wendler, 1938) have shown that such factors as flexibility, speed of movement, agility, balance, and endurance are general qualities that individuals have in different proportions which are important in accounting for individual differences in performance attainments. Certain of these factors, such as speed of movement, balance, and endurance, are believed to be composed, in and of themselves, of separate and distinct factors. For example, balance is generally held to consist of two independent factors, static and dynamic balance. Endurance is probably not all-inclusive, since it is clear that what is generally held to be muscular endurance is distinct from cardio-respiratory endurance, the latter permitting prolonged sustained effort of the entire organism, the former involving maximum functioning of specific muscle groups over a relatively brief time interval.

The changing relationship among factors within a factor structure as a motor task is learned is shown by the research of Fleishman and Hempel (1954) who found that with practice, a complex motor task became less complex factorially as practice continued. There was a substantial change in the variance attributable to the several factors from the early to the later stages of practice. Thus, the relative contribution of the various factors in the performance of a particular skill changes materially as proficiency in the skill improves.

Factor Structure of Motor Abilities of Normal Children

Only limited attention has been given to identifying the basic components of motor abilities of children. Barry and Cureton (1961) isolated three motor performance and five physique factors in a sample of prepubescent boys, ages 7–11 years. The three motor performance factors were identified as (1) power, dominated by measures of jumping performance; (2) endurance; and (3) dynamic shoulder strength. In a factor analysis of motor performance and related variables in kindergarten, first-grade, and second-grade children, Peterson, Reuschlein, and Seefeldt (1974) identified such physical growth and motor performance factors as body size, body structure, hand-eye coordination, gross motor coordination, dynamic balance, static balance, and grip strength. Ismail and Cowell (1961), in a factor analytic study of the motor aptitude of preadolescent boys, extracted five factors from a battery of 25 test items, namely, factors identified as speed, growth and maturity, kinesthetic memory of the arms, body balance on objects, and body balance on the floor. These studies clearly show that there are well-defined basic components that underlie the motor performance of children. However, none of the studies published to date has included within its scope a range of variables broad enough to encompass a major part of the motor domain of children.

Factor Structure of Motor Abilities of Retarded Children

A few studies have used factor analysis in studying the nature of motor abilities and perceptual-motor functions in the retarded. Vandenberg (1964), using the Lincoln Oseretsky Test with a mixture of institutionalized and public school retardates and normal children, isolated eight factors, including such components as speed of movement, balance, dynamic coordination, and age. Rarick (1968), in a recent factor analysis of motor performance data on educable mentally retarded children in which factors of static strength, explosive muscular force, coordination, and physical maturity were identified, found that the factor structure of the abilities assessed was highly similar across the age span 8 to 14 years and was almost identical for the two sexes. Further evidence of the relative constancy of the factor structure of perceptual-motor abilities among groups of retarded children of different ages is shown by the work of Clausen (1966), who isolated some 12 factors from a large number of perceptual-motor tasks. Seven of the factors (general ability, intellectual-perceptual ability, spatially related intellectual ability, visual acuity, auditory acuity, reactive motor speed, and cutaneous space discrimination) were identified in all of the groups.

While the above studies have been limited either in the number of variables used in their analyses or in the type of variables selected (too greatly oriented to fine perceptual-motor tests), they do clearly show the value of the factor analytic approach. Factor analysis has proved to be a highly effective methodological approach in studying the motor behavior of humans, and from past experience we believe it will be an equally effective procedure with the mentally retarded.

Purpose of the Investigation

The central purpose of this investigation was to determine the factor structure of motor abilities of educable mentally retarded (EMR) boys and girls in the age ranges 6 to 9 years and 10 to 13 years, respectively, and to ascertain the extent to which the factor structure differed by chronological age and sex.

A second purpose was to determine if the factor structure of motor abilities of educable mentally retarded children differed from that of intellectually normal children of the same age and sex.

The third purpose was to provide baseline data from which the motor performance of educable mentally retarded children and normal children could be compared by age and sex.

A fourth purpose was to determine the extent to which mixed groups of educable mentally retarded and normal boys and girls might be homogeneously grouped on the basis of similar motor performance profiles.

A fifth purpose was to identify those motor performance variables which most clearly differentiated educable mentally retarded from normal children and those which differentiated the sexes most effectively.

The final purpose of the study was to utilize the findings to draw inferences regarding the physical activity needs of educable mentally retarded boys and girls.

Hypothesized Factor Structure of Motor Abilities

The theoretical frame of reference upon which this study was developed was based on the premise that there are certain well-defined general components of motor performance upon which the broad range of physical activities of our culture rests. To hypothesize a factor structure for these varied abilities is not an easy task. In the light of the findings of the many early factor analytic studies, however, and in view of what experience and observation tell us about the performance of the skills used in the physical activities of children and youth, it is possible to postulate a framework which encompasses many of the basic components required in the execution of these skills. For example, most of the more common physical activities of children require proficiency in the locomotor skills (or modifications of them). Many require the ability to start and stop quickly and to change the orientation of the body in space. Many require muscular strength and power as well as speed of movement. Others demand hand-eye coordination in the projection, retrieval, or striking of objects moving freely in space. Most skills require that the body be sensitive to its orientation in space and be capable of maintaining this orientation under a variety of circumstances. Some call upon the body's energy reserves in activities of long duration, whereas others make extreme demands in short bursts of activity. Almost all are dependent upon physical and intellectual maturation.

The hypothesized factor structure which follows is an attempt to piece together from the findings of earlier research and from logical considerations the basic components of the gross motor abilities of human beings, with particular reference to children. It is recognized that the success of factor analysis as a research tool is dependent upon the wisdom and knowledge used in formulating an hypothesized factor structure and the care with which the test items are selected. The following constitutes an hypothesized factor structure which, it is believed, embraces the domain of motor behavior of man and which should provide a logical beginning for identifying the basic components of motor performance of educable mentally retarded boys and girls:

I. Static Muscular Strength
II. Explosive Muscular Strength
III. Muscular Strength-Endurance
IV. Gross Body Coordination
V. Cardio-Respiratory Endurance
VI. Limb-Eye Coordination
VII. Manual Dexterity
VIII. Static Balance
IX. Dynamic Balance
X. Kinesthesis
XI. Flexibility
XII. Speed and Coordination of Gross Limb Movements
XIII. Body Fat
XIV. Body Size

Chapter 2 / Methodology

General Plan of the Investigation

The initial step in the investigation was the formulation of an hypothesized factor structure which would, in theory, encompass those basic abilities that are needed in the execution of the broad range of motor skills characteristically used by children in our culture. The second step was the selection of tests which, according to previous research, had been shown to load high on the factors in the hypothesized factor structure or which might logically (by nature of the task) be expected to do so. The third step was to administer the tests to a sample of educable mentally retarded children on a pilot basis to ascertain the administrative feasibility of each test and to obtain preliminary data on the reliability of the tests. The fourth was to identify the sample of children to be tested, arrange with school authorities in the San Francisco Bay area for the administration of the test battery, and set up a time schedule for testing. The fifth was to administer the tests to the children in the several school districts. The final step included the processing and analyzing of the data.

Subjects

The design of the study called for two age groups of educable mentally retarded boys and girls: a young group with a chronological age range of 6 through 9 years, and an older group in the age range of 10 through 13 years. The decision to add a group of intellectually normal boys and girls in the age range 6 through 9 years only was based on the premise that this procedure would provide a sample of children, for comparative purposes, that would be similar in chronological age to the young retarded group and similar in mental age to the group of older retarded children.

A total of 406 children completed all tests: 135 young retardates, 126 older retardates, and 145 normal children. The number of children by age categories, sex, and intellectual level is given in Table 2.1. The frequency

Table 2.1

DISTRIBUTION OF SUBJECTS BY AGE CATEGORIES, SEX, AND INTELLECTUAL LEVEL

	Boys	*Girls*
Young Retardates	71	64
Older Retardates	65	61
Normals	71	74
Total	207	199

in each category is entirely adequate for the type of analysis planned. The numerical distribution by age, sex, and intellectual level of the entire population tested is shown in Table 2.2.

Table 2.2

DISTRIBUTION OF SUBJECTS BY CHRONOLOGICAL AGE, SEX, AND INTELLECTUAL LEVEL

	Boys		*Girls*	
Age	*Normals*	*Retardates*	*Normals*	*Retardates*
6	8	7	5	9
7	21	16	19	16
8	14	21	19	11
9	28	27	31	28
10		18		18
11		32		20
12		11		15
13		4		8

Categorizing the children by chronological age resulted in an unequal number in each chronological age group, distorting the frequencies particularly at the upper and lower ages. In all groups, the number of children at the 6 and the 13 year age levels was small. As will be pointed out later, the method of statistical treatment of the data made appropriate adjustments for the distorted frequencies within age levels and the 4-year age span within the two major age categories.

The educable mentally retarded subjects came from eight school districts in the San Francisco Bay area. Children from 26 classes in 21 schools participated. The intellectually normal subjects were pupils attending a single elementary school in an East Bay Unified School District. The geographical region from which the samples of children came is shown in Figure 2.1.

The chronological age of each subject was taken as his age in months calculated from the date of the initial testing. The means and standard deviations of the chronological ages of the normal and the retarded subjects by age category and sex are given in Table 2.3. These values are highly similar across age and disability at the younger age level. While the mean

Table 2.3

MEANS AND STANDARD DEVIATIONS OF THE CHRONOLOGICAL AGES OF SUBGROUPS OF NORMAL AND MENTALLY RETARDED SUBJECTS

	Retarded				*Normal*			
	Boys		*Girls*		*Boys*		*Girls*	
	Mean	*S.D.*	*Mean*	*S.D.*	*Mean*	*S.D.*	*Mean*	*S.D.*
Young	102.1	11.96	100.6	14.21	100.7	13.59	102.8	13.52
Older	137.6	11.07	140.6	13.28				

chronological age of the older retarded girls is slightly greater than that of the older retarded boys, it is evident from the standard deviations that the difference is of little consequence. The similarity in mean chronological age among the groups is further indicated by the mean ages of the subjects when they are grouped according to chronological age (see Table 2.4).

Table 2.4

MEANS AND STANDARD DEVIATIONS OF THE CHRONOLOGICAL AGES IN MONTHS OF THE NORMAL AND EDUCABLE MENTALLY RETARDED CHILDREN GROUPED INTO AGE CATEGORIES

Age	*EMR Boys*	*EMR Girls*	*Normal Boys*	*Normal Girls*
6	80.14 ± 2.47	78.44 ± 4.66	79.25 ± 2.86	77.40 ± 1.62
7	91.69 ± 3.57	89.21 ± 3.41	89.14 ± 3.22	88.37 ± 3.22
8	101.14 ± 4.10	104.55 ± 3.33	102.00 ± 4.04	101.89 ± 3.34
9	114.59 ± 3.14	114.23 ± 3.81	114.79 ± 4.28	116.19 ± 3.53
10	125.38 ± 3.76	125.89 ± 3.16		
11	137.47 ± 3.94	137.35 ± 3.51		
12	147.45 ± 4.08	149.93 ± 3.99		
13	165.75 ± 7.13	163.67 ± 4.47		

The I.Q.'s of all of the mentally retarded subjects except those from one school district were made available. Unfortunately, the school district which did not conform represented a sizable proportion of the total sample, namely,

Fig. 2.1 Map of the San Francisco Bay area showing locations of participating schools and the number of retarded children tested in each school.

44 subjects, 27 boys and 17 girls. Of the total number of children for whom I.Q. scores were available, the number of subjects by tests was as follows: WISC, 172; Stanford-Binet, 33; WPPSI, 6; Leiter, 2; Peabody, 3; and CTMMI, 1.

A breakdown of the means and ranges of the I.Q.'s for the WISC and the Stanford-Binet by age level and sex is given in Table 2.5. As may be seen,

Table 2.5

MEANS AND RANGES OF I.Q.'s OF EDUCABLE MENTALLY RETARDED CHILDREN BY AGE LEVEL AND SEX ON THE WISC AND THE STANFORD-BINET SCALE OF INTELLIGENCE

		Stanford-Binet			*WISC*	
Group	*N*	*Mean*	*Range*	*N*	*Mean*	*Range*
Young EMR Boys	13	66.7692	41–81	39	66.2632	44–88
Young EMR Girls	9	61.6667	52–69	46	65.3913	46–80
Older EMR Boys	6	67.0000	61–74	45	68.5556	46–95
Older EMR Girls	5	67.8000	58–77	42	66.8810	46–82

the mean I.Q.'s on the two tests did not differ materially by age level or sex. I.Q.'s from the other four tests were similar, ranging from 49 to 80. Note in Table 2.5 that the range of the I.Q.'s in the case of the WISC extended from the mid-40's to the high 80's and the mid-90's. Except for a few isolated cases, however, the I.Q.'s of the subjects were well within what is generally held to be the I.Q. range of the educable retarded.

The school districts in which the testing was done draw children largely from what is commonly termed the middle-to-upper-middle-class socio-economic segment of society. The number of children from minority-group families was small. Hence, the sample upon which the data were collected cannot be considered to be characteristic of the California population as a whole. For the purpose of this investigation this was perhaps good, since it reduced the possibility of including sizable numbers of intellectually mis-classified children.

Test Administration

Each child was tested at the school which he attended. The total time required to test a given subject was approximately 3 hours. The number of tests given to a particular child during each testing session depended upon the nature of the test, the physical demands it imposed, and the response capabilities of the child. Normally, only one to three tests were given to a child during one testing session.

The testing schedule was arranged so that the children had ample opportunity to rest between tests. The testing procedures were set up so that a child could observe the test being administered to his classmates prior to taking the test himself. This served two purposes. First, it oriented him to the task and tended to reduce the apprehension he might have had about a particular test; and second, it provided a period of rest for the children between tests. No more than three or four children were in a testing station at any one time. The children not being tested remained quiet and were in no sense a distractive influence on the subject being tested. Care was taken that the child fully understood the nature and demands of the test before the test was administered.

The tests were basically of two types, namely, tests that could be best administered indoors and tests suitable only for outdoor administration. The latter were tests that required considerable space, such as track-and-field type tests or those that necessitated the use of bulky equipment. The indoor tests were administered in a three-room mobile unit, measuring 10 feet by 55 feet, that could be moved from school to school. A schematic drawing of the mobile unit is shown in Figure 2.2. The testing operation was set up so that five testing stations—three in the mobile unit and two outdoors—were in operation continuously. This meant that six persons were involved in the testing, one at each testing station and a supervisor who was responsible for overseeing and coordinating the testing procedures.

The testers were all college graduates with considerable experience in working with children. Without exception, they were quickly able to gain the confidence of the children. Once assigned to a test and to a testing station, the testers retained this assignment almost without exception. There is every reason to believe that the testing operation was very nearly ideal for a field project of this kind.

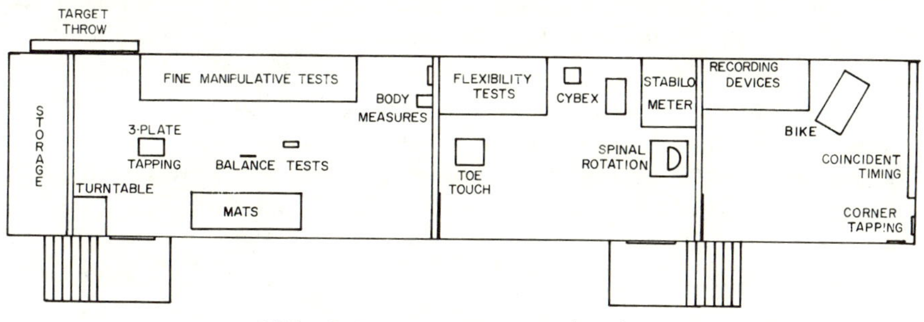

Fig. 2.2 Schematic drawing of interior of mobile unit showing location of test areas.

Description of Tests and Testing Procedures

As pointed out in an earlier section, the design of the investigation required that each test selected for use depends primarily upon a basic component for its successful execution. Thus, certain tests placed demands on the subject's capacity to exert maximum muscular force, some taxed primarily the subject's ability to maintain his balance under different but well-defined conditions, and others placed demands on still other primary abilities. Such tests would logically be expected to correlate highly with the basic ability characteristic of that particular test. After considerable preliminary investigation, 61 tests were selected which could logically be grouped according to the basic components encompassed by the hypothesized factor structure. These tests, appropriately grouped within the framework of the hypothesized factor structure, are given in Table 2.6.

The following are descriptions of the tests on which sufficiently reliable data were obtained for the test scores to be included in the final analysis. Certain tests which were employed in the pilot study were dropped because of their unreliability or because they did not prove to be appropriate for retarded children. For example, the test of kinesthesis, although administered to the entire population of retarded subjects, did not have reliability coefficients high enough to be retained; hence, a description of this test and others not retained in the final test battery is not included.

All indoor tests were conducted with children wearing their usual school attire. Tennis shoes were worn by the children while participating in tests of an athletic nature. All tests performed against time were timed to tenths of a second by stopwatch unless the equipment was connected to electric timers.

Grip Strength

Right grip and left grip were measured by a hand dynamometer with an adjustable grip (Lafayette Instrument Co., Lafayette, Indiana, Model No. 4205E). The dynamometer was placed in the hand of the seated subject and the initial adjustment for hand size was made by the tester. Any body position was acceptable as long as the gripping hand and arm did not make contact with the subject's body. The score for right grip was the mean of three trials with the right hand, and for left grip the mean of three trials with the left hand. Readings were taken to the nearest kilogram.

Knee Flexion Strength, Knee Extension Strength, Elbow Flexion Strength, Elbow Extension Strength

The Cybex II Isokinetic System, consisting of a Cybex dynamometer, a speed selector, and a recorder, allowed torque measurements to be determined for each of the above four joint actions at a predetermined speed of rotation. The nature of the instrumentation makes it possible to record torque in foot-pounds over a range of speeds from 0 degrees per second (isometric) to 210 degrees per second. The four torque measures taken were recorded at 30 degrees per second, a medium rate of rotation. The subject's task was to exert maximum force through 90 degrees of rotation when the joint of the limb tested (knee or elbow) was aligned with, and fixed at, the axis

Table 2.6

TESTS GROUPED ACCORDING TO HYPOTHESIZED FACTORS

I. *Static Muscular Strength*
1. Grip Strength Right
2. Grip Strength Left
3. Cybex Elbow Flexion
4. Cybex Elbow Extension
5. Cybex Knee Flexion
6. Cybex Knee Extension

II. *Explosive Muscular Strength*
1. Vertical Jump
2. Standing Broad Jump
3. 35-Yard Dash (5–35)
4. Light Medicine Ball Throw*
5. Bicycle Ergometer With Resistance (10 seconds)
6. Bicycle Ergometer Without Resistance (10 seconds)
7. Softball Throw (Velocity)

III. *Muscular Strength-Endurance*
1. Sit-ups
2. Trunk Raise for Time
3. Leg Raise for Time
4. Bicycle Ergometer Total (90 seconds)

IV. *Gross Body Coordination*
1. Shuttle Run*
2. Edgren Test*
3. Scramble
4. Mat Crawl
5. Tire Run

V. *Cardio-Respiratory Endurance*
1. Physical Work Capacity (170)
2. 150-Yard Dash
3. Bicycle Drop-off*
4. Drop-off Index (Run)*

VI. *Limb-Eye Coordination*
1. Pursuit Rotor at 20 RPM*
2. Pursuit Rotor at 40 RPM
3. Target Throw Horizontal
4. Target Throw Vertical
5. Visual Coincidence Timing*

VII. *Manual Dexterity*
1. Minnesota Manipulative Test
2. Purdue Pegboard Test
3. 2-Plate Tapping Test
4. Ring Stacking Test
5. Golfball Placement Test
6. Steadiness Groove*

VIII. *Static Balance*
1. Bass Test
2. Stabilometer
3. Stork Test

IX. *Dynamic Balance*
1. Railwalk Forward
2. Railwalk Backward
3. Railwalk Sideways

X. *Kinesthesis*
1. Angle Reproduction*
2. Comparative Hand Adjustment*
3. Force Estimation*

XI. *Flexibility*
1. Toe Touch
2. Spinal Extension
3. Spinal Rotation
4. Lateral Spinal Extension

XII. *Speed and Coordination of Gross Limb Movements*
1. 3-Plate Foot Tapping*
2. Corner Plate Tapping*
3. Turntable*

XIII. *Body Fat*
1. Triceps Skinfold
2. Subscapular Skinfold
3. Abdominal Skinfold

XIV. *Body Size*
1. Bi-Acromial Breadth
2. Bi-Iliac Breadth
3. Calf Girth*
4. Height (cm)
5. Weight (kg)

**Not used in factor analysis.*

of rotation of the Cybex dynamometer. A readout in foot-pounds gave a continuous record of the torque exerted at each trial. Each subject was given three trials on each of the four Cybex tests. The mean peak torque in foot-pounds of the three trials was used as the subject's score for each of the four tests.

KNEE EXTENSION AND KNEE FLEXION. The subject sat comfortably on the corner of a padded table so that the axis of rotation of the Cybex dynamometer could be aligned with, and in contact with, the apex of the right knee joint. The lever arm length was adjusted to match the length of the subject's lower limb. The subject's right foot was then mounted in the foot support with the apex of the right knee joint at the axis of rotation of the Cybex dynamometer. A wide belt secured the subject's hip and thigh to the table to prevent movement of these parts during testing. The subject was then directed to move the leg upward with maximum force through a range of motion of 90 degrees from an initial position perpendicular to the floor. Knee flexion strength was determined by having the subject move the lower limb with maximum force from the horizontal position downward through the full range of flexion.

ELBOW EXTENSION AND ELBOW FLEXION. The subject assumed the supine position on the testing table so that the apex of the right elbow was aligned with, and in contact with, the axis of rotation of the Cybex dynamometer. The lever arm length was adjusted to match the length of the forearm, allowing the subject to grasp comfortably the lever arm stop while maintaining the set position of the elbow at the axis of rotation of the dynamometer. The subject's upper right arm was secured with two belts to render movement of the upper arm impossible. The measurement of elbow extension strength was obtained while the subject was moving the forearm from its vertical starting position to the horizontal. Elbow flexion strength was measured while the subject was moving the forearm from the horizontal starting position to the vertical.

Vertical Jump

With the subject standing adjacent, and at right angles, to a wall on which was mounted a measuring board placed slightly above his head, the subject's stretch height (standing height plus maximum arm reach) was determined. From this position, the subject then jumped to touch as high a point as possible on the measuring board with the fingers of the arm nearest the board. The score was the difference in inches between the subject's stretch height and the jump height. Four trials were given, the score used in the analysis being the mean of four trials.

Standing Broad Jump

The subject stood with feet slightly apart and with the toes just behind a clearly marked take-off line. The subject was directed to jump as far as possible, using a two-foot take-off, and to land on both feet simultaneously. The jump was measured from the take-off line to the point nearest to the take-off line where the heels first touched the floor. Measurement was to the nearest 1/2 inch. In the case of a mistrial—e.g., if the subject fell backward—the trial was repeated. The score was the mean of four trials.

35-Yard Dash (5–35)

Four pairs of photoelectric cells (Sigma Division, Sigma Instruments, Inc., Braintree, Mass., Model No. 8P3-115 Photo Relay) were positioned at different points on the 35-yard course, one at the starting line, others at points 5 yards, 10 yards, and 35 yards from the starting line (see Figure 2.3).

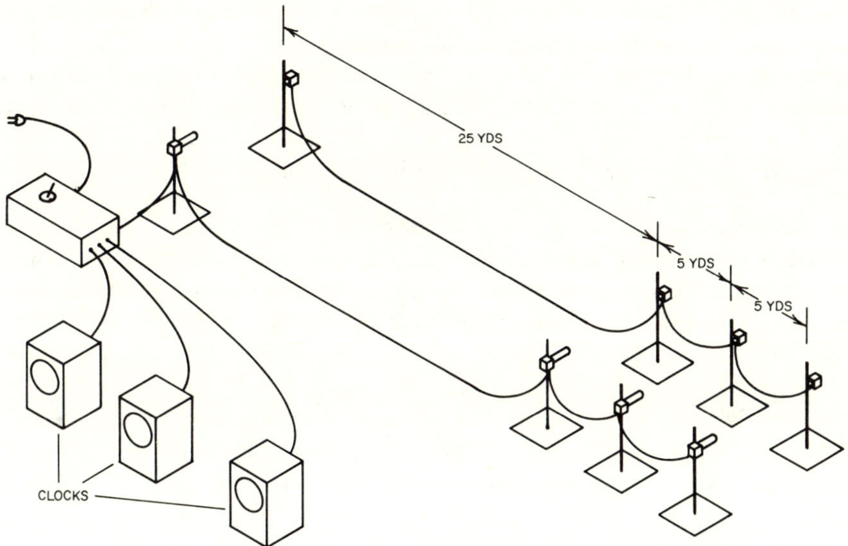

Fig. 2.3 Schematic drawing of photoelectric timing apparatus.

In each case, the light beam was set at head height of the runner. As the subject moved from his starting position, the light, which had been interrupted by his body, became continuous, thus starting the first electric timer. The other timers were triggered as the light beams were interrupted by the subject at the points 5, 10, and 35 yards from the starting line. The positioning of the photoelectric cells made it possible to determine the net time it took the runner to cover the distances 0–5 yards, 0–10 yards, 5–10 yards, and 5–35 yards. On the command "Go," the subject was directed to run as fast as possible on the straight 35-yard course. For the purposes of this investigation, the subject's running speed was taken as the time required to negotiate the 5–35-yard distance. The mean time of three trials was used as the score.

Tests Using the Bicycle Ergometer

Three tests were administered using a standard bicycle ergometer which was connected to an automatic counter (Lafayette Instrument Co., Lafayette, Indiana, Model No. 5809). In each instance, the height of the seat was adjusted appropriately for the leg length of the child.

BICYCLE ERGOMETER WITHOUT RESISTANCE. When comfortably seated on the bicycle ergometer, the subject was directed to pedal as fast as possible for a period of 10 seconds. The number of revolutions in 10 seconds constituted the trial score. The score used in the analysis was the mean of three trials.

BICYCLE ERGOMETER WITH RESISTANCE. This was a test identical to the above test except the subjects pedaled against a standard resistance. The young retarded girls and boys, the normal girls and boys, and the older retarded girls pedaled against a 1-1/2-kilopond resistance. The older retarded boys pedaled against a resistance of 2-1/2 kiloponds. These resistances were decided upon after preliminary testing in the pilot study.

BICYCLE ERGOMETER TOTAL (90 SECONDS). The subject's task was to pedal as fast as possible for 90 seconds. The resistance used for each subject was the same as that employed in the bicycle ergometer with resistance task. The score was the total number of revolutions pedaled in 90 seconds. One trial only was given.

Softball Throw

The subject threw a regulation 7-inch softball as far as possible. Only one forward step was allowed during the throw. A time score in hundredths of a second measured from the point of release to the point where the ball landed and a distance score measured to the nearest 1/4 foot provided data from which a velocity score in feet per second could be computed by simple trigonometry. The score was the mean velocity of three trials. Two practice throws were permitted as a warm-up.

Sit-ups

The subject assumed a supine position on a gymnasium mat with legs extended and feet approximately shoulder width apart. Fingers were interlaced and the hands placed at the back of the neck. The tester held down the subject's ankles, keeping the heels in contact with the floor at all times. The subject then sat up, turning the trunk to the left, and touched the right elbow to the left knee before returning to the supine position. This cycle was repeated, alternating sides, until the subject had performed as many sit-ups as possible in 1 minute. One trial was administered.

Trunk Raise for Time

The subject was positioned facedown on a board measuring 3 feet by 5 feet and 3 inches in height, with the upper body above the iliac crests protruding beyond the edge of the board. The subject, with interlaced fingers placed below, and in contact with, the chin, and with elbows pointed outward, hyperextended the back and attempted to hold that position for as long as possible. The subject's calves were held down throughout the test. The test began when the subject first attained the required position and terminated when that position was broken. The score was the mean in seconds of two trials.

Leg Raise for Time

The purpose of this test was to determine how long the subject, while in the supine position, could hold his fully extended legs in a position in which his heels remained elevated 1 foot above a gymnasium mat. The equipment for this test was a trip wire mounted horizontally on supports in such a way that any force from above would cause a buzzer to sound (see Figure 2.4). The subject's task was to maintain the ankles above the trip wire for as long as possible while retaining the position described above. The test started when the tester, who had lifted the subject's legs to a position immediately above the trip wire, released the legs. Care was taken to be sure that the legs of the subject were straight at all times, that the subject's hands never were in a position to support the legs, and that the ankles of the subject never moved higher than 2 to 3 inches above the trip wire. When the ankles

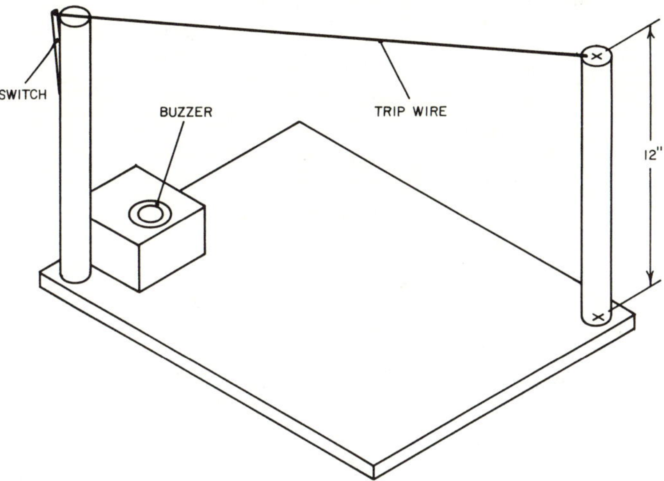

Fig. 2.4 Schematic drawing of the apparatus used in the Leg Raise Test.

dropped to make contact with the trip wire a buzzer sounded, terminating the test. The score was the time in seconds (stopwatch) that the legs were held unsupported above the trip wire. Only one trial was given.

Scramble

The subject lay in a supine position on a standard gymnastic mat with the hands placed at the sides of the body. A 4-inch by 1-inch by 1-inch wooden baton was placed on its long axis 10 feet away from the subject's feet. The subject's task was to move as quickly as possible from the supine position to the vertical, run to the baton, retrieve it, and return to the starting supine position. The score was the mean stopwatch time of three trials. On each trial, care was taken to ensure that the subject returned to, and assumed, the starting supine position.

Mat Crawl

The subject assumed a starting position on hands and knees and retained this position throughout the test. On the command "Go," the subject's task was to crawl as quickly as possible from the starting place to a pylon 8 feet away, around the pylon, and then to the finish line. The score was the mean of three trials timed in seconds by stopwatch.

Tire Run

This test required that the subject run as fast as possible from a start-finish line to a second line 15 feet away and then return to the start-finish line (see Figure 2.5). During the run, the subject was required to step in sequence from one tire to the next in negotiating the distance to the second line, continuing this procedure on the return. If a subject stepped on a tire the trial was allowed, but if a tire was missed that trial was taken again. The score used was the mean time in seconds of three trials.

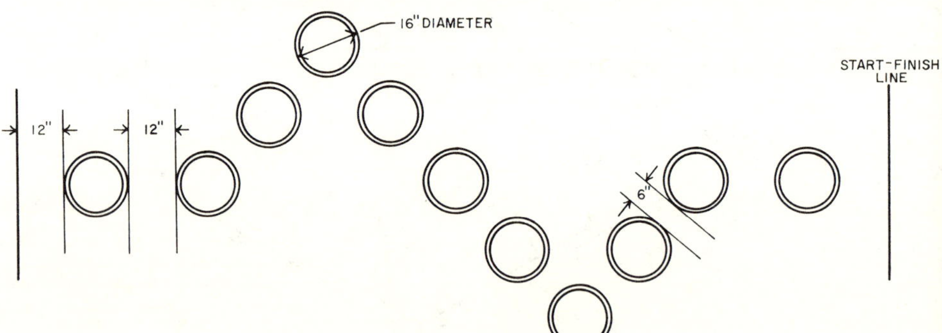

Fig. 2.5 Layout of the Tire Run.

Physical Work Capacity at a Heart Rate of 170 Beats Per Minute (PWC_{170})

The test, adapted from the research of Sjostrand (1947), has been used to assess the work capacity of children and adults. It is a submaximal test based on the principle that the heart rate varies in proportion to the work load. While it is not as good an index of functional work capacity as are tests of maximal oxygen consumption, it provides a useful measure for comparing the work capacity of children of the same age and sex.

The test was administered on a standard Monark Bicycle Ergometer, (Quinton Instruments, Seattle, Washington) modified by using a pendulum bob of 168 grams rather than the normal bob of approximately 817 grams. Subects were instructed to pedal at a rate of 60 revolutions per minute for a total of 12 minutes, or 4 minutes at each of three progressively heavier work loads. Each subject's heart rate was continuously monitored by telemetric equipment (Signatron Model No. 4200 Telemetric Receiver, Signatron Model No. 201 Transmitter, Signatron Model No. 1100 VCO, and Signatron Differential Amplifier ECG 2120, Signatron, Inc., Gardena, California) and an oscilloscope (Tektronix 564B Storage Oscilloscope, Tektronix, Inc., Beaverton, Oregon). Heart beats were recorded near the end of each minute on a fast response electronic recorder (Clevite Brush Mark 200, Clevite Corporation, Cleveland, Ohio). The heart rate at the end of the 4th, 8th, and 12th minutes was plotted against the respective work loads and a regression line was calculated to determine the physical work capacity at a heart rate of 170 beats per minute. Recommended resistances by age, sex, and weight necessary to produce a heart rate of approximately 170 beats per minute after 12 minutes of cycling are given by a publication of the Canadian Association for Health, Physical Education, and Recreation (1968).

150-Yard Dash

This test was selected as a measure of cardio-respiratory endurance. While it does not meet the criteria of placing heavy demands on the aerobic work capacity of children, it is a task sufficiently strenuous for untrained children to call on their energy reserves while at the same time being well within their tolerance limitations.

The subjects were directed to run the distance in as short a time as possible. The starter used the commands "Ready" and "Go." The latter was accompanied by a downward sweep of the starter's arm to give a visual signal to the timer who was standing at the finish line. One subject ran at a time. The 150 yards were clearly marked by flags and typically were run as a straightaway on a hard-top playground, although some subjects ran on dry adobe. All children ran in tennis shoes. Only one trial was given, with the score being the time in seconds (stopwatch) for negotiating the 150 yards.

Pursuit Rotor at 40 Revolutions per Minute

In performing this task, the subject stood in front of the photoelectric rotary pursuit apparatus (Lafayette Instrument Co., Lafayette, Indiana, Model 2203) and with a stylus tip (containing a photoelectric cell) tracked a light source circling at 40 revolutions per minute. Tracking time per trial was for a period of 15 seconds. Each trial began as the pursuit rotor was started and the stylus manned by the subject was in contact with the light source. A 1/100 of a second timer (Lafayette Instrument Co., Lafayette, Indiana, Model 5809) recorded the time the stylus tip was on the rotating target light. The time on target for the 15-second time interval was the score per trial. The score used was the mean time in seconds of four trials.

Target Throw Horizontal and Target Throw Vertical

The subject threw a tennis ball at a 6-foot-square target, the bottom edge of which was 3 feet above the ground. The target was divided by parallel lines into 15 divisions of 4.8 inches each. The body of the target was painted white, the parallel lines were black, and the centermost division was red to highlight the zone at which the subject aimed (see Figure 2.6). A ball that struck the centermost zone scored 8 points; the zones on either side of the centermost area scored 7 points; and with each successive zone beyond, the score was lessened by 1 point, the outermost divisions scoring 1 point. A

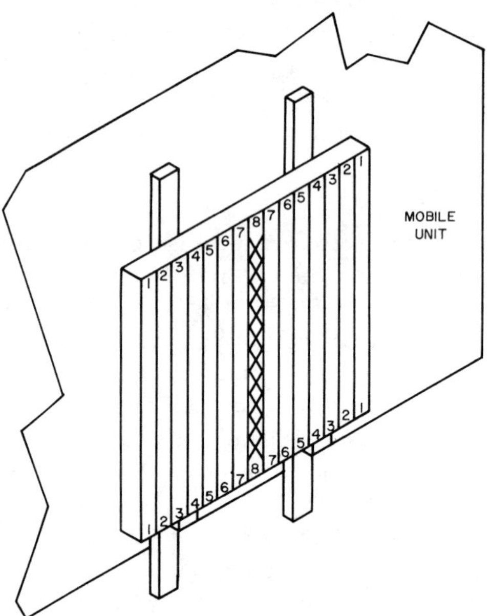

Fig. 2.6 Schematic drawing of target used in the Test of Throwing Accuracy.

throw missing the target was given a 0 score. After five practice throws, the subjects threw 30 times at the target with the parallel divisions running horizontally (target throw vertical) and 30 times with the parallel divisions running vertically (target throw horizontal). The score on each test was the mean of the 30 throws. Subjects threw from different distances, depending upon age and sex. The target was placed 10 feet from the young EMR and normal girls; 15 feet from the young EMR and normal boys; 20 feet from the older EMR girls; and 25 feet from the older EMR boys.

Adapted Minnesota Manipulative Test

The Minnesota Manipulative Test is a standardized test of manual dexterity. The test was considered too long to be suitable for use with retarded children. Hence, it was reduced in length. In the administration of the test, the subject was seated comfortably at a table directly in front of the portion of the test boards containing 16 circular blocks, 4 blocks in each of four rows. The blocks were 1/2-inch thick and 1-1/2 inches in diameter, resting in indented slots 1/4-inch deep and of only slightly greater diameter than the disks. On the command "Go," the subject turned over the 16 circular blocks and replaced them as rapidly as possible in the slots where they had originally rested. Each subject completed four trials, two trials with the preferred hand and two with the nonpreferred hand. Scores for each hand were the mean times in seconds of the two trials required to turn and replace the 16 circular blocks.

Purdue Pegboard

This is a standardized test of fine manipulative skill. The objective of the test is for the subject to take small, cylindrical metal pegs singly from the peg container on the test board and place them one by one, as rapidly as possible, in small holes in a standardized arrangement on the pegboard. In the administration of the test, the subject was seated comfortably at a table in front of the pegboard. He was then directed to place as many pegs as possible in the appropriate row within a time period of 30 seconds. Three trials, with 30-second intertrial rest periods, were given for the preferred hand. This was followed by three trials with the nonpreferred hand, then three 30-second trials using both hands simultaneously. Three scores resulted, namely, the mean of the three trials with the preferred hand only, the mean of the three trials with the nonpreferred hand, and the mean of the three trials using both hands simultaneously.

Two-Plate Tapping

This test required that the subject hold a small stylus as he would hold a pencil and alternately tap two metal plates (2 inches by 2 inches square) placed 11.25 inches apart. The metal plates and the stylus were wired to an electric counter which registered each contact the metal stylus made with the plate. The subject was seated comfortably at a table with the tapping apparatus (Lafayette Instrument Co., Lafayette, Indiana, Model No. 32012) in front of him. At reduced speed the tester demonstrated the task, clearly indicating the proper contact of the stylus with the tapping plate and the stepped-up total registered by the electric counter. The subject was allowed two practice trials, one with the preferred hand and one with the nonpreferred. The test consisted of six trials, alternately using the preferred hand and the nonpreferred hand, beginning with the preferred hand. Each trial was of 10 seconds duration. The score was the mean number of taps in 10 seconds for the three trials of the preferred hand and of the nonpreferred hand, respectively.

Ring Stacking

The object of this test, as specified in the test instructions, was for the subject to remove the eight rings one by one from their initial position on the test board and place them, one at a time and as rapidly as possible, over the post. When using the right hand, the subject was directed to stack the rings over the post on the left side of the board. When the left hand was used, he was directed to stack the rings over the post on the right side (see Figure 2.7).

The subject was seated comfortably directly in front of the ring stacking board. After one practice trial with each hand, the subject was given three

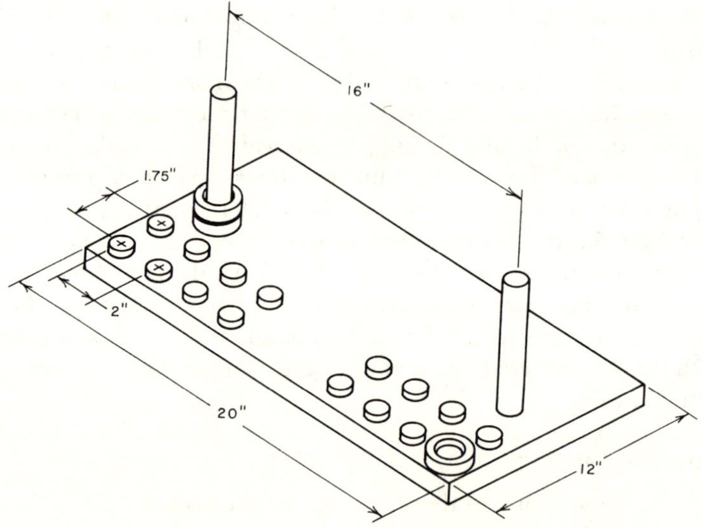

Fig. 2.7 Schematic drawing of the Ring Stacking apparatus.

trials with each hand, beginning with the preferred hand and alternating with the nonpreferred. The score was the mean in seconds of the three trials with the preferred hand and the mean of the three trials with the nonpreferred hand. If a subject fumbled badly, dropped a ring, or picked up more than one ring at a time, the trial was declared a mistrial and the subject was allowed another trial.

Golfball Placement

The task required that the subject transfer golfballs (diameter 1.68 inches) from an open container (4 inches by 8 inches by 9 inches) to a second container placed 27 inches from the first, as quickly as possible. The subject was directed to place the golfballs, one by one, through an opening 1.75 inches in diameter in the top of the second container. After one practice trial with each hand, the subject was given three trials with each hand, beginning with the preferred hand and alternating trials with the nonpreferred hand. The trial length was 15 seconds. The score for each hand was the mean number of golfballs transferred during the three trials for that hand. When the right hand was being used, the ball reservoir was on the subject's right and the balls were placed to the left. When the left hand was placing the balls, the apparatus was reversed so that the ball reservoir was on the subject's left and the golfballs were placed to the subject's right.

Adapted Bass Test of Static Balance

The subject was instructed to balance for as long as possible while standing on the preferred foot on the long axis of a 1-inch by 1-inch by 12-inch board. The test began when the subject raised the nonsupporting foot from the floor and terminated when the subject touched the floor for the second time with any part of the body. Two practice trials were allowed. The score in seconds was the mean of two trials. All subjects were tested in tennis shoes.

Stabilometer

The stabilometer is a balancing board with a central pivot mounted on an axis above the board (see Figure 2.8). A work-adder, scaled in arbitrary but equal units, records the magnitude of the rotary movements of the board around the pivot. A clock records the time in seconds that the subject is freely balanced on the stabilometer. When the board on which the subject is balancing makes contact with the floor of the stabilometer, the clock is automatically stopped. Breakage of the electric contacts between the edge of the balancing board and the floor of the stabilometer automatically restarts the clock. The work-adder in conjunction with the circuit breakers provides the means of determining the amount of angular rotation while the balancing board is unsupported for a defined period of time.

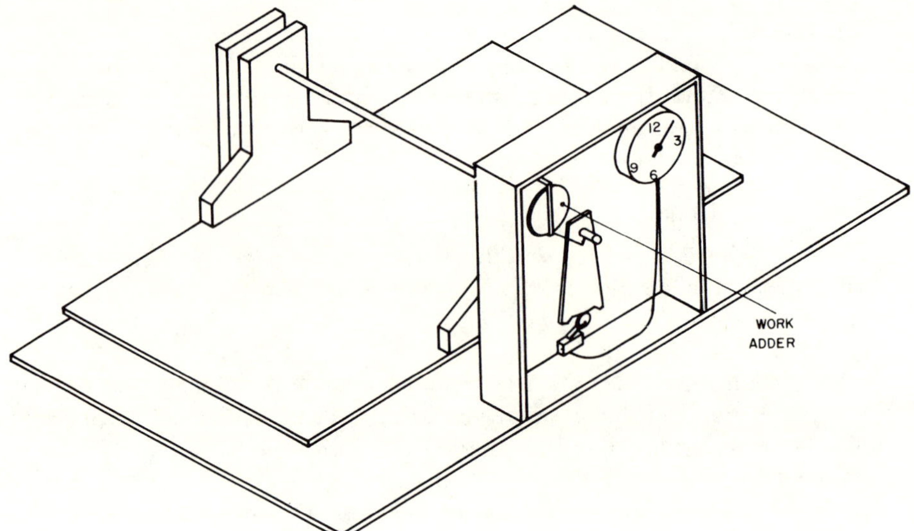

Fig. 2.8 Schematic drawing of the stabilometer.

In taking the test the subject stood on the board with the feet comfortably placed, shoulder width apart, on either side of the pivot. The score was the total of the work-adder units summed over five 15-second free-balancing trials. No practice was allowed save for a brief initial familiarization with the stabilometer and its actions. Intertrial rest was set at thirty seconds.

Stork Test

This test required that the subject retain his balance on one leg for as long as possible while standing with the support foot on a 12 inch by 3-1/4 inch by 3/4 inch footboard. Each subject, blindfolded, balanced under three conditions: (a) free standing, (b) hands on hips, (c) hands on hips with the nonbalancing foot tucked behind and in contact with the calf of the supporting leg. The test was terminated when any part of the subject's body touched the floor or if the subject failed to maintain the position described in parts (b) and (c) of the test. The maximum score was 45 seconds, 15 seconds for each of the three conditions. A trial consisted of a sequence of conditions (a) through (c). If the subject failed to retain his balance during the first 15 seconds of condition (a), the trial was terminated at the time he lost his balance and he was not allowed to progress to conditions (b) and (c). If he negotiated (a) successfully but failed to retain his balance during the 15 seconds of (b), the trial was terminated at that point. The score per trial was the total time in balance (seconds) according to the conditions stipulated above (maximum score of 45). One practice trial was allowed. The score used in the analysis of the data was the mean in seconds of two trials. All subjects were tested in tennis shoes.

Railwalking

Three tests were administered on the balance beams, namely, railwalk forward, railwalk backward, and railwalk sideways. The railwalking apparatus consisted of five beams each 10 feet long, firmly supported so that the top or walking surface of the beam was 6 inches above ground level. The walking surfaces of the five beams had widths of 3 inches, 2-1/2 inches, 2 inches, 1-1/2 inches, and 1 inch, respectively. On all three balance beam tasks, the subject attempted to walk the broadest beam first, and if successful, he proceeded to beams of progressively narrower width. The subject was permitted one step-off, the test being ended at the point of the second step-off. Subjects were instructed to take 10 steps per beam, heel to toe, in the forward and backward railwalking tasks. In the railwalk sideways test, the subject also took 10 steps per beam, the trailing foot being brought into contact with the leading foot before the next step was taken. In the latter test, the subject's feet were at right angles to the length of the beam. The scoring system was the same for all railwalking tasks. Subjects were credited with the number of steps taken before the second step-off occurred. The maximum score attainable was 50, 10 steps for each of the 5 beams. Only one trial under each of the three conditions was administered.

Toe Touch

Standing barefoot on the toe touch apparatus, shown in Figure 2.9, with the toes of both feet touching the vertical flange and the knees fully extended, the subject reached with both hands as far down the front of the flange as possible. No support was given the subject other than to help retain the subject's knees in full extension. The score (in centimeters) was the mean of three trials.

Spinal Extension and Lateral Spinal Extension

Both tests were administered on a specially constructed table that enabled the tester to immobilize the body of the subject below the pelvis.

SPINAL EXTENSION. The subject was positioned on his left side, facing and in contact with the vertical flange of the testing table. The lower extremities were secured to the flange of the table by straps across the legs (calf region) and in the region of the iliac crests, so that no movement away from the vertical flange by the lower body was possible. The subject's task was to extend the trunk as far as possible away from the vertical flange. When

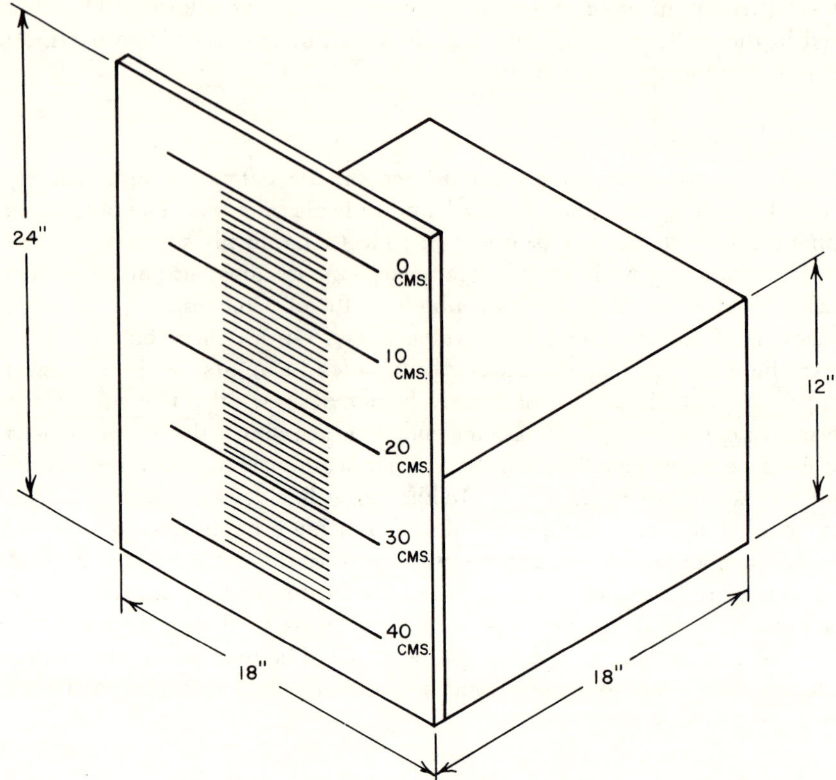

Fig. 2.9 Schematic drawing of the apparatus used for the Toe Touch Test.

the subject had achieved maximum extension, the tester measured the perpendicular distance between the supra-sternal notch and the vertical flange. In addition, the distance was measured from the anterior spine of the ilium to the point on the vertical flange which was coincidental with the perpendicular dropped from the supra-sternal notch to the flange. The angle of extension was determined by solving for the right triangle thus formed. The score in degrees was the mean of three trials. At no time during the test were the subjects allowed to push with the arms or hands in an effort to increase the range of motion.

Lateral Spinal Extension. The subject was positioned facedown on the testing table and was firmly secured to the vertical flange by straps around the calves and by a strap around the pelvis. The subject's task was to extend the upper body sideward as far as possible. No body twist was allowed, nor was the use of hands and arms permitted. As with the spinal extension test, the score was the mean of three trials in degrees computed by simple trigonometry, using the measurements from the perpendicular distances between the seventh cervical vertebra and the vertical flange and between the point located by this procedure and the anterior superior spine of the ilium (see Figure 2.10).

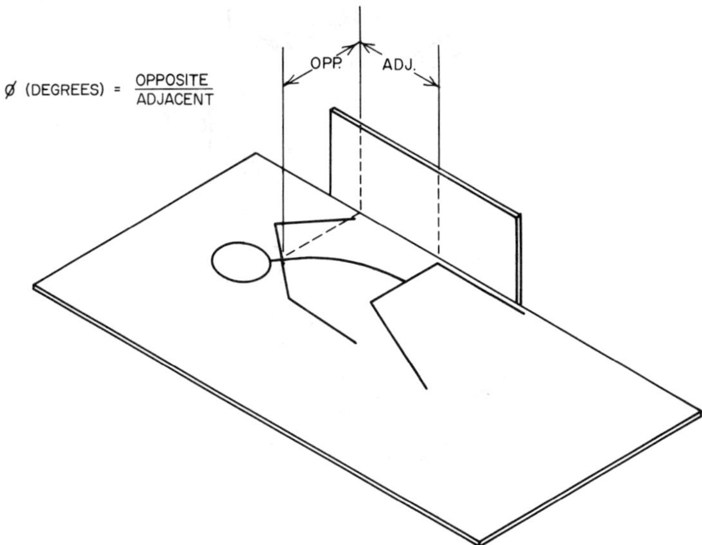

Fig. 2.10 Schematic drawing of the method of assessing lateral spinal flexibility.

Spinal Rotation

The subject was seated in the apparatus designed for measuring spinal rotation. An adjustable leg stop, a seat belt stabilizing the hips, and two shoulder belts attaching the upper arms to the horizontal rotating bar fixed the subject so that rotation of the subject's upper body was a function solely of rotation of the spine (see Figure 2.11). Rotary movement of the trunk rotated the entire assembly to which the horizontal bar was attached, thus moving the dial on the protractor which measured in degrees the angle of rotation. After one practice trial, the subject was instructed to turn as far as possible to the left, then as far as possible to the right. The total range of movement in degrees was read from the protractor above the subject's head. The score was the mean of three trials.

Skinfold Measures

A Lange skinfold caliper was used to secure all skinfold measurements. A fold of the subject's skin at the points where the measurements were taken was firmly grasped between thumb and forefinger and lifted. The

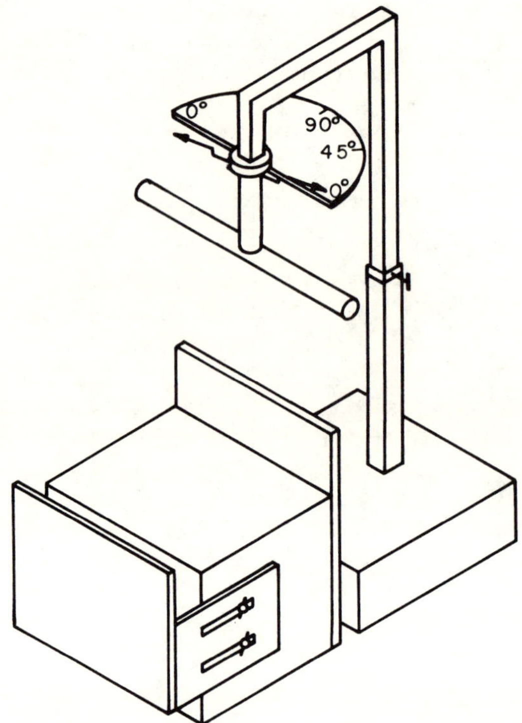

Fig. 2.11 Schematic drawing of apparatus used in measuring spinal rotation.

contact surfaces of the caliper were placed about 1 centimeter below the tester's fingers. The caliper was released so that the full spring pressure of the calipers was applied to the skinfold. Readings were taken to the nearest 1/2 millimeter. Three readings were taken at each site. The final value was the mean of the three readings. All measures were taken on the right side of the body.

Triceps. The skinfold measurement was taken on the posterior aspect of the right arm midway between the elbow and the acromium. The subject's arm was allowed to hang freely. The skinfold was lifted parallel to the long axis of the arm.

Subscapular Skinfold. The skinfold was lifted 1 inch below and medial to the inferior angle of the right scapula, parallel to the long axis of the body.

Abdominal Skinfold. The skinfold was lifted 2 inches to the right of the umbilicus parallel to the long axis of the body.

Body Breadth Measurements

The subject's bi-acromial and bi-iliac breadths were measured with an anthropometer. Measurements were taken to the nearest millimeter. The tester held the anthropometer so that the blades were positioned at the bony protuberances of the part to be measured. To minimize the effects of individual differences in subcutaneous tissue, considerable pressure was exerted on the blades by the tester.

BI-ILIAC BREADTH. The subject stood upright with arms held slightly away from the body. The tester, facing the subject, located the crest of the ilium. One blade of the anthropometer was placed at one iliac crest and the other blade was moved inward to rest on the other iliac crest. The measurement was taken in centimeters.

BI-ACROMIAL BREADTH. The measurement was taken with the subject standing and with the tester positioned behind him. The lateral edge of the acromial processes was located and one blade of the anthropometer was fixed at one acromial process and the other blade brought inward until it rested on the other process. The measurement was read in centimeters.

Weight

The subjects were weighed on a Continental Health-0-Meter. Boys wore only trousers, girls wore skirts and tops or dresses. Measurements were taken to the nearest quarter of a pound. The values were later converted to kilograms.

Height

Height was measured by means of a stadiometer. Measurements were taken to the nearest 1/2 centimeter.

Chronological Age

Chronological age of all subjects was calculated in months as of the initial month of testing. Testing of the retardates began in September 1970 and chronological age was calculated as of August 31, 1970. Testing of the normal subjects was initiated in October 1971 and chronological age for this group was calculated as of September 30, 1971.

Reliability of the Tests

The reliabilities of the tests were determined by using within-day test-retest scores. In instances where only two trials were given, the scores on trial one were correlated with the scores on trial two. In cases where more than two trials were given, correlations were run between the sum of the scores of the even-numbered trials and the sum of the scores of the odd-numbered trials.

It should be noted that the nature of certain tests was such that it was not feasible to administer more than one trial per day on these tests. The following are the tests for which reliabilities were not obtained: sit-ups, leg raise for time, bicycle ergometer total (90 seconds), physical work capacity 170, 150-yard dash, railwalk forward, railwalk backward, and railwalk sideways.

The test-retest reliabilities stepped up by the Spearman-Brown prophesy formula are shown in Appendix A. The majority of the coefficients in each of the six groups are in the 80's and 90's. Less than a fourth of the tests in any one of the six groups of subjects are in the 70's. The only tests in which the reliabilities are consistently low are the three that were developed to measure kinesthesis. Because of the low reliabilities of these tests with the retarded children, they were not administered to the normal children and the scores from these tests were not used in any of the analyses. All tests with the exception of the above three had reliabilities acceptable for grouped data analysis.

The reliabilities reported here are not materially different from those obtained on normal children and for the most part are equal to, or higher than, those reported in other investigations on the motor performance of retarded children (Francis and Rarick, 1959; Clausen, 1966).

Of the 61 measures originally selected for use, 39 motor performance tests, 7 physical growth measures, and chronological age were retained. These measures have already been described. Three were dropped because of low reliabilities. The remainder were not retained because the pilot study indicated that these tests either were not appropriate for use with retarded children or they added little information not provided by those which were retained.

Analysis of the Data

The purposes of the investigation and the nature of the data required that a rather broad range of statistical approaches be used in the treatment of the data. Various univariate and multivariate analyses were employed to assess the differences by disability and sex between the intellectually normal and the retarded children, and to clarify the relationships among the variables within the six groups of subjects and between the components (factors) that were common to these groups.

The following briefly outlines the major methods of treating the data:

(1) Zero-order correlations were used to determine the relationships among the 47 variables within each of the six subgroups, and first order partial correlations were employed to remove the possible confounding effect of variations in chronological age on these intercorrelations.

(2) Factor analysis was employed to extract the basic components or factors from the residual intercorrelation matrices (chronological age held constant) of the physical growth and motor performance variables. The factor analytic method used here followed the strategy proposed by Harris and Harris (1971) in which several different computing algorithms are employed for the initial solutions to obtain both orthogonal and oblique solutions. The initial component and factor methods included the Incomplete Principal Components (Hotelling, 1933), Alpha (Kaiser and Caffrey, 1965), and Rao's Canonical Factor Analysis (1955).

The above three factor analytic methods provide two component solutions (Incomplete Principal Components and Rao's Canonical), each having a statistical base, and one factor solution (alpha) with a psychometric base. Orthogonal solutions employed the Kaiser normal varimax procedures (Kaiser, 1958) in each of the three initial solutions. In all initial oblique solutions the default value (δ) was set at zero. More specific details regarding the rationale for employing these procedures and the techniques that were followed in comparing the factor structure across groups of subjects are given in Chapter 4.

(3) Variance analysis was used to identify those physical growth and motor performance variables for which there were statistically significant differences between intellectually normal and educable mentally retarded children of similar chronological ages.

(4) Differences expressed in standard deviation units were used to denote the magnitude of the differences between the normal and the mentally retarded children in the several physical growth and motor performance measures.

(5) The procedure for developing what has been defined as person-clusters (Tryon, 1967) was used to sort retarded and intellectually normal children of the same chronological age into groups or clusters of individuals who showed similar profiles of motor performance scores. The specific procedures that were followed are described in Chapter 5.

(6) Discriminant analysis was used as a means of discriminating between paired groups of subjects (EMR boys, EMR girls, normal boys, and normal girls) on the basis of selected motor performance scores. This type of analysis also made it possible to identify those variables which had the greatest discriminating power between subject groups. The procedures are outlined in Chapter 6.

Summary

The procedural steps that were followed in the collection and analysis of the data were described in this chapter. The study, which was designed primarily to determine the factor structure of motor abilities of educable mentally retarded and normal children, involved the administration of a large number of motor performance tests and measures of physical growth to 135 educable mentally retarded boys and girls and 126 normal boys and girls ages 6 to 9 years, and to 145 educable mentally retarded boys and girls ages 10 to 13 years. After the reliabilities and the appropriateness of these measures for further use were determined, the scores obtained on 39 motor performance and 7 physical growth measures were retained for data analysis.

Chapter 3 / Group Differences in Anthropometric and Motor Performance Variables

This chapter presents comparative data on selected anthropometric and motor performance measures of educable mentally retarded and normal boys and girls. Means and standard deviations of 47 anthropometric and motor performance variables obtained on the six groups of subjects are shown in Table 3.1. On most measures other than those of body size, skinfolds, and strength, the normal boys and girls had mean scores superior to those of the older retarded boys and girls. This was particularly true in tests requiring speed and precision of movement. Similarly, the older retarded boys and girls had mean scores substantially greater than the means of the young retarded children.

Comparisons Between the Normal and the Young Educable Mentally Retarded Children on Measures of Body Size and Tests of Motor Performance

The preceding section presented comparative findings on measures of body size and motor performance of the entire sample of educable mentally retarded and normal children categorized by chronological age and sex. In order to examine more thoroughly the significance of these findings, the data on the four groups of young children were treated by two-way variance analysis to determine if the observed differences in the means of the four groups on each of the 46 measurements (age excluded) could be attributed to factors other than chance. Thus, for each

Table 3.1

MEANS AND STANDARD DEVIATIONS OF MOTOR PERFORMANCE AND ANTHROPOMETRIC DATA OBTAINED ON EDUCABLE MENTALLY RETARDED AND NORMAL CHILDREN

	YOUNG EMR BOYS		*YOUNG EMR GIRLS*		*OLDER EMR BOYS*		*OLDER EMR GIRLS*		*NORMAL BOYS*		*NORMAL GIRLS*	
Variable	*Mean*	*S.D.*	*Mean*	*S.D.*	*Mean*	*S.D.*	*Mean*	*S.D.*	*Mean*	*S.D.*	*Mean*	*S.D.*
35-Yard Dash (sec.)	5.73	.70	6.23	.91	5.19	.60	5.57	.72	5.31	.57	5.42	.51
Tire Run (sec.)	10.15	2.16	12.12	3.17	9.11	2.16	9.85	2.50	8.55	1.16	8.32	1.01
Railwalk Forward (ft.)	35.61	11.55	31.77	11.99	38.42	12.56	36.30	12.71	46.56	6.58	47.58	4.44
Railwalk Backward (ft.)	24.68	12.71	17.34	10.24	26.20	13.72	23.43	12.57	34.30	11.56	37.73	11.50
Railwalk Sideways (ft.)	30.39	10.02	23.69	10.04	29.72	10.92	28.28	12.55	35.89	7.99	37.36	8.90
Target Throw Horizontal (pts.)	5.85	.75	5.68	1.01	5.38	.74	5.13	.85	6.30	.80	6.40	.54
Target Throw Vertical (pts.)	5.99	.69	6.06	.79	5.36	.78	5.46	.89	6.36	.84	6.69	.41
Vertical Jump (in.)	6.61	1.89	5.68	1.92	8.09	2.59	7.43	2.43	8.65	1.83	7.94	1.51
Mat Crawl (sec.)	4.99	.79	5.95	1.35	4.81	.84	5.65	1.29	4.17	.60	4.42	.68
Standing Broad Jump (in.)	44.41	9.27	37.98	9.73	50.64	10.97	46.30	11.11	52.35	7.92	50.86	6.10
Scramble (sec.)	5.75	.97	6.37	1.13	5.71	1.06	6.26	.99	5.21	.62	5.31	.51
150-Yard Dash (sec.)	32.18	5.55	35.83	6.54	28.68	4.38	30.95	5.35	28.87	3.65	29.32	3.09
Cybex Knee Flexion (ft-lb.)	23.34	8.57	19.35	8.54	36.94	14.23	33.56	14.46	29.40	8.74	28.80	6.82
Cybex Knee Extension (ft-lb.)	25.12	9.06	23.25	10.03	44.43	18.50	45.90	19.69	31.06	12.73	35.59	11.36
Cybex Elbow Flexion (ft-lb.)	6.19	1.72	6.09	4.53	10.01	6.09	9.33	3.64	5.92	2.23	5.17	1.36
Cybex Elbow Extension (ft-lb.)	9.72	3.01	9.09	3.16	15.23	9.23	15.27	10.84	9.31	2.70	8.71	2.42
Triceps Skinfold (mm.)	10.60	4.90	13.91	7.87	10.79	5.78	14.44	7.17	5.99	2.18	7.26	3.07
Subscapular Skinfold (mm)	6.71	5.34	8.66	5.34	9.58	7.06	12.19	6.92	4.42	1.90	6.05	3.33
Abdominal Skinfold (mm)	8.33	6.78	12.12	7.60	13.49	11.64	15.38	9.34	4.95	3.34	7.03	4.16
Bi-Acromial Breadth (cm)	30.67	2.90	31.07	2.69	33.42	3.58	33.96	3.71	30.28	1.86	30.39	1.85

Bi-Iliac Breadth (cm)	21.99	2.65	22.73	3.02	24.46	3.07	26.18	3.76	21.14	1.24	21.41	1.67
Height (cm)	130.50	7.66	131.20	8.60	148.10	10.66	145.90	10.88	133.10	8.76	132.90	8.80
Weight (kg)	28.81	5.74	29.49	7.44	41.44	11.37	43.09	11.84	29.21	5.56	29.47	5.43
Grip Strength Right (kg)	14.86	3.36	12.73	3.66	20.89	6.29	19.27	6.90	19.04	3.66	17.92	2.48
Grip Strength Left (kg)	14.25	3.02	12.12	3.54	20.32	6.76	17.80	6.31	18.66	3.56	17.06	2.36
Bicycle With Resistance (rev.)	10.51	3.57	8.75	3.66	13.41	3.68	12.83	3.95	14.62	3.51	14.16	2.72
Bicycle Without Resistance (rev.)	17.10	2.99	14.42	3.84	20.35	3.35	16.85	3.68	20.48	2.90	19.29	2.67
Sit-ups (no/min.)	16.76	7.83	11.72	7.48	21.86	8.55	17.13	9.25	22.59	8.08	21.24	6.50
Trunk Raise (sec.)	40.37	30.02	35.34	27.23	52.92	40.40	52.07	34.65	85.46	42.02	95.57	40.61
Leg Raise (sec.)	24.87	14.43	26.88	26.95	21.49	17.88	25.64	21.04	61.38	41.55	59.64	34.01
Pursuit Rotor at 40 RPM (sec.)	2.77	1.60	1.90	1.29	3.79	2.29	3.78	1.99	3.44	1.50	3.49	1.40
Minnesota Manipulative (sec.)	23.15	5.42	23.92	4.96	19.82	3.67	19.33	3.80	18.88	2.58	18.40	2.88
Ring Stacking (sec.)	13.97	2.69	14.39	2.62	12.19	2.22	11.88	2.06	11.52	1.44	10.85	1.30
Golfball Placement (no.)	8.63	1.50	8.11	1.57	9.98	1.68	10.00	1.58	10.44	1.25	10.82	1.33
Bass Test (sec.)	7.45	7.04	6.63	6.03	12.73	18.93	9.34	9.08	31.21	107.30	37.19	60.53
Stabilometer (wk. add. unit)	142.90	36.98	162.20	43.87	150.80	43.38	170.40	54.33	122.70	28.88	121.90	28.90
Stork Test (sec.)	17.36	9.72	15.59	8.75	20.52	11.37	18.93	8.86	23.72	9.55	28.80	10.59
Toe Touch (cm)	16.91	6.10	15.27	6.31	15.80	7.34	16.73	7.00	20.49	5.52	21.90	5.57
Spinal Extension (deg.)	46.45	6.71	42.80	6.97	43.90	8.09	42.91	6.90	47.50	7.52	50.85	7.19
Spinal Rotation (deg.)	125.00	20.19	119.00	23.26	128.00	22.77	118.80	22.58	144.70	17.61	141.20	20.65
Lateral Spinal Extension (deg.)	58.97	6.22	55.04	7.23	57.55	8.07	55.83	6.91	63.53	8.10	65.12	7.87
Physical Work Capacity (kpm/min.)	306.70	90.85	266.80	107.60	458.30	161.50	368.60	115.10	347.30	143.00	269.20	78.82
Bicycle Ergometer Total (rev.)	82.49	18.09	68.37	23.16	96.03	23.34	101.40	27.17	110.30	23.78	103.60	18.82
2-Plate Tapping Test (no.)	22.51	5.48	21.70	5.42	27.73	5.67	29.95	6.18	25.38	4.62	28.26	5.48
Softball Throw (ft./sec.)	41.47	9.78	30.47	7.45	47.41	10.75	37.07	9.03	49.40	8.69	35.66	4.99
Purdue Pegboard Test (no.)	10.33	1.98	9.51	2.40	12.08	4.76	11.97	1.96	13.88	2.11	14.63	1.88
Chronological Age (mo.)	102.10	11.96	100.60	14.21	137.60	11.07	140.60	13.28	100.70	13.59	102.80	13.52

of the physical growth and motor performance variables the effects of disability and sex on the several variables could be determined, as well as the possible sex by disability interactions.

Measures of Body Size, Flexibility, and Skinfold Thickness

A tabular comparison of the means of the normal and EMR boys and girls on the several measures of body size, flexibility, and skinfold thickness is shown in Table 3.2. There were no significant sex differences on

Table 3.2

DIFFERENCES BETWEEN YOUNG EDUCABLE MENTALLY RETARDED AND NORMAL BOYS AND GIRLS ON MEASURES OF BODY SIZE, SKINFOLD THICKNESS, AND FLEXIBILITY

	MEANS				*MAIN EFFECTS* F *RATIO*		*INTER-ACTIONS* F *RATIO*
Variable	*Young EMR Boys*	*Young EMR Girls*	*Normal Boys*	*Normal Girls*	*Disability*	*Sex*	*Disability by Sex*
Height (cm)	130.5	131.2	133.1	132.9	4.59*	.10	.21
Weight (kg)	28.8	29.5	29.2	29.5	.07	.42	.08
Bi-Acromial Breadth (cm)	30.7	31.1	30.3	30.4	3.54	.67	.26
Bi-Iliac Breadth (cm)	22.0	22.7	21.1	21.4	15.90*	2.90	.77
Triceps Skinfold (mm)	10.6	13.9	6.0	7.3	90.60**	12.00**	2.99
Abdominal Skinfold (mm)	8.3	12.1	5.0	7.0	38.00**	16.20**	1.56
Subscapular Skinfold (mm)	6.7	8.7	4.4	6.1	23.50**	11.26**	.10
Spinal Rotation (deg.)	125.0	119.0	145.0	141.0	72.50**	2.55	.26
Spinal Extension (deg.)	46.0	43.0	48.0	51.0	27.50**	.03	16.70**
Lateral Spinal Extension (deg.)	59.0	55.0	64.0	65.0	66.40**	.81	9.60**
Toe Touch (cm)	16.9	15.3	20.5	21.9	51.40**	.03	4.60*

**5 percent Level of Significance = 3.84*
***1 percent Level of Significance = 6.63*
1 and 276 Degrees of Freedom

any of the four measures of body size: height, weight, and bi-iliac and bi-acromial breadths. On the other hand, the height of the normal children was significantly greater than that of the retardates ($p < .05$). Since there was no significant difference in weight, it is evident that the retarded children were relatively heavy for their height. In terms of measures of body breadth, while there was no significant difference between the normal and the retarded in bi-acromial breadth, the difference in the means of bi-iliac breadth favoring the retarded was highly significant ($p < .01$). Since the bi-iliac breadth was taken in a region where fat accumulates, these findings (in view of the relatively greater weight of the retarded) indicated that the measurement included fat tissue. This observation is supported by the highly significant differences ($p < .01$) in skinfold thickness of the retarded at all three measurement sites. Significant sex differences favoring the girls are in line with the findings of other research on retarded and normal boys and girls (Lombard, 1950; Stuart and Sobel, 1946; Reynolds, 1944; Rarick et al., 1966).

The normal children were superior to the retarded children on all four measures of flexibility ($p < .01$), the retarded boys being superior to the retarded girls on each of the four tests.

Measures of Strength and Muscular Endurance

Table 3.3 provides a tabular comparison of the means of the four groups of children on the measures of strength and muscular endurance. In both right and left grip strength, there is a significant sex difference favoring the boys in both the normal and the retarded sample. The normal children as a group were significantly superior to the retarded on these two measures (see Table 3.3). The results of both the trunk raise and the leg raise tests were similar in that the normal children as a group were signif-

Table 3.3

DIFFERENCES BETWEEN YOUNG EDUCABLE MENTALLY RETARDED AND NORMAL BOYS AND GIRLS ON TESTS OF STRENGTH AND MUSCULAR ENDURANCE

	MEANS				*MAIN EFFECTS* F *RATIO*		*INTER-ACTIONS* F *RATIO*
Variable	*Young EMR Boys*	*Young EMR Girls*	*Normal Boys*	*Normal Girls*	*Disability*	*Sex*	*Disability by Sex*
Knee Flexion (ft-lb.)	23.34	19.35	29.40	28.80	61.39**	3.92*	2.95
Knee Extension (ft-lb.)	25.12	23.25	31.06	35.59	47.79**	1.83	5.92*
Elbow Flexion (ft-lb.)	6.19	6.09	5.92	5.17	3.34	2.02	.99
Elbow Extension (ft-lb.)	9.72	9.09	9.31	8.71	1.36	3.44	.00
Grip Strength Right (kg)	14.86	12.73	19.04	17.92	137.12**	13.19**	1.59
Grip Strength Left (kg)	14.25	12.12	18.66	17.06	152.11**	19.91**	.51
Trunk Raise (sec.)	40.37	35.34	85.46	95.57	148.23**	1.20	3.08
Leg Raise (sec.)	24.87	26.88	61.38	59.64	85.95**	.12	.25
Bicycle With Resistance (rev.)	10.51	8.75	14.62	14.16	136.36**	5.06*	2.59
Bicycle Without Resistance (rev.)	17.10	14.42	20.48	19.29	120.14**	22.10**	3.95*
Bicycle Ergometer Total (rev.)	82.49	68.37	110.30	103.60	153.58**	12.98**	2.15
Sit-ups (no. per min.)	16.76	11.72	22.59	21.24	71.80**	10.00**	4.19*

**5 percent Level of Significance = 3.84*
***1 percent Level of Significance = 6.63*

1 and 276 Degrees of Freedom

icantly superior to the retarded, although there were no statistically significant sex differences in the performance of either test. Thus, for this group of normal and retarded children, the normal boys and girls were superior to the retarded children in both manual and trunk-thigh strength, with sex differences favoring the boys only in manual strength.

In the four measures of arm and leg strength the picture is mixed. Statistically significant differences favoring the normal children were obtained in both knee flexion and knee extension strength, although only in the knee flexion strength were the boys, on the average, superior to the girls (see Table 3.3). A significant sex by disability interaction occurred in knee extension strength, in which the retarded boys were superior to the retarded girls; but the normal girls had greater knee extension strength than the normal boys. In elbow flexion and elbow extension strength, no statistically significant differences in mean strength of the four groups were found.

The results of the bicycle ergometer with resistance test, in performances for both the 10-second interval and the 90-second interval (Table 3.3), disclosed differences in favor of the males over the females and the normal children over the retarded. It is evident that on the tests of dynamic strength, the performance of normal children is superior to that of retarded children and boys exhibit greater dynamic strength than girls.

The bicycle ergometer without resistance test was used to determine speed of movement of the legs as assessed by the number of revolutions the child could pedal in an interval of 10 seconds. As may be noted in Table 3.3, there were significant differences favoring the normal over the retarded children and the boys over the girls.

Measures of Muscular Power and Coordination

Effective throwing performance calls upon components of muscular power and precise muscular coordination, depending upon the requirements of the throwing task. To sort out the effects of these two components, two types of throwing tasks were used, one a power throw (softball velocity), the other an accuracy throw (target throw horizontal and target throw vertical). As may be noted in Table 3.4, the two types of tasks produced different results. The power throw resulted in clear-cut differences favoring the normal over the retarded children and also significant sex differences, the boys proving to be superior to the girls. This finding is in no sense new, since without exception other studies have reported similar results.

In the tasks requiring precision rather than power in throwing performance, the results were different. In the target throw horizontal, the normal children on the average outperformed the retarded, but there were no sex differences in performance. In the target throw vertical, the normal children were again superior to the retarded, with the girls in this case proving to be significantly superior to the boys (Table 3.4). It is interesting

Table 3.4

DIFFERENCES BETWEEN YOUNG EDUCABLE MENTALLY RETARDED AND NORMAL BOYS AND GIRLS ON TESTS OF MUSCULAR POWER AND GROSS BODY COORDINATION

	MEANS				*MAIN EFFECTS* F *RATIO*		*INTER-ACTIONS* F *RATIO*
Variable	*Young EMR Boys*	*Young EMR Girls*	*Normal Boys*	*Normal Girls*	*Disability*	*Sex*	*Disability by Sex*
Target Throw Horizontal (pts.)	5.85	5.68	6.30	6.40	38.35**	.00	1.92
Target Throw Vertical (pts.)	5.99	6.06	6.36	6.69	35.03**	7.06**	2.37
5–35-Yard Dash (sec.)	5.73	6.23	5.31	5.42	54.70**	11.16**	5.85*
Tire Run (sec.)	10.15	12.12	8.55	8.32	121.18**	9.09**	20.50**
Mat Crawl (sec.)	4.99	5.95	4.17	4.42	118.27**	26.33**	10.96**
Scramble (sec.)	5.75	6.37	5.21	5.31	61.50**	10.14**	6.62*
Vertical Jump (in.)	6.61	5.68	8.65	7.94	99.50**	11.97**	.26
Standing Broad Jump (in.)	44.41	37.98	52.35	50.86	106.84**	12.18**	6.08*
150-Yard Dash (sec.)	32.18	35.83	28.87	29.32	69.96**	9.69**	7.50**
Physical Work Capacity (170) (kpm/min.)	306.70	266.80	347.30	269.20	2.68	20.17**	2.04
Softball Throw (Velocity) (ft./sec.)	41.47	30.47	49.40	35.66	47.57**	163.34**	2.08

**5 percent Level of Significance = 3.84* — *1 and 276 Degrees of Freedom*
***1 percent Level of Significance = 6.63*

to note that where the goal is precision of throwing performance as compared to power, the differences between the retarded and the normal diminish and the sex differences do not necessarily favor boys. It should be kept in mind that on the two accuracy tests, the distances of the throws were short and hence the component of muscular power was reduced to a minimum.

The 30-yard dash (net) and the 150-yard dash were used to assess running performance, the one task placing limited demands on the cardio-respiratory system, the other placing heavier demands on the child's cardio-respiratory functions. Reference to Table 3.4 discloses that the findings on the two were similar. On both tasks the differences were statistically significant, the performance of the normal children being superior to that of the retarded and the performance of the boys being superior to that of the girls. The significant sex by disability interaction clearly demonstrated the relatively low level of performance of the retarded girls as compared to the normal girls.

Five tasks—the tire run, the mat crawl, the scramble, the vertical jump, and the standing broad jump—all require elements of gross body coordination, agility, and muscular power. By the nature of the tasks, the vertical jump and standing broad jump place a premium upon explosive muscular power, whereas the tire run, the mat crawl, and the scramble tap elements of balance and agility. The variance analyses provided similar results in all five tasks (see Table 3.4). The general superiority of the boys over the girls is evidenced by the significant *F* ratios on all five tasks. The performance of the normal children was significantly higher than that of the retarded on all five tasks. With the exception of the vertical jump, there were significant sex by disability interactions which once again indicated the relatively poor performance of the retarded girls as compared to the normal girls.

The variance analysis of the data on the physical work capacity test provided something of a surprise. While the overall sex difference favoring the boys over the girls was as anticipated, the statistically insignificant difference between the performance of the normal and retarded children on this task was not expected. While there was no significant sex by disability interaction, a visual comparison of the means as tabled shows that, on the average, the normal boys performed substantially better than the retarded boys, with little difference between the normal and the retarded girls. This observed difference must be viewed in the light of the insignificant sex by disability interaction.

Fine Visual-Motor Coordination and Balance

The results of the variance analyses of the seven tests of fine visual-motor coordination and the five balance tests are shown in Table 3.5. The results obtained from the data on the Minnesota Manipulative, the Purdue pegboard, ring stacking, and golfball placement tests were highly similar. There were no sex differences in the performance of these tests. There were, however, highly significant differences favoring the normal children over the retarded. There was a significant sex by disability interaction on the Purdue pegboard, ring stacking, and golfball placement tests. As may be noted in Table 3.5, the performance of the retarded girls on these three tasks was inferior to that of the retarded boys, whereas the normal girls performed better than the normal boys.

On the pursuit rotor, the average performance of the boys was superior to that of the girls and the normal children, on the average, performed better than the retarded. The significant sex by disability interaction again focuses attention on the relatively poor performance of the retarded girls. The same picture emerged in the analysis of the data on the two-plate tapping test. In summary, it is evident that on fine visual-motor coordination tasks the retarded children perform well below the level of normal children, this being more particularly true of the retarded girls than of the retarded boys.

The variance analyses of the data obtained on the six balance tests followed much the same pattern as was noted on the tasks requiring fine visual-motor coordination. While performance on the stabilometer showed no significant sex differences, the normal children performed significantly better than the retarded. The significant sex by disability interaction is once

Table 3.5
DIFFERENCES BETWEEN YOUNG EDUCABLE MENTALLY RETARDED AND NORMAL BOYS AND GIRLS ON TESTS OF FINE VISUAL-MOTOR COORDINATION AND BALANCE

	MEANS				*MAIN EFFECTS* F *RATIO*		*INTER-ACTIONS* F *RATIO*
Variable	*Young EMR Boys*	*Young EMR Girls*	*Normal Boys*	*Normal Girls*	*Disability*	*Sex*	*Disability by Sex*
Minnesota Manipulative (sec.)	23.15	23.92	18.88	18.40	96.76**	.01	1.59
Purdue Pegboard Test (no.)	10.33	9.51	13.88	14.63	171.41**	.99	6.09*
Ring Stacking (sec.)	13.97	14.39	11.52	10.85	140.00**	.97	4.68*
Golfball Placement (no.)	8.63	8.11	10.44	10.82	174.35**	.03	7.11**
2-Plate Tapping Test (no.)	22.51	21.70	25.38	28.26	54.62**	4.05*	8.47**
Pursuit Rotor at 40 RPM (sec.)	2.77	1.90	3.44	3.49	40.79**	4.17*	6.90**
Stabilometer (wk. add. unit)	142.90	162.20	122.70	121.90	51.03**	3.41	5.65*
Stork Test (sec.)	17.36	15.59	23.72	28.80	69.05**	3.34	8.55**
Bass Test (sec.)	7.45	6.63	31.21	37.19	12.92**	.24	.20
Railwalk Forward (ft.)	35.61	31.77	46.56	47.58	147.83**	.59	4.90*
Railwalk Backward (ft.)	24.68	17.34	34.30	37.73	114.41**	.76	14.91**
Railwalk Sideways (ft.)	30.39	23.69	35.89	37.36	72.75**	3.62	13.45**

**5 percent Level of Significance = 3.84* *1 and 276 Degrees of Freedom*
***1 percent Level of Significance = 6.63*

again a function of the relatively poor performance of the EMR girls as compared to that of the normal girls. Similar findings were obtained in the analysis of the data for the stork test. On the Bass Test and the three railwalking tests, there were statistically significant differences favoring the normal over the retarded children. However, there were no significant sex differences in the means of these tasks. In all three railwalking tests, there were significant sex by disability interactions, a reflection of the poor performance of the retarded girls as compared to the normal girls.

Age and Sex Differences Between Younger and Older EMR Children on Measures of Motor Performance

In view of what is known about age as a factor positively affecting motor performance in both normal and retarded children, it was anticipated that the differences in the performance measures would consistently favor the older over the younger retardates. In order to test this hypothesis with this population of children, two-way variance analyses were used for each of the motor performance variables. The only physical growth variables included in this analysis were the three skinfold measures.

Measures of Strength and Muscular Endurance

The results of the several variance analyses of the data from the tests of strength and muscular endurance are shown in Table 3.6. As would be expected, the older children were significantly superior to the younger children on these tests. The only exception was the leg raise. Sex differences in performance, however, were not consistent. On three of the six strength tests and three of the measures of muscular endurance, the differences were not statistically significant. Where significant differences were found, they favored the boys.

Table 3.6

AGE AND SEX DIFFERENCES IN EDUCABLE MENTALLY RETARDED CHILDREN ON TESTS OF STRENGTH AND MUSCULAR ENDURANCE

	MEANS				*MAIN EFFECTS* F *RATIO*		*INTER-ACTIONS* F *RATIO*
Variable	*Young EMR Boys*	*Young EMR Girls*	*Older EMR Boys*	*Older EMR Girls*	*Sex*	*Age*	*Sex by Age*
Knee Flexion (ft-lb.)	23.34	19.35	36.94	33.56	5.90*	90.29**	.04
Knee Extension (ft-lb.)	25.12	23.25	44.43	45.90	.01	125.97**	.80
Elbow Flexion (ft-lb.)	6.19	6.09	10.01	9.33	.43	44.33**	.29
Elbow Extension (ft-lb.)	9.72	9.09	15.23	15.27	.07	40.72**	.14
Grip Strength Right (kg)	14.86	12.73	20.89	19.27	7.78**	92.36**	.16
Grip Strength Left (kg)	14.25	12.12	20.32	17.80	12.48**	84.62**	.09
Trunk Raise (sec.)	40.37	35.34	52.92	52.07	.47	12.20**	.25
Leg Raise (sec.)	24.87	26.88	21.49	25.64	1.40	.85	.17
Bicycle With Resistance (rev.)	10.51	8.75	13.41	12.83	6.27*	55.92**	1.61
Bicycle Without Resistance (rev.)	17.10	14.42	20.35	16.85	49.56**	43.37**	.90
Bicycle Ergometer Total (rev.)	82.49	68.37	96.03	101.40	2.41	63.58**	11.53**
Sit-ups (no. per min.)	16.76	11.72	21.86	17.13	21.88**	25.78**	.02

**5 percent Level of Significance = 3.84*
***1 percent Level of Significance = 6.63*

1 and 257 Degrees of Freedom

Measures of Muscular Power and Gross Motor Coordination

Table 3.7 summarizes the results of the several variance analyses on the measures of muscular power and gross body coordination. Highly significant age differences were found on all tests except the mat crawl and

Table 3.7

AGE AND SEX DIFFERENCES IN EDUCABLE MENTALLY RETARDED CHILDREN ON TESTS OF MUSCULAR POWER AND GROSS BODY COORDINATION

	MEANS				*MAIN EFFECTS* F *RATIO*		*INTER-ACTIONS* F *RATIO*
Variable	*Young EMR Boys*	*Young EMR Girls*	*Older EMR Boys*	*Older EMR Girls*	*Sex*	*Age*	*Sex by Age*
Target Throw Horizontal (pts.)	5.85	5.68	5.38	5.13	3.91*	23.40**	.16
Target Throw Vertical (pts.)	5.99	6.06	5.36	5.46	.60	39.57**	.01
5–35-Yard Dash (sec.)	5.73	6.23	5.19	5.57	22.61**	41.32**	.41
Tire Run (sec.)	10.15	12.12	9.11	9.85	18.74**	26.72**	3.84*
Mat Crawl (sec.)	4.99	5.95	4.81	5.65	43.76**	2.98	.20
Scramble (sec.)	5.75	6.37	5.71	6.26	20.53**	.32	.05
Vertical Jump (in.)	6.61	5.68	8.09	7.43	8.03**	33.75**	.25
Standing Broad Jump (in.)	44.41	37.98	50.64	46.30	17.40**	31.84**	.67
150-Yard Dash (sec.)	32.18	35.83	28.68	30.95	18.33**	36.68**	1.01
Physical Work Capacity (170) (kpm/min.)	306.70	266.80	458.30	368.60	17.17**	71.35**	2.72
Softball Throw (Velocity) (ft./sec.)	41.47	30.47	47.41	37.07	82.61**	28.75**	.08

**5 percent Level of Significance = 3.84* *1 and 257 Degrees of Freedom*
***1 percent Level of Significance = 6.63*

the scramble. These tasks, by their very nature, are perhaps more appropriate both psychologically and physically for younger than for more mature children, thus countering the greater strength and presumably greater muscle coordination of the older children. On all but one of the tasks, the boys were significantly better than the girls. The greatest sex difference in performance was in the softball throw for velocity, the relative magnitude of this difference being similar to what is seen in normal boys and girls.

Measures of Fine Visual-Motor Coordination and Balance

A summary of the results of the several variance analyses on the measures of fine visual-motor coordination and balance is given in Table 3.8. On the fine visual-motor tests, the older children performed significantly better than the younger ones. No significant sex differences were observed on these test items. The differences between the younger and the older children on the balance tests, while for the most part favoring the older children, were not as dramatic as for the fine visual-motor tasks. This might suggest that in the age range of these subjects, age carries with it factors such as maturity or experience which appear to account for relatively greater

Table 3.8

AGE AND SEX DIFFERENCES IN EDUCABLE MENTALLY RETARDED CHILDREN ON TESTS OF FINE VISUAL-MOTOR COORDINATION AND BALANCE

	MEANS				*MAIN EFFECTS F RATIO*		*INTER-ACTIONS F RATIO*
Variable	*Young EMR Boys*	*Young EMR Girls*	*Older EMR Boys*	*Older EMR Girls*	*Sex*	*Age*	*Sex by Age*
Minnesota Manipulative (sec.)	23.15	23.92	19.82	19.33	.04	47.75**	1.23
Purdue Pegboard Test (no.)	10.33	9.51	12.08	11.97	1.50	31.07**	.87
Ring Stacking (sec.)	13.97	14.39	12.19	11.88	.03	49.48**	1.45
Golfball Placement (no.)	8.63	8.11	9.98	10.00	1.50	66.53**	1.96
2-Plate Tapping Test (no.)	22.51	21.70	27.73	29.95	1.03	88.41**	4.54**
Pursuit Rotor at 40 RPM (sec.)	2.77	1.90	3.79	3.78	3.78	39.49**	3.62
Stabilometer (wk. add. unit)	142.90	162.20	150.80	170.40	12.17**	2.05	.00
Stork Test (sec.)	17.36	15.59	20.52	18.93	1.82	7.12**	.01
Bass Test (sec.)	7.45	6.63	12.73	9.34	2.01	8.03**	.81
Railwalk Forward (ft.)	35.61	31.77	38.42	36.30	3.81	5.70*	.32
Railwalk Backward (ft.)	24.68	17.34	26.20	23.43	10.84**	5.75*	2.17
Railwalk Sideways (ft.)	30.39	23.69	29.72	28.28	9.29**	1.85	3.74

**5 percent Level of Significance = 3.84* *1 and 257 Degrees of Freedom*
***1 percent Level of Significance = 6.63*

Table 3.9

AGE AND SEX DIFFERENCES IN EDUCABLE MENTALLY RETARDED CHILDREN ON MEASURES OF FLEXIBILITY AND SKINFOLD THICKNESS

	MEANS				*MAIN EFFECTS F RATIO*		*INTER-ACTIONS F RATIO*
Variable	*Young EMR Boys*	*Young EMR Girls*	*Older EMR Boys*	*Older EMR Girls*	*Sex*	*Age*	*Sex by Age*
Triceps Skinfold (mm)	10.60	13.91	10.79	14.44	18.41**	.19	.05
Abdominal Skinfold (mm)	8.33	12.12	13.49	15.38	6.74**	14.31**	.72
Subscapular Skinfold (mm)	6.71	8.66	9.58	12.19	8.86**	17.02**	.18
Spinal Rotation (deg.)	125.00	119.00	128.00	118.80	7.38**	.29	.33
Spinal Extension (deg.)	46.45	42.80	43.90	42.91	7.00**	2.03	2.20
Lateral Spinal Extension (deg.)	58.97	55.04	57.55	55.83	10.37**	.16	1.54
Toe Touch (cm)	16.91	15.27	15.80	16.73	.23	.02	2.34

***1 percent Level of Significance = 6.63* *1 and 257 Degrees of Freedom*

differences in fine visual-motor coordination than in the mechanisms that control body balance.

Measures of Flexibility and Skinfold Thickness

Age differences in the four measures of flexibility were not found (see Table 3.9). Sex differences, however, were noted in three of the four flexibility tests, the boys at both ages showing greater flexibility than the girls. Highly significant sex differences in body fat, as assessed by the three skinfold measurements, were found, the girls consistently having the greater skinfold measurements. Both abdominal and subscapular skinfolds were significantly greater in the older than the younger children. The observed differences in subcutaneous tissue are in agreement with other studies on normal and mentally retarded boys and girls (Lombard, 1950; Rarick et al., 1966).

Magnitude of Retardation of EMR Children Expressed in Standard Deviation Units

In order to bring into focus the relative magnitude of the differences in physical growth and motor performance between the retarded and the normal children, the differences by sex between the means of the young EMR children and the normal children on each variable have been expressed in standard deviation units. This score represents the number of standard deviations, or fractional parts thereof, that the mean score of the retarded on a particular variable differs from the mean score of the normal children of the same sex on that variable.

Measures of Physical Growth

The magnitude of the differences within sex between the respective means of the EMR children and the normal children is shown in Figure 3.1. In height and weight the differences are not great, the retarded of both sexes being somewhat shorter in height than the normal children, but of almost the same weight. In skinfold thickness, on the other hand, the retarded girls ranged from .79 to 2.17 standard deviation units above the mean of the normal girls, the retarded boys from 1.01 to 2.12 standard deviation units greater than the normal boys. The relatively greater bi-iliac diameter of the retarded boys and girls is also indicative of substantial fat deposits in the hips. These data clearly point up a strong tendency toward obesity in this population of EMR boys and girls.

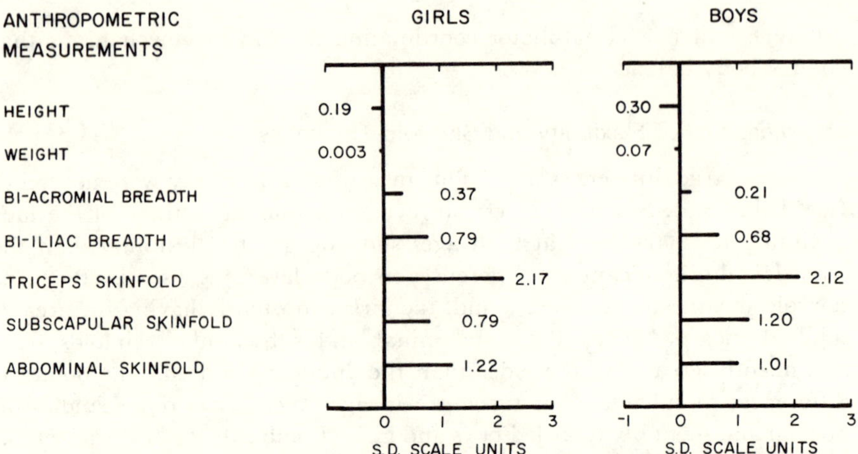

Fig. 3.1 Differences expressed in S.D. Scale Units between young EMR and normal children on anthropometric measurements (zero = mean values of normal boys and girls)

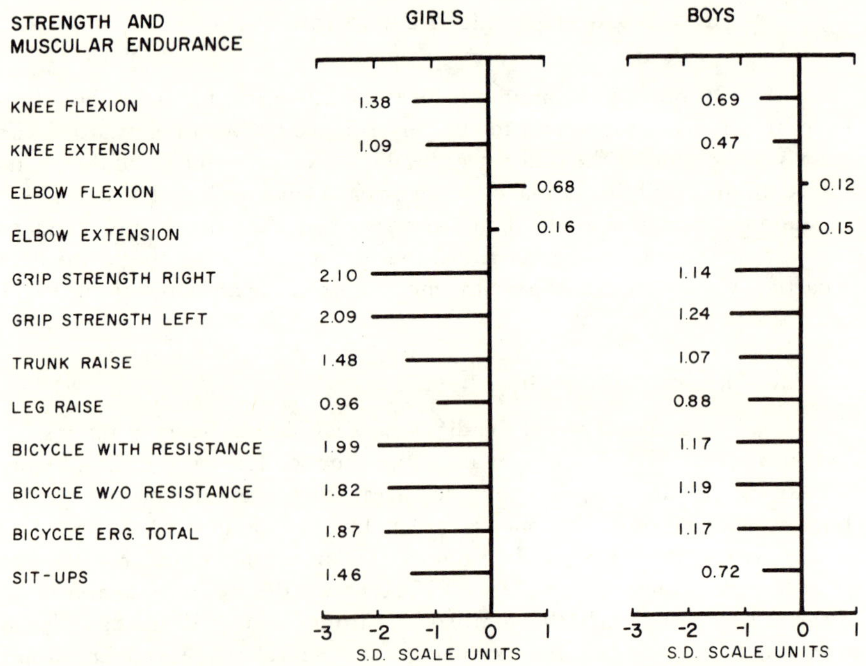

Fig. 3.2 Differences expressed in S.D. Scale Units between young EMR and normal children on tests of strength and muscular endurance (zero = mean values of normal boys and girls)

Strength and Muscular Endurance

The differences between the retarded and the normal children on the 12 measures of strength and muscular endurance are shown in Figure 3.2. On two measures, elbow flexion and elbow extension, the retarded boys and girls were slightly superior to their normal counterparts. On all other measures the performance of the retarded children was decidedly inferior, the performance of the retarded girls being relatively poorer than that of the retarded boys.

Muscular Power and Coordination

On all but one of the tests of power and gross body coordination, the performance of the retarded children was markedly poorer than that of the normal children (see Figure 3.3). Only on the test of physical work capacity did the retardates compare favorably with the normal children. The performance of the retarded girls was relatively poorer than that of the retarded boys on all of the measures other than the PWC_{170}. This difference is further illustrated by the observation that on 7 of the 11 measures, the retarded girls were, on the average, more than 1.5 standard deviation units below the means

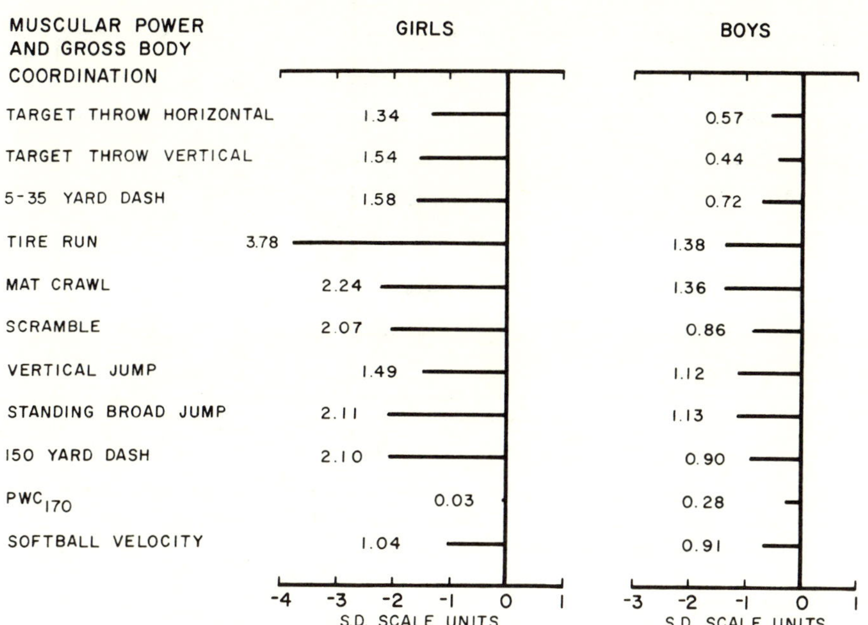

Fig. 3.3 Differences expressed in S.D. Scale Units between young EMR and normal children on tests of muscular power and gross body coordination (zero = mean values of normal boys and girls)

of their normal counterparts, whereas the retarded boys had no measure in which the mean was more than 1.38 standard deviation units below that of the normal boys.

Fine Visual-Motor Coordination and Balance

The magnitude of the retardation of the EMR boys and girls on the measures of fine visual-motor coordination and balance is shown in Figure 3.4. Again, the retarded girls show relatively poorer performances than do the retarded boys. On all but one of the tests, the retarded girls were, on the average, more than 1 standard deviation unit below the means of the normal girls, whereas on a comparable basis this was true with the retarded boys on only 5 of the 12 tests.

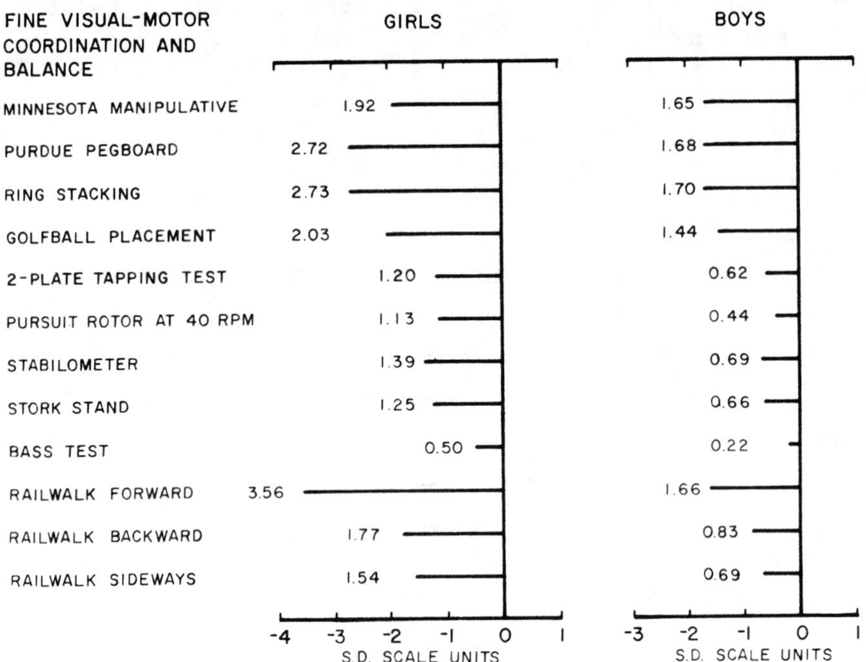

Fig. 3.4 Differences expressed in S.D. Scale Units between young EMR and normal children on tests of fine visual-motor coordination and balance (zero = mean values of normal boys and girls)

Flexibility

Figure 3.5 shows the magnitude of the differences between the retarded and the normal children on the measures of flexibility. The retarded children were consistently below the mean values of the normal children of

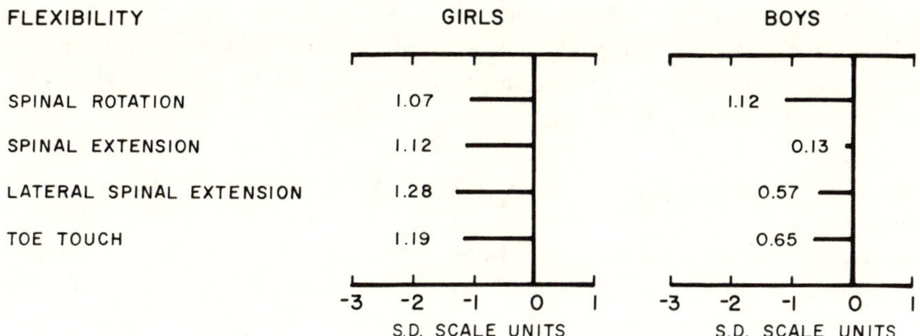

Fig. 3.5 Differences expressed in S.D. Scale Units between young EMR and normal children on measures of flexibility (zero = mean values of normal boys and girls)

the same sex, the retarded girls having relatively poorer average performances than the retarded boys. On all four measures, the retarded girls were, on the average, more than 1 standard deviation unit below the means of the normal girls.

Summary Comments

The magnitude of the differences between the retarded and the normal girls in the motor domain is indicated by the fact that on 34 of the 39 motor tests, the mean scores of the retarded girls were more than 1 standard deviation below the test means of the normal girls. On 9 of the 39 tasks, the mean scores of the retarded girls were more than 2 standard deviations below the means of the normal girls, and on two of the tasks they were more than 3.5 standard deviations below the normal girls' means. The magnitude of the retardation of the girls was particularly great on the measures of fine motor control, grip strength, and the gross motor coordination tasks that require considerable muscular power. In isokinetic arm strength, the young retarded girls were from .15 to .68 standard deviation units above the mean of the normal girls.

The deficit in motor performance of the retarded girls is reflected in the fact that the average of the standard deviation units for the 39 motor tasks placed them 1.56 standard deviations below the mean of the normal girls. Thus, the average of their performance on these 39 motor tasks was exceeded by 94 percent of the normal girls. On the other hand, the retarded girls were, on the average, .73 of a standard deviation above the mean of the normal girls on the seven anthropometric measures, largely a reflection of skinfold thickness.

The magnitude of the overall motor deficit of the young retarded boys, while substantial, was not as great as that of the young EMR girls. In no case was the mean of the young retarded boys as much as 2 standard deviations below the mean of the normal boys, and in only 16 of the 39 motor performance tests were the means of the retarded boys more than 1 standard deviation below those of the normal boys. In general, the magnitude of the retardation was relatively small in the isokinetic strength tests (in two of these, no retardation) and relatively large in the tests of fine visual-motor control.

The overall mean of the young EMR boys on the 39 tests was .91 standard deviations below the mean of the normal boys. Thus, their performance was, on the average, exceeded by approximately 84 percent of the normal boys. On all anthropometric measures except height and weight, the means of the young EMR boys ranged from .21 to 2.12 standard deviation units above the means of the normal boys. The average of the seven anthropometric measures placed the young retarded boys .69 of a standard deviation above the mean of the normal boys. In the case of the retarded boys, this value was largely a reflection of the skinfold measurements which ranged from 1.01 to 2.12 standard deviation units above the mean of the normal boys.

The disadvantage that these EMR children face in attempting to function motorically is indeed great. While their intellectual performance, as measured by I.Q. tests, can be expected to be exceeded by approximately 98 percent of normal children, the motor deficit is nevertheless sizable. The reason for the apparently greater retardation in the motor performance of the retarded girls as compared to the retarded boys is only conjecture at this time. It might be that more boys than girls are placed in classes for the retarded because of behavioral probems or learning difficulties, rather than for clear-cut evidence of mental retardation. On the other hand, it may be that retarded boys find motor pursuits to be more satisfying than retarded girls do, and as a result the boys devote more of their time and energy to this end.

Frequency and Percentage of EMR Children with Scores Equal to or Above Selected Percentile Scores of Normal Subjects

Comparisons of means and standard deviations of test results of different groups of subjects may occasionally give a distorted picture of the similarities or differences among these groups. It has already been shown that the differences between normal and retarded subjects of similar chronological age on tests of strength and motor coordination were, in almost all instances, statistically significant. However, one might ask if the performance of retarded children is invariably low, or if some of these children might be well above the average or even at the level of the best performance of normal children. If such were the case, it would indicate that superior motor performance is within the reach of some EMR children. To ascertain this, the investigators determined the number and percentage of young EMR boys and young EMR girls who had scores on the respective growth and motor performance variables equal to, or above, selected percentile values of normal children of the same sex.

Table 3.10 shows the number and percentage of young EMR boys with physical growth and motor performance scores at or above the 5th, 25th, 75th, and 95th percentiles of normal boys. If the frequency distribution of the scores of the 71 retarded boys followed the expected frequencies, then one would expect 68 cases to be above the 5th percentile, 53 cases to be above the 25th percentile, 35 cases to be above the 50th percentile, 18 cases to be above the 75th percentile, and 3 cases to be above the 95th percentile. It is clear from a quick survey of Table 3.10 that on all performance measures except one (elbow flexion strength), far less than 50 percent of the retarded boys were at or above the 50th percentile of the normal boys. On measures of skinfold thickness, well over 80 percent were above the median of the normal boys. In fact, on these measures, from 14 percent to 16.9 percent were above the 95th percentile of the normal boys. On 18 of the 39 measures of motor performance, one or more retarded boys scored at or above the 95th percentile of the normal subjects; and there were only three of the performance tests in which one or more retarded boys did not achieve the 75th percentile of the normal boys. While it is true that the proportion of retarded subjects failing to reach even the middle percentile values of the normal subjects was relatively low, the findings suggest that the higher performance levels of the normal boys are not out of reach of educable mentally retarded boys.

Table 3.11 presents similar data on the sample of young EMR girls. Other than for the measures of skinfold thickness and bi-iliac breadth, the percentage of the young retarded girls achieving performance levels equal to or above the median of the normal girls was low. In fact, none of the retarded girls reached the median of the normal girls on the vertical jump or the Purdue pegboard test. On the other hand, the 95th percentile of the normal girls was achieved by one or more retarded girls on 21 of the 39 tests of motor performance, and the 75th percentile was achieved by one or more on 32 of the 39 tests. As in the case of the retarded boys, this suggests that the upper levels of performance of normal children are not necessarily out of reach of the retarded.

Table 3.10

NUMBER AND PERCENT OF YOUNG EDUCABLE MENTALLY RETARDED BOYS WITH SCORES EQUAL TO, OR HIGHER THAN, SELECTED PERCENTILE VALUES OF NORMAL BOYS

Variable	*5th Percentile No.*	*%*	*25th Percentile No.*	*%*	*50th Percentile No.*	*%*	*75th Percentile No.*	*%*	*95th Percentile No.*	*%*
35-Yard Dash (5–35)	(62)	87.4	(43)	60.2	(18)	25.0	(6)	8.4	(0)	0
150-Yard Dash	(60)	84.5	(39)	54.9	(14)	19.7	(7)	9.9	(1)	1.4
Tire Run	(45)	63.4	(21)	29.6	(12)	16.9	(11)	15.4	(1)	1.4
Target Throw Horizontal	(64)	90.1	(29)	40.8	(11)	15.5	(6)	8.5	(3)	4.2
Target Throw Vertical	(69)	97.1	(39)	54.9	(11)	15.5	(7)	9.9	(1)	1.4
Softball Throw	(50)	70.4	(35)	49.3	(11)	15.5	(7)	9.9	(1)	1.4
Vertical Jump	(37)	52.0	(27)	38.0	(14)	19.7	(4)	5.6	(0)	0
Standing Broad Jump	(49)	69.0	(31)	43.7	(10)	14.1	(3)	4.2	(1)	1.4
Mat Crawl	(48)	67.6	(22)	31.0	(12)	16.9	(2)	2.8	(0)	0
Scramble	(51)	71.8	(37)	52.1	(18)	25.4	(8)	11.3	(3)	4.2
Cybex Knee Flexion	(58)	81.7	(34)	47.9	(15)	21.1	(11)	15.5	(0)	0
Cybex Knee Extension	(63)	88.7	(47)	66.2	(19)	26.8	(8)	11.3	(0)	0
Cybex Elbow Flexion	(70)	98.6	(60)	84.5	(46)	64.8	(19)	26.8	(3)	4.2
Cybex Elbow Extension	(69)	97.1	(59)	83.1	(32)	45.0	(24)	33.8	(5)	7.0
Grip Strength Right	(60)	84.5	(22)	31.0	(8)	11.3	(3)	4.2	(0)	0
Grip Strength Left	(51)	71.8	(19)	26.8	(5)	7.0	(1)	1.4	(0)	0
Triceps Skinfold	(70)	98.6	(66)	93.0	(63)	88.7	(58)	81.7	(18)	25.4
Subscapular Skinfold	(70)	98.6	(65)	91.5	(62)	87.3	(50)	70.4	(12)	16.9
Abdominal Skinfold	(71)	100.0	(70)	98.6	(57)	80.3	(44)	62.0	(10)	14.0
Bi-Acromial Breadth	(64)	90.1	(53)	74.6	(37)	52.1	(20)	28.0	(11)	15.5
Bi-Iliac Breadth	(64)	90.1	(51)	71.8	(41)	57.7	(37)	52.1	(20)	28.0
Height	(68)	95.8	(43)	60.6	(26)	36.6	(9)	12.7	(1)	1.4
Weight	(70)	98.6	(49)	69.0	(38)	53.5	(13)	18.3	(3)	4.2
Bicycle With Resistance	(46)	64.8	(23)	32.4	(10)	14.1	(4)	5.6	(0)	0
Bicycle Without Resistance	(59)	83.1	(23)	32.4	(8)	11.3	(1)	1.4	(0)	0
Bicycle Ergometer Total	(53)	74.6	(13)	18.3	(5)	7.0	(0)	0	(0)	0
Sit-ups	(69)	97.2	(27)	38.0	(14)	19.7	(6)	8.5	(2)	2.8
Trunk Raise	(46)	64.8	(19)	26.8	(8)	11.3	(2)	2.8	(0)	0
Leg Raise	(55)	77.5	(22)	31.0	(0)	0	(0)	0	(0)	0
Pursuit Rotor at 40 RPM	(55)	77.5	(43)	60.6	(20)	28.0	(14)	19.7	(3)	4.2
Purdue Pegboard Test	(33)	46.5	(15)	21.1	(1)	1.4	(0)	0	(0)	0
Minnesota Manipulative	(46)	64.8	(27)	38.0	(10)	14.1	(3)	4.2	(0)	0
Ring Stacking	(43)	60.6	(27)	38.0	(14)	19.7	(3)	4.2	(0)	0
Golfball Placement	(43)	60.6	(28)	39.4	(9)	12.7	(2)	2.8	(0)	0
2-Plate Tapping Test	(53)	74.6	(38)	53.5	(28)	39.4	(7)	9.9	(5)	7.0
Bass Test	(41)	57.7	(16)	22.5	(9)	12.7	(6)	8.5	(0)	0
Stabilometer	(61)	85.9	(39)	54.9	(18)	25.4	(9)	12.7	(1)	1.4
Stork Test	(53)	74.6	(31)	43.7	(16)	22.5	(7)	9.9	(3)	4.2
Railwalk Forward	(49)	69.0	(16)	22.5	(12)	16.9	(12)	16.9	(12)	16.9
Railwalk Backward	(53)	74.6	(29)	40.8	(17)	23.9	(9)	12.7	(4)	5.0
Railwalk Sideways	(60)	84.5	(33)	46.5	(25)	35.2	(11)	15.5	(6)	8.5
Toe Touch	(52)	73.2	(38)	53.5	(24)	33.8	(8)	11.3	(0)	0
Spinal Extension	(64)	90.1	(50)	70.4	(31)	43.6	(15)	21.1	(1)	1.4
Spinal Rotation	(48)	67.6	(28)	39.4	(11)	15.5	(4)	5.6	(0)	0
Lateral Spinal Extension	(66)	92.0	(31)	43.7	(19)	26.8	(3)	4.2	(0)	0
Physical Work Capacity	(67)	94.4	(53)	74.6	(28)	39.4	(10)	14.1	(0)	0
Chronological Age	(68)	95.8	(61)	85.9	(39)	54.9	(22)	31.0	(0)	0

Table 3.11

NUMBER AND PERCENT OF YOUNG EDUCABLE MENTALLY RETARDED GIRLS WITH SCORES EQUAL TO, OR HIGHER THAN, SELECTED PERCENTILE VALUES OF NORMAL GIRLS

Variable	*5th Percentile No.*	*%*	*25th Percentile No.*	*%*	*50th Percentile No.*	*%*	*75th Percentile No.*	*%*	*95th Percentile No.*	*%*
35-Yard Dash (5–35)	(44)	68.7	(24)	37.5	(10)	15.6	(2)	3.1	(1)	1.6
150-Yard Dash	(31)	48.4	(17)	26.6	(5)	7.8	(0)	0	(0)	0
Tire Run	(13)	20.3	(9)	14.1	(1)	1.6	(1)	1.6	(1)	1.6
Target Throw Horizontal	(42)	65.6	(25)	39.1	(14)	21.9	(6)	9.4	(2)	3.1
Target Throw Vertical	(42)	65.6	(26)	40.6	(13)	20.3	(5)	7.8	(1)	1.6
Softball Throw	(48)	75.0	(23)	35.9	(10)	15.6	(7)	10.9	(4)	6.3
Vertical Jump	(35)	54.7	(18)	28.1	(0)	0	(0)	0	(0)	0
Standing Broad Jump	(30)	46.9	(17)	26.6	(5)	7.8	(1)	1.6	(1)	1.6
Mat Crawl	(27)	42.2	(12)	18.8	(2)	3.1	(1)	1.6	(0)	0
Scramble	(32)	50.0	(15)	23.4	(9)	14.1	(4)	6.3	(2)	3.1
Cybex Knee Flexion	(37)	57.8	(15)	23.4	(13)	20.3	(5)	7.8	(1)	1.6
Cybex Knee Extension	(42)	65.6	(17)	26.6	(12)	18.8	(3)	4.7	(0)	0
Cybex Elbow Flexion	(59)	92.2	(45)	70.3	(36)	56.3	(32)	50.0	(7)	10.9
Cybex Elbow Extension	(58)	90.6	(52)	81.3	(36)	56.3	(20)	31.3	(6)	9.4
Grip Strength Right	(26)	40.6	(9)	14.1	(4)	6.3	(4)	6.3	(1)	1.6
Grip Strength Left	(21)	32.8	(13)	20.3	(5)	7.8	(3)	4.7	(0)	0
Triceps Skinfold	(62)	96.8	(61)	95.3	(59)	92.2	(43)	67.2	(33)	51.6
Subscapular Skinfold	(64)	100.0	(59)	92.2	(42)	65.6	(33)	51.6	(16)	25.0
Abdominal Skinfold	(64)	100.0	(59)	92.2	(50)	78.2	(38)	59.4	(18)	28.1
Bi-Acromial Breadth	(61)	95.3	(50)	78.1	(30)	46.9	(21)	32.8	(9)	14.1
Bi-Iliac Breadth	(59)	92.2	(54)	84.4	(46)	71.8	(27)	42.2	(14)	21.9
Height	(54)	84.4	(42)	65.6	(23)	35.9	(11)	17.2	(5)	7.8
Weight	(56)	87.5	(43)	67.2	(31)	48.4	(19)	29.7	(7)	10.9
Bicycle With Resistance	(26)	40.6	(10)	15.6	(5)	7.8	(2)	3.1	(0)	0
Bicycle Without Resistance	(35)	54.7	(15)	23.4	(5)	7.8	(2)	3.1	(1)	1.6
Bicycle Ergometer Total	(32)	50.0	(11)	17.2	(1)	1.6	(1)	1.6	(0)	0
Sit-ups	(37)	57.8	(17)	26.6	(11)	17.2	(2)	3.1	(0)	0
Trunk Raise	(32)	50.0	(7)	10.9	(2)	3.1	(0)	0	(0)	0
Leg Raise	(34)	53.1	(15)	23.4	(8)	12.5	(4)	6.3	(1)	1.6
Pursuit Rotor at 40 RPM	(37)	57.8	(18)	28.1	(10)	15.6	(4)	6.3	(1)	1.6
Purdue Pegboard Test	(14)	21.9	(7)	10.9	(0)	0	(0)	0	(0)	0
Minnesota Manipulative	(32)	50.0	(19)	29.7	(5)	7.8	(3)	4.7	(0)	0
Ring Stacking	(21)	32.8	(12)	18.7	(3)	4.7	(1)	1.6	(0)	0
2-Plate Tapping Test	(36)	56.3	(19)	29.7	(11)	17.2	(3)	3.1	(0)	0
Golfball Placement	(22)	34.4	(13)	20.3	(5)	7.8	(1)	1.6	(0)	0
Bass Test	(26)	40.6	(6)	9.4	(3)	4.7	(1)	1.6	(0)	0
Stabilometer	(40)	62.5	(23)	35.9	(11)	17.2	(5)	7.8	(1)	1.6
Stork Test	(35)	54.7	(16)	25.0	(7)	10.9	(0)	0	(0)	0
Railwalk Forward	(18)	28.9	(13)	20.3	(2)	3.1	(2)	3.1	(2)	3.1
Railwalk Backward	(38)	59.4	(7)	10.9	(1)	1.6	(1)	1.6	(1)	1.6
Railwalk Sideways	(36)	56.2	(15)	23.4	(4)	6.3	(3)	4.7	(1)	1.6
Toe Touch	(44)	68.7	(17)	26.6	(5)	7.8	(0)	0	(0)	0
Spinal Extension	(42)	65.6	(19)	29.7	(12)	18.8	(1)	1.6	(0)	0
Spinal Rotation	(44)	68.7	(23)	35.9	(9)	14.1	(3)	4.7	(0)	0
Lateral Spinal Extension	(46)	71.9	(13)	20.3	(7)	10.9	(0)	0	(0)	0
Physical Work Capacity	(61)	95.3	(44)	68.7	(23)	35.9	(13)	20.3	(10)	15.6
Chronological Age	(59)	92.2	(46)	71.8	(32)	50.0	(12)	18.8	(1)	1.6

While it is evident that a few retarded girls demonstrated high levels of motor performance on a sizable number of motor tasks, the percentage reaching the lower percentile values was low. For example, only 20 percent achieved the 5th percentile on the tire run, and only 29 percent on the railwalk forward. Of the motor performance variables, only on the Cybex strength tests were frequency distributions of the retarded girls comparable to those of the normal girls.

The findings suggest that factors other than intelligence are in no small measure responsible for the poor motor performance of educable mentally retarded children. The fact that on most of the motor performance tests several of the retarded boys and girls achieved the 75th percentile of the normal children indicates that factors other than mental retardation per se may be at work.

Variability in Physical Growth and Motor Performance

The range of individual differences in measures of physical growth and motor performance of mentally retarded children has received only limited attention, yet this is a factor of considerable significance in planning the learning experiences of these children. To provide comparable data on the variability of normal and educable retarded children in the physical growth and motor domains, the coefficient of variation was employed. Table 3.12 shows the coefficients of variation of the physical growth and motor performance variables included in the investigation.

With the exception of a few measures, such as height and spinal flexibility, the retarded boys and girls were much more variable than the normal children. In weight and skinfold measures, the retardates showed approximately 50 percent greater variability than the normal children of equivalent chronological age. While this is primarily a reflection of the tendency for a large number of retarded children to be overweight, nevertheless some were substantially underweight for their height.

The marked variability in motor performance of the retarded is seen primarily in the railwalking tests and in the tests of fine visual-motor coordination. In tests of muscular power and muscular endurance, the variability was from 25 percent to 50 percent greater than in the normal children. What this means, as has been previously pointed out, is that some of the retarded performed well within the normal range, but the number and range of poor scores were considerably greater among the retarded than among the normal children.

Table 3.12

COEFFICIENTS OF VARIATION OF THE 47 PHYSICAL GROWTH AND MOTOR PERFORMANCE VARIABLES OF THE TWO GROUPS OF NORMAL CHILDREN AND FOUR GROUPS OF EDUCABLE MENTALLY RETARDED CHILDREN

Variable	*Normal Boys*	*Normal Girls*	*Young EMR Boys*	*Young EMR Girls*	*Older EMR Boys*	*Older EMR Girls*
35-Yard Dash (5–35)	10.70	9.46	12.22	14.64	11.53	12.97
150-Yard Dash	12.65	10.54	17.24	18.24	15.26	17.30
Tire Run	13.52	12.09	21.27	26.15	23.67	25.33
Target Throw Horizontal	12.65	8.37	12.79	17.73	13.81	16.63
Target Throw Vertical	13.27	6.08	11.48	13.03	14.48	16.37
Softball Throw	17.58	13.99	23.57	24.46	22.67	24.36
Vertical Jump	21.09	19.03	28.62	13.81	31.99	32.68
Standing Broad Jump	15.12	11.98	20.88	25.62	21.66	24.00
Mat Crawl	14.39	15.40	15.83	22.77	17.52	22.80
Scramble	11.92	9.56	16.93	17.76	18.55	15.85
Cybex Knee Flexion	29.71	23.68	36.70	44.13	38.52	43.09
Cybex Knee Extension	40.99	31.92	36.05	43.14	41.64	42.90
Cybex Elbow Flexion	37.75	26.34	27.72	74.50	60.81	39.03
Cybex Elbow Extension	28.97	27.77	30.98	34.78	60.58	70.99
Grip Strength Right	19.21	13.81	22.16	28.73	30.13	35.79
Grip Strength Left	19.09	13.85	21.20	29.22	33.27	35.45
Triceps Skinfold	36.31	42.29	46.22	56.56	53.57	49.62
Subscapular Skinfold	43.05	55.00	79.51	61.62	73.70	56.74
Abdominal Skinfold	67.54	59.13	81.29	62.74	86.29	60.75
Bi-Acromial Breadth	6.14	6.08	9.47	8.65	10.71	10.93
Bi-Iliac Breadth	5.88	7.80	12.06	13.28	12.55	14.35
Height	6.58	6.62	5.87	6.56	7.20	7.46
Weight	19.03	18.44	19.91	25.24	27.44	27.48
Bicycle With Resistance	24.00	19.20	33.95	41.77	27.43	30.81
Bicycle Without Resistance	14.17	13.86	17.46	26.66	16.47	21.86
Bicycle Ergometer Total	21.56	18.17	21.93	33.87	24.30	26.79
Sit-ups	35.75	30.59	46.74	63.81	39.10	54.01
Trunk Raise	49.17	42.49	74.36	77.05	76.34	66.55
Leg Raise	67.69	57.03	58.02	100.26	83.20	82.06
Pursuit Rotor at 40 RPM	43.60	40.12	57.76	67.90	60.42	52.65
Purdue Pegboard Test	15.20	12.85	19.17	25.24	39.40	16.37
Minnesota Manipulative	13.68	15.64	23.42	20.74	18.54	19.67
Ring Stacking	12.48	11.94	19.27	18.23	18.20	17.31
Golfball Placement	11.97	12.33	17.37	19.38	16.79	15.79
2-Plate Tapping Test	18.20	19.39	24.35	24.98	20.45	20.63
Bass Test	343.80	162.76	94.39	90.86	148.70	97.26
Stabilometer	23.54	23.71	25.88	27.05	28.77	31.88
Stork Test	40.24	36.77	56.01	56.14	55.41	46.83
Railwalk Forward	14.14	9.34	32.43	37.74	32.69	35.01
Railwalk Backward	33.70	30.48	51.50	59.05	52.37	53.65
Railwalk Sideways	22.27	23.82	32.97	42.38	36.74	44.38
Toe Touch	26.95	25.41	36.10	41.34	46.47	41.82
Spinal Extension	15.84	14.14	14.15	16.29	18.42	16.08
Spinal Rotation	12.17	14.62	16.15	19.45	17.79	19.01
Lateral Spinal Extension	12.74	12.09	10.54	13.13	14.02	12.37
Physical Work Capacity	41.17	29.28	29.62	40.33	35.24	31.23
Chronological Age	13.50	13.15	11.71	14.13	8.05	9.45

Table 3.13

CORRELATION COEFFICIENTS OF I.Q.'s WITH THE TEST SCORES FOR EDUCABLE MENTALLY RETARDED BOYS AND GIRLS

Variable	*Young EMR Boys*	*Young EMR Girls*	*Older EMR Boys*	*Older EMR Girls*
35-Yard Dash (5–35)*	−.30	−.17	−.19	−.16
150-Yard Dash*	−.36	−.10	−.31	−.22
Tire Run*	−.26	−.24	−.42	−.29
Target Throw Horizontal	.40	.11	.23	.25
Target Throw Vertical	.38	.04	.23	.16
Softball Throw	.46	.26	.54	.22
Vertical Jump	.41	.36	.36	.11
Standing Broad Jump	.26	.31	.32	.23
Mat Crawl*	−.27	−.14	−.33	−.22
Scramble*	−.18	.14	−.16	−.21
Cybex Knee Flexion	.40	.25	.51	.03
Cybex Knee Extension	.41	.15	.33	.04
Cybex Elbow Flexion	.18	−.01	.40	−.01
Cybex Elbow Extension	.30	.07	.31	.11
Grip Strength Right	.40	.14	.24	.06
Grip Strength Left	.40	.14	.17	.07
Bicycle With Resistance	.52	.05	.36	.18
Bicycle Without Resistance	.47	.19	.56	.16
Bicycle Ergometer Total	.21	.21	.48	.19
Sit-ups	.09	.16	.26	.12
Trunk Raise	.11	.13	.20	−.03
Leg Raise	.02	−.05	.12	.10
Pursuit Rotor at 40 RPM	.50	.28	.46	.20
Purdue Pegboard Test	.34	.29	.27	.36
Minnesota Manipulative*	−.35	−.42	−.40	−.40
Ring Stacking*	−.27	−.24	−.39	−.25
Golfball Placement	.42	.28	.42	.19
2-Plate Tapping Test	.31	.10	.36	.22
Bass Test	.18	.35	.22	.31
Stabilometer*	−.32	−.11	−.26	−.14
Stork Test	.30	.39	.18	.20
Railwalk Forward	.19	.40	.13	.29
Railwalk Backward	.32	.42	.27	.40
Railwalk Sideways	.40	.40	.28	.48
Toe Touch	.25	.14	.18	.11
Spinal Extension	.18	.31	.25	.13
Spinal Rotation	.30	.34	.39	.20
Lateral Spinal Extension	.33	.12	.23	.26
Physical Work Capacity	.09	.03	.17	.20
Height	.22	.14	.18	−.10

**Note: These tests are scored so that the lower score is the better score; hence, a negative correlation reflects a positive relationship.*

Relationship Between I.Q. and Test Performance

Product-moment correlation coefficients between I.Q.'s of the four groups of retarded children and scores on the strength and motor performance tests are shown in Table 3.13. For the most part the coefficients are low, ranging from 0 to .30. The correlations vary considerably by age and sex for a given variable; hence, no one test item shows a substantial correlation in all four groups. The variables that consistently give the highest correlations in all four groups are the balance items and the tests of fine visual-motor coordination. With the boys, the bicycle ergometer with resistance and the Cybex knee extension and knee flexion tests give moderate correlations with I.Q. While the correlations, almost without exception, are positive, they nevertheless are low-to-moderate. For the most part they fall within the range reported by other investigators (Dingman and Silverstein, 1964; Ellis and Sloan, 1957; Rarick et al., 1970; Rabin, 1957).

Summary

Clear-cut and consistent differences in motor performance between the normal children and the EMR children were found. The normal children, on the average, performed significantly better than the retarded, the boys performing better than girls on most tests and the performances of the EMR girls being particularly poor. Comparisons of age and sex difference within the EMR samples showed that the older children performed significantly better than the younger ones, the boys performing better than the girls on the majority of the tests. While the performance of the retarded was generally inferior to that of the normal children, a few of the retardates performed well above the average on most of the tests. When comparable units of measures were employed, it was evident that the degree of motor retardation within sex was much greater for the girls than for the boys. Similarly, the variability in weight, skinfold thickness, and measures of motor performance was substantially greater in the mentally retarded than in the normal children. The relationships between I.Q. and the measures of motor performance were generally positive but, for the most part, were low.

Chapter 4 / Basic Components and Similarities of Factor Structures

This chapter describes the factor analytic procedures that were used to identify the basic components of motor performance of the two groups of normal children and the four groups of educable mentally retarded children. The results which came from the several factor analyses are presented, as are the findings on the similarities and differences in the factor structures of the six groups.

Procedural Steps

The 47 variables in each of the six groups constituted the basic data for the computation of the six intercorrelation matrices* needed for the several factor analyses. Because of the 4-year age span within each of the age groups, it was first necessary to remove the possible confounding effect of chronological age on the zero order correlations by the use of partial correlation. The resulting residual intercorrelation matrices were used in all six factor analyses.

The factor analytic methods that were employed followed the strategy proposed by Harris and Harris (1971). This procedure extracts the common factors from an intercorrelation matrix in which several different computing algorithms for the initial solution are used to obtain both orthogonal and oblique solu-

*Tables of intercorrelations are in Appendix B, Tables 12.1 to 12.6, inclusive.

tions. It is now widely recognized that a single factor analytic method is not an appropriate procedure (Harris, 1967; Kaiser, 1964; Glass and Taylor, 1966).

The factoring techniques used in the analysis of the data bases included two statistical models, namely, canonical component analysis (Rao, 1955) and incomplete principal component analysis (Harmon, 1967), and also a psychometric method, alpha factor analysis (Kaiser and Caffrey, 1965). Each of the three initial solutions was rotated orthogonally by the normal varimax procedures (Kaiser, 1958) and obliquely by the Harris-Kaiser (1964) approach to produce six derived solutions. For the three initial solutions, only those factors with eigen values greater than 1.00 were rotated. For the oblique rotation, the delta value was set at zero.

The approach used in identifying the factors that were common across solutions followed closely that outlined by Harris and Harris (1971). The procedure rests on the premise that there should be substantial agreement among the several solutions in respect to the commonality of variables that load on a given factor. This necessitated the selection of one derived solution to be used as a template against which the factors of the remaining five solutions could be compared for similarity on the basis of a similar profile of factor loadings. The incomplete principal component solution with varimax rotation was chosen as the starting base because it included more variables with substantial loadings on a particular component than any other derived solution.

Beginning with the first rotated factor of the incomplete principal component solution, a search was made among the five remaining derived solutions for a factor in each solution that was similar to it with reference to the pattern of factor loading. Once this was accomplished, this factor was eliminated from future searches. Following the same procedure, subsequent searches were made for additional factors—specifically, those in which the loadings on the other five derived solutions were similar to the loadings on the incomplete principal component solution. Thus, the identification of factors common to the six derived solutions yielded what have been called comparable common factors, comparable specific factors, and noncomparable factors. For the purposes of this study, a comparable common factor was defined as one having three or more variables with rotated loadings greater than .40 on at least four of the six derived solutions. A comparable specific factor was defined as one having one or two variables with loadings greater than .40 on at least four of the six derived solutions. A noncomparable specific factor was defined as one that did not have at least one variable with loadings of .40 or higher on at least four of the solutions.

The results of the factor analyses of the residual intercorrelation matrices of each of the six groups of subjects appear in the next section. In each instance, an attempt has been made to label or name the comparable factors.

(This is a somewhat hazardous undertaking for it involves some subjectivity.) The labeling of a factor is done on the basis of the pattern of variables which have high loadings on that particular factor, with consideration being given to the kinds of abilities these variables require. Thus, if only measures of strength load on a factor, this could logically be considered a strength factor. To the extent that comparable factors are robust across the different solutions, some confidence can be placed in the validity of these factors. However, it should be understood that the labels ascribed to these factors are tentative and should be interpreted as an attempt to identify the nature of the common abilities associated with the variables of that particular comparable factor.

Results of the Factor Analyses

Factor Structure of the Normal Boys

Six comparable common and four comparable specific factors were extracted from the residual intercorrelation matrix of the normal boys (see Table 4.1). The variables with substantial loadings on Comparable

Table 4.1

ROTATED FACTOR MATRIX OF PHYSICAL GROWTH AND MOTOR PERFORMANCE VARIABLES (NORMAL BOYS)

	Orthogonal Solutions			*Oblique Solutions*		
Factors	*Principal Components*	*Alpha*	*Rao*	*Principal Components*	*Alpha*	*Rao*
Comparable Common Factor 1						
Bicycle With Resistance	87	88	87	61	42	
Height	85	85	86	50	56	47
Knee Flexion	86	84	82	71		
Grip Strength Right	83	78	80	78		80
Bi-Acromial Breadth	77	78	78		58	
Weight	75	76	77	40	49	
Grip Strength Left	76	71	72	73		80
Knee Extension	74	74	71	43	55	
Elbow Flexion	71	66	66	72		50
Bicycle Without Resistance	70	70	71	51	43	
Elbow Extension	70	66	63	73		
Comparable Common Factor 2						
Target Throw Horizontal	81	80	79	80	78	80
Target Throw Vertical	81	79	77	77	75	73
Softball Throw	75	70	71	72	68	69
Mat Crawl	71	60	49	44	44	
Tire Run	51	52	52	47	49	45

Table 4.1 Continued

	Orthogonal Solutions			*Oblique Solutions*		
Factors	*Principal Components*	*Alpha*	*Rao*	*Principal Components*	*Alpha*	*Rao*
Comparable Common Factor 3						
Purdue Pegboard	81	76	76	72	78	75
Minnesota Manipulative	73	70	72	71	60	67
Ring Stacking	72	69	70	55	63	61
Golfball Placement	68	65	62	41	58	45
2-Plate Tapping	67	63	66	68	62	69
Tire Run	62	63	62	52	56	54
Pursuit Rotor at 40 RPM	58	58	54	47	50	43
Comparable Common Factor 4						
Abdominal Skinfold	94	95	92	98	99	94
Subscapular Skinfold	93	92	92	95	94	94
Triceps Skinfold	86	79	82	82	81	85
Weight	50	49	49	46	48	46
Comparable Common Factor 5						
Railwalk Sideways	75	70		52	64	
Stork Test	59	45	66	67	49	71
Railwalk Backward	59	50		43	42	
Comparable Common Factor 6						
Scramble	41	57	61		62	72
35-Yard Dash		57	66	59	66	63
150-Yard Dash		52	57	49	63	57
Comparable Specific Factor 1						
Leg Raise	86	79	69	73	78	59
Trunk Raise	43	53	57	53	56	71
Comparable Specific Factor 2						
Lateral Spinal Extension	83	79	74	83	81	79
Spinal Extension	75	60	64	60	62	63
Comparable Specific Factor 3						
Bass Test	91	89		90	92	
Comparable Specific Factor 4						
Toe Touch	56		63	68	53	67

Note: Figures have been rounded to two places and decimal points have been omitted.

Common Factor 1 are predominantly those that stress muscular strength, muscular power, and such correlates of strength and power as height and weight. It is apparent that there is no clear-cut separation of measures of static strength (grip strength right hand, grip strength left hand) and isokinetic strength (knee flexion, knee extension strength, elbow flexion, and elbow extension strength) from those of dynamic strength (bicycle ergometer with resistance) or from those of body size. In this sample of boys, these measures seem closely bound together in what might be termed a *Strength-Power-Body Size* factor.

Comparable Common Factor 2 includes a nucleus of test items that stress those abilities perhaps best described as *Gross Limb-Eye Coordination.* Tests of throwing accuracy and throwing power have high loadings on this factor. In addition, two variables requiring quick changes in body orientation load on this factor.

Comparable Common Factor 3 is clearly a factor of *Fine Visual-Motor Coordination*, for six of the seven variables with the highest factor loadings are tasks which require fine manipulative skill and precise hand-eye coordination. It is interesting that a test item requiring elements of balance, namely, the tire run, also has a substantial loading on this factor.

Comparable Common Factor 4, with high loadings of skinfold measures, can logically be called a *Fat* or *Dead Weight* factor. The three balance variables that comprise Comparable Common Factor 5 identify this as a *Balance* factor. There is no clear-cut separation of the measure of static balance (stork test) from those items generally held to measure dynamic balance (railwalking).

Comparable Common Factor 6, with three variables loading on five of the six factor solutions, can perhaps best be termed a component of *Leg Power and Coordination.* All three of these tasks require power and coordinated action of the lower extremities.

Comparable Specific Factor 1 is clearly a factor of muscular endurance of the thigh flexors and the extensor muscles of the spine. A general factor of flexibility did not emerge, as evidenced by the loading of the measures of lateral spinal extension and spinal extension on Comparable Specific Factor 2 and the loading of the toe touch on Comparable Specific Factor 4. That balance in this sample of boys cannot be categorized into elements of static and dynamic balance or as a factor of static balance per se is evidenced by the loading of the Bass Test on a factor (Comparable Specific Factor 3) in isolation from the stork test.

Factor Structure of the Normal Girls

Seven comparable common and three comparable specific factors were extracted from the normal girls' residual intercorrelation matrix (see Table 4.2). In view of the substantial loadings of the six strength measures, the power test on the bicycle, and the measures of body size, Comparable Common Factor 1 is clearly a Strength-Power-Body Size factor. Comparable Common Factor 2, made up predominantly of throwing tasks, is perhaps best labeled Gross Limb-Eye Coordination. The pattern of variables loading on Comparable Common Factor 3 establishes this factor as Fine Visual-Motor Coordination. Comparable Common Factor 4 is clearly a factor of Fat or Dead Weight. Comparable Common Factor 5 is made up of three dynamic balance items, namely, the railwalking tests and one item of static balance, the stork test. Clearly, this is a factor of *Balance*. Comparable Common Factor 6, with loadings on the two running and two jumping

Table 4.2

ROTATED FACTOR MATRIX OF PHYSICAL GROWTH
AND MOTOR PERFORMANCE VARIABLES
(NORMAL GIRLS)

	Orthogonal Solutions			*Oblique Solutions*		
Factors	*Principal Components*	*Alpha*	*Rao*	*Principal Components*	*Alpha*	*Rao*
Comparable Common Factor 1						
Grip Strength Right	72	73	48	43	69	88
Elbow Flexion	72	72	63	58		62
Grip Strength Left	70	71	44		79	89
Bicycle With Resistance	68	66	71	77		45
Bicycle Ergometer Total	68	65	65	58		49
Elbow Extension	62	63	69	60		45
Knee Flexion	62	60	60	53		47
Knee Extension	59	58	56	45		47
Bi-Acromial Breadth	56	58	58	40		47
Bicycle Without Resistance	54	49	48	56		40
Physical Work Capacity (170)	46	60	53	51		42
Height	51	47	44	42		
Comparable Common Factor 2						
Target Throw Horizontal	68	55	56	52		53
Softball Throw	63	66	75	70	58	79
Tire Run	64	63	54	44		60
Target Throw Vertical	40	40	46	52		46
Comparable Common Factor 3						
Minnesota Manipulative	76	73	76	80	77	77
Ring Stacking	76	73	69	63	68	68
Purdue Pegboard	73	64	66	70	60	71
Golfball Placement	60	60	55	55	48	53
2-Plate Tapping	56	53	53	46	43	47
Comparable Common Factor 4						
Subscapular Skinfold	91	90	91	93	94	92
Abdominal Skinfold	90	87	88	89	91	90
Triceps Skinfold	87	83	87	86	84	89
Weight	78	77	77	90	70	84
Bi-Iliac Breadth	67	64	66	76	58	73
Bi-Acromial Breadth	59	56	56	66	54	60
Scramble	48	47	57	55		57

Table 4.2 Continued

	Orthogonal Solutions			*Oblique Solutions*		
Factors	*Principal Components*	*Alpha*	*Rao*	*Principal Components*	*Alpha*	*Rao*
Comparable Common Factor 5						
Railwalk Sideways	71	62	67	68	62	71
Railwalk Forward	61	56	58	59	54	64
Railwalk Backward	60	56	58	62	54	65
Stork Test	60	54	50	58	51	55
Target Throw Vertical	57	48	44	47	52	48
Comparable Common Factor 6						
35-Yard Dash	81	79	82	84	76	77
150-Yard Dash	76	73	74	86	79	70
Vertical Jump	73	68	70	62	53	71
Standing Broad Jump	62	59	53	74	62	54
Scramble	50	49	41	69	43	
Mat Crawl	49	43		66	50	
Comparable Common Factor 7						
Sit-ups	72	69		80		78
Trunk Raise	65	49	72	61	73	40
Leg Raise	62	59	43	55	49	
Comparable Specific Factor 1						
Spinal Extension	78	63		65	66	
Comparable Specific Factor 2						
Bass Test	74	59	70	67	77	74
Knee Extension	65	70	63	84	64	83
Comparable Specific Factor 3						
Toe Touch	79	69	48	71	72	45
Spinal Rotation	58	43		53	50	

Note: Figures have been rounded to two places and decimal points have been omitted.

activities, plus the scramble and the mat crawl, is logically a factor of Leg Power and Coordination.

It is difficult to attach a meaningful label to Comparable Common Factor 7. Most logically, it is a factor of muscular endurance, as all three items loading high on this factor require this capability.

Comparable Specific Factors 1 and 3 would appear to be factors of flexibility with high loadings of spinal extension (CSF1) and toe touch and spinal rotation (CSF3). Comparable Specific Factor 2 is composed of two variables that logically do not belong together; the Bass Test is a test of static balance and the knee extension is a test of strength.

Young EMR Boys' Factor Structure

The rotated factor loadings of the six derived solutions of the young EMR boys are shown in Table 4.3. Six comparable common and four comparable specific factors were recognized. Comparable Common Factor 1, with substantial loadings on manual strength, leg strength, power measurements, and height, is logically a factor of Strength-Power-Body Size. Comparable Common Factor 2, with loadings of the three throwing events, would appear to be a factor of Gross Limb-Eye Coordination. Com-

Table 4.3

ROTATED FACTOR MATRIX OF PHYSICAL GROWTH AND MOTOR PERFORMANCE VARIABLES (YOUNG EMR BOYS)

	Orthogonal Solutions			*Oblique Solutions*		
Factors	*Principal Components*	*Alpha*	*Rao*	*Principal Components*	*Alpha*	*Rao*
Comparable Common Factor 1						
Knee Flexion	80	74	79	87	85	77
Bicycle With Resistance	69	59	60	61	64	55
Knee Extension	68	61	60	66	66	61
Grip Strength Left	57		43	47	41	
Height	49		45	41	46	
Comparable Common Factor 2						
Target Throw Vertical	87	81	87	86		83
Target Throw Horizontal	68	65	62	57	42	62
Softball Throw	61	63	51		44	87
Pursuit Rotor at 40 RPM	60	53	50			48
Comparable Common Factor 3						
Minnesota Manipulative	75	53		49	54	
Ring Stacking	71	41		40	46	
2-Plate Tapping	59	67		57	63	
Comparable Common Factor 4						
Bi-Iliac Breadth	90	91	89	90	90	81
Bi-Acromial Breadth	86	84	86	78	77	73
Triceps Skinfold	84	78	79	85	86	84
Abdominal Skinfold	82	82	84	83	83	83
Weight	80	82	83	68	67	63
Subscapular Skinfold	75	73	78	73	72	78
Bicycle Ergometer Total	53	53	51	41		
Comparable Common Factor 5						
Railwalk Forward	50	74	72	89	70	75
Railwalk Backward		77	52	58	64	51
Purdue Pegboard		56	53	54		68

Table 4.3 Continued

	Orthogonal Solutions			*Oblique Solutions*		
Factors	*Principal Components*	*Alpha*	*Rao*	*Principal Components*	*Alpha*	*Rao*
Comparable Common Factor 6						
Scramble	84	87	85	86	87	79
35-Yard Dash	78	80	80	63	61	67
150-Yard Dash	78	80	79	59	55	67
Mat Crawl	72	69	71	59	52	61
Standing Broad Jump	67	63	59	43	44	41
Tire Run	61	64	64	55	53	52
Bicycle With Resistance	57	60	61			42
Comparable Specific Factor 1						
Leg Raise	82	86	80	85	88	68
Trunk Raise	65	42	43	49	42	50
Comparable Specific Factor 2						
Toe Touch	78	78	74	74		74
Spinal Extension	67	49	59	59		41
Comparable Specific Factor 3						
Bass Test	74		75	70		76
Stork Test	65		55	59		56
Comparable Specific Factor 4						
Lateral Spinal Extension	85	68		82	75	

Note: Figures have been rounded to two places and decimal points have been omitted.

parable Common Factor 3 is clearly a factor of Fine Visual-Motor Coordination. Comparable Common Factor 4 is designated as a factor of Fat or Dead Weight, although it might perhaps be more logically called a body size/dead weight factor in view of the high loadings of measures of body size and measures of skinfold thickness.

Comparable Common Factor 5 is a Balance factor with substantial loadings of two of the three railwalking tests. Comparable Common Factor 6 is a well-defined factor, and in view of the pattern of loadings it would logically be identified as Leg Power and Coordination.

Comparable Specific Factor 1, with loadings of the leg raise and trunk raise tests (measures that stress muscular endurance), might best be considered a factor of Muscular Endurance. Comparable Specific Factors 2 and 4 are flexibility factors. Comparable Specific Factor 3 includes the Bass Test and the stork test, tasks that have similar requirements, and hence the factor would appear to be one of static balance.

Young EMR Girls' Factor Structure

Table 4.4 gives the rotated factor loadings of the six comparable common and seven comparable specific factors extracted from the residual intercorrelation matrix of the young EMR girls. Comparable Common Factors 1 through 6 are similar in their composition of variables to those reported for the three subject groups previously mentioned. Thus, they are labeled: CCF1 = Strength-Power-Body Size, CCF2 = Gross Limb-Eye

Table 4.4

ROTATED FACTOR MATRIX OF PHYSICAL GROWTH AND MOTOR PERFORMANCE VARIABLES (YOUNG EMR GIRLS)

	Orthogonal Solutions			*Oblique Solutions*		
Factors	*Principal Components*	*Alpha*	*Rao*	*Principal Components*	*Alpha*	*Rao*
Comparable Common Factor 1						
Knee Extension	79	71	75	67	40	72
Knee Flexion	78	81	72	66	46	53
Elbow Extension	58	62	42	58		46
Comparable Common Factor 2						
Target Throw Horizontal	86	67	73	70	71	76
Target Throw Vertical	76	80	78	90	90	82
Softball Throw	56	51	47	54	55	46
Pursuit Rotor at 40 RPM	45	42	44	45	45	41
Comparable Common Factor 3						
Minnesota Manipulative	75	72	65			67
Ring Stacking	59	61	55			50
Pursuit Rotor at 40 RPM	52	56	46			43
Comparable Common Factor 4						
Abdominal Skinfold	89	86	90	90	90	93
Triceps Skinfold	88	89	86	88	85	86
Bi-Acromial Breadth	88	88	86	76	75	73
Subscapular Skinfold	87	86	87	93	93	93
Bi-Iliac Breadth	80	79	77	67	65	63
Weight	80	77	80	68	68	67
Bicycle Ergometer Total	58	53	54	47	48	
Bicycle With Resistance	56	50	54	44	45	
Comparable Common Factor 5						
Bass Test	72		66	62	64	
Railwalk Sideways	71		71	63	72	
Railwalk Backward	66		67	51	63	
Railwalk Forward	58		58	41	57	
Stork Test	40		47	51	40	

Table 4.4 Continued

Factors	*Orthogonal Solutions* Principal Components	Alpha	Rao	*Oblique Solutions* Principal Components	Alpha	Rao
Comparable Common Factor 6						
150-Yard Dash	80	80	80		50	
Scramble	79	79	76		47	
Mat Crawl	76	79	71	43		45
35-Yard Dash	70	70	80		56	
Bicycle Without Resistance	68	68	67	50	51	64
Tire Run	64	62	60			46
Bicycle With Resistance	50	58	51		54	
Railwalk Forward	45		42	42		41
Bicycle Ergometer Total	43	43	44		49	
Comparable Specific Factor 1						
Trunk Raise	82	70	74	70	66	48
Stabilometer	64	54	40	59	43	73
Comparable Specific Factor 2						
Spinal Extension	80	72	68	82	60	42
Comparable Specific Factor 3						
Grip Strength Left	86	87	87	99	99	95
Grip Strength Right	79	74	81	84	85	87
Comparable Specific Factor 4						
Toe Touch	84	73	77	59	82	85
Spinal Rotation	54	50	43	47		45
Comparable Specific Factor 5						
Physical Work Capacity (170)	91	82	49	93	90	49
Comparable Specific Factor 6						
Sit-ups	80	67	57	80	81	77
Comparable Specific Factor 7						
Elbow Flexion	86	69		73	77	45

Note: Figures have been rounded to two places and decimal points have been omitted.

Coordination, CCF3 = Fine Visual-Motor Coordination, CCF4 = Fat or Dead Weight, CCF5 = Balance, and CCF6 = Leg Power and Coordination.

Of the seven comparable specific factors recognized, two—CSF2 (loading of spinal extension) and CSF4 (loading of toe touch and spinal rotation)—are factors of flexibility. Comparable Specific Factor 1 is an odd mixture of one variable (trunk raise) that logically represents muscular endurance and another (stabilometer) that stresses balance abilities. Comparable Specific Factor 3 is a factor of manual strength. Comparable Specific Factor 5 is one of physiological efficiency as evidenced by the physical work capacity test.

Comparable Specific Factor 6 is a factor of muscular endurance specific to sit-ups and CSF7 is a strength factor specific to elbow flexion strength.

Factor Structure of Older EMR Boys

Seven comparable common factors and three comparable specific factors emerged from the intercorrelation matrix of the data on the older EMR boys (see Table 4.5). In view of the patterns of loadings, Com-

Table 4.5

ROTATED FACTOR MATRIX OF PHYSICAL GROWTH AND MOTOR PERFORMANCE VARIABLES (OLDER EMR BOYS)

	Orthogonal Solutions			*Oblique Solutions*		
Factors	*Principal Components*	*Alpha*	*Rao*	*Principal Components*	*Alpha*	*Rao*
Comparable Common Factor 1						
Grip Strength Left	87	87	87	91	90	87
Grip Strength Right	85	84	85	82	82	82
Physical Work Capacity (170)	78	74	73	67	68	67
Height	76	75	75	64	63	65
Bi-Acromial Breadth	74	71	68	55	56	53
Bicycle Ergometer Total	73	73	67	46	49	43
Knee Extension	71	70	70	56	57	51
Bicycle With Resistance	67	67	61			41
Weight	66	67	66	54	55	50
Knee Flexion	61	61	60	42	44	
Comparable Common Factor 2						
Target Throw Vertical	81	67	62	77	83	75
Target Throw Horizontal	77	74	76	92	89	90
Softball Throw	49	46	48	52	51	55
Comparable Common Factor 3						
Golfball Placement	84	83	85			49
Ring Stacking	82	80	85	52	44	64
Minnesota Manipulative	80	75	79	47		59
2-Plate Tapping	75	70	71			45
Tire Run	74	74	76			41
Purdue Pegboard	41		48	74	76	64
Comparable Common Factor 4						
Abdominal Skinfold	91	90	89	94	92	94
Subscapular Skinfold	89	88	88	90	88	90
Triceps Skinfold	85	82	84	83	84	83
Bi-Iliac Breadth	65	64	70	65	63	66
Weight	65	65	65	60	59	60

Table 4.5 Continued

Factors	Orthogonal Solutions Principal Components	Alpha	Rao	Oblique Solutions Principal Components	Alpha	Rao
Comparable Common Factor 5						
Bass Test	48			56	64	53
Pursuit Rotor at 40 RPM	44			43	51	41
Bicycle With Resistance	42			46	46	45
Comparable Common Factor 6						
Lateral Spinal Extension	77	73	65	64	63	67
Leg Raise	70	61	65	66	68	65
Trunk Raise	58	56	55	53	51	54
Scramble	58	56		41	42	42
Comparable Common Factor 7						
Toe Touch	75	52	50	57	59	53
Knee Flexion	42			43	41	48
Knee Extension	40			44	42	49
Comparable Specific Factor 1						
Elbow Extension	91	91	88	98	98	95
Elbow Flexion	90	88	87	97	96	95
Comparable Specific Factor 2						
Railwalk Sideways			44	74	60	75
Comparable Specific Factor 3						
Spinal Rotation	79	62	58	53	60	54

Note: Figures have been rounded to two places and decimal points have been omitted.

parable Common Factors 1, 2, 3, and 4 are recognizable as factors of Strength-Power-Body Size, Gross Limb-Eye Coordination, Fine Visual-Motor Coordination, and Fat or Dead Weight, respectively. The patterns of variables loading on these factors are similar to those noted on the other four groups mentioned previously.

Comparable Common Factor 5 cannot be logically named, for it is a strange mix of a balance item (Bass Test), a fine visual-motor item (pursuit rotor), and a strength-endurance item (bicycle with resistance). Nor can Comparable Common Factor 6 be labeled, for it contains two muscular endurance tasks (the trunk and leg raise variables), a flexibility test (lateral spinal extension), and an agility item (the scramble).

Comparable Specific Factor 1 seems clearly to be a factor of strength specific to the elbow joint. Comparable Specific Factor 2 is specific to the railwalk sideways variable, while CSF3 is specific to spinal rotation.

Factor Structure of Older EMR Girls

Five comparable common and six comparable specific factors were extracted from the intercorrelation matrix of the older EMR girls (see Table 4.6).

Comparable Common Factor 1 is clearly a strength factor, with measures of manual strength and arm and leg strength having high loadings on this factor. Comparable Common Factor 2 here is very similar to CCF6 in the other subject groups and is labeled Leg Power and Coordination. Compa-

Table 4.6

ROTATED FACTOR MATRIX OF PHYSICAL GROWTH AND MOTOR PERFORMANCE VARIABLES (OLDER EMR GIRLS)

	Orthogonal Solutions			*Oblique Solutions*		
Factors	*Principal Components*	*Alpha*	*Rao*	*Principal Components*	*Alpha*	*Rao*
Comparable Common Factor 1						
Grip Strength Left	89	90	89	89	79	84
Grip Strength Right	85	83	84	71	63	71
Knee Extension	73	69	67	52	44	52
Knee Flexion	72	68	69	52		56
Elbow Flexion	70	65	65	49	53	54
Comparable Common Factor 2						
Sit-ups	75	69	70		67	60
Scramble	71	69	69		86	55
150-Yard Dash	68	61	69		63	64
Mat Crawl	68	59	64		57	47
Standing Broad Jump	62	56	63		54	52
Vertical Jump	62	54	58	59	43	63
Tire Run	57	51	55		51	
35-Yard Dash	52	46	52	52		55
Comparable Common Factor 3						
Purdue Pegboard	77	78	69	47		42
Minnesota Manipulative	72	76	79	60		74
Ring Stacking	63	72	73	63	52	52
2-Plate Tapping	62	63	61	42		51
Golfball Placement	53	64	62	60	51	49
Knee Extension	42	46	50			44
Comparable Common Factor 4						
Subscapular Skinfold	88	88	87	89	91	85
Triceps Skinfold	87	87	86	83	87	78
Abdominal Skinfold	79	75	77	82	81	85
Bi-Iliac Breadth	76	74	78	56	61	57
Weight	59	61	62	49	53	45

Table 4.6 Continued

Factors	*Orthogonal Solutions*			*Oblique Solutions*		
	Principal Components	*Alpha*	*Rao*	*Principal Components*	*Alpha*	*Rao*
Comparable Common Factor 5						
Bi-Acromial Breadth	65	59	56	67	60	68
Bicycle Ergometer Total	63	66	64	78	79	71
Height	55	55	60	64	74	67
Bi-Iliac Breadth	47	41		54	40	52
Bicycle With Resistance	44	47	46	56	61	53
Comparable Specific Factor 1						
Leg Raise	81	71	67		61	60
Comparable Specific Factor 2						
Trunk Raise	82	72	70	85	82	73
Comparable Specific Factor 3						
Spinal Extension	82	60	75	63	72	81
Lateral Spinal Extension	69	77	51	73	73	55
Comparable Specific Factor 4						
Stork Test	73	65	73	80	77	84
Bass Test	67	54	58	66	65	60
Comparable Specific Factor 5						
Elbow Extension	81	63	44	50	64	54
Target Throw Vertical	41	54	74	77		77
Comparable Specific Factor 6						
Spinal Rotation	90	70		65	73	

Note: Figures have been rounded to two places and decimal points have been omitted.

rable Common Factor 3 has substantial loadings of variables requiring fine motor control and is clearly a factor of Fine Visual-Motor Coordination. Comparable Common Factor 4 corresponds to the factor of Fat or Dead Weight identified in the other groups. In view of the loadings of measures of body size and muscular power (bicycle with resistance) on Comparable Common Factor 5, this factor would appear to be a factor of body size and muscular power. Thus, Factor 1 in the other groups, strength-power-body size, appeared in the case of the older EMR girls to be split into two factors, one a factor of strength, the other a factor of power and body size.

The Comparable Specific Factors 3 and 4 would appear to be factors of flexibility and balance, respectively. The other comparable specific factors are specific to the task, and hence no attempt has been made to label them.

Similarity of Factor Structures Among Groups

This investigation is unique in that it has sampled a wide range of variables believed to encompass most aspects of the motor domain of both normal and mentally retarded children. It is also unique, with the exception of the study by Rarick (1968), in that the factor structures of different subject groups have been described and can consequently be compared for similarities and/or differences.

Visual inspection of the tables of comparable common and comparable specific factors of the six subject groups has revealed some strong similarities among the factor structures. Any attempt to make generalizations regarding the factor structures of different subject groups solely by visual inspection, however, is hazardous.

Recently, a procedure for assessing similarities and differences among factor structures of several groups of subjects, when the same variables have been factored in each, has been developed by Kaiser, Hunka, and Bianchini (1971). The quantified comparisons of the factor structures of the six groups of subjects utilized this method, applying it to the orthogonally rotated incomplete principal components solution. The results provided a quantitative estimate of similarity among the respective comparable common and comparable specific factors of all subject groups. It should be understood that these coefficients are not correlation coefficients per se; rather, they are cosines between factor axes, the latter identifiable by the definers (factor loadings) within the respective comparable common and comparable specific factors in each subject group. They can, however, be conceptually interpreted as correlation coefficients with a theoretical range of 1.00 to −1.00.

As is reflected by Tables 4.1 to 4.6, the varimax rotated principal components solution generally reflects the comparable common and comparable specific factors identified by the other solutions. It was appropriate, therefore, to use this algorithm as the base upon which to assess the similarities of factor structures across all subject groups. The sections that follow provide a brief account of the results of this analysis within the framework of the respective comparable common and comparable specific factors.

Comparable Common Factor 1

The magnitude of the interrelationships (cosines) among the six groups of subjects in respect to Comparable Common Factor 1 is shown in Table 4.7. All cosines are .50 or higher, the majority being above .75. In all groups the definers stress the qualities of strength and power, and in the case of the three groups of boys and the normal girls, measures of body size

Table 4.7

COSINES AMONG FACTOR AXES—COMPARABLE COMMON FACTOR 1

GROUPS	*Normal Boys*	*Normal Girls*	*Young EMR Boys*	*Young EMR Girls*	*Older EMR Boys*
Normal Girls	.953				
Young EMR Boys	.783	.790			
Young EMR Girls	.654	.500	.757		
Older EMR Boys	.922	.894	.735	.509	
Older EMR Girls	.863	.838	.824	.662	.830

DEFINERS BY GROUPS IN DESCENDING ORDER OF FACTOR LOADINGS

Normal Boys	*Normal Girls*	*Young EMR Boys*	*Young EMR Girls*	*Older EMR Boys*	*Older EMR Girls*
Bicycle With Resistance	Grip Strength Right	Knee Flexion*	Knee Extension*	Grip Strength Left	Grip Strength Left
Height	Elbow Flexion	Bicycle With Resistance	Knee Flexion*	Grip Strength Right	Grip Strength Right
Knee Flexion*	Grip Strength Left	Knee Extension*	Elbow Extension	Physical Work Capacity (170)	Knee Extension*
Grip Strength Right	Bicycle With Resistance	Grip Strength Left		Height	Knee Flexion*
Bi-Acromial Breadth	Bicycle Ergo-meter Total	Height		Bi-Acromial Breadth	Elbow Flexion
Weight	Elbow Extension			Bicycle Ergo-meter Total	
Grip Strength Left	Knee Flexion*			Knee Extension*	
Knee Extension*	Knee Extension*			Bicycle Without Resistance	
Elbow Flexion	Bi-Acromial Breadth			Weight	
Bicycle Without Resistance	Bicycle Without Resistance			Knee Flexion*	
Elbow Extension	Physical Work Capacity (170)				
	Height				
	Bi-Iliac Breadth				

**Definers common across all groups.*

are included among the definers. Note the substantial cosines between the normal boys and normal girls (.95), between the normal boys and older EMR boys (.92), and between the normal girls and older EMR girls. The agreement among groups is less strong where the young EMR girls are involved, the cosines ranging from .50 to .76. As indicated by the limited number of definers for the young EMR girls, this component is less clearly defined in them than in the other groups.

Comparable Common Factor 2

Quantification of the similarity among the six subject groups in respect to Comparable Common Factor 2 is shown in Table 4.8. For the most part the agreement is substantial, with 9 of the 15 cosines being about .70 and all but 3 above .60. As indicated by the pattern of definers, perhaps this can best be considered a factor of Gross Limb-Eye Coordination. The

Table 4.8

COSINES AMONG FACTOR AXES—COMPARABLE COMMON FACTOR 2

GROUPS	*Normal Boys*	*Normal Girls*	*Young EMR Boys*	*Young EMR Girls*	*Older EMR Boys*
Normal Girls	.733				
Young EMR Boys	.765	.606			
Young EMR Girls	.836	.799	.976		
Older EMR Boys	.857	.815	.833	.945	
Older EMR Girls	.706	.359	.600	.649	.356

DEFINERS BY GROUPS IN DESCENDING ORDER OF FACTOR LOADINGS

Normal Boys	*Normal Girls*	*Young EMR Boys*	*Young EMR Girls*	*Older EMR Boys*	*Older EMR Girls*
Target Throw Horizontal	Target Throw Horizontal	Target Throw Vertical*	Target Throw Horizontal	Target Throw Vertical*	Target Throw Vertical*
Target Throw Vertical*	Softball Velocity	Target Throw Horizontal	Target Throw Vertical*	Target Throw Horizontal	Elbow Extension
Softball Velocity	Tire Run	Softball Velocity	Softball Velocity	Softball Velocity	
Mat Crawl	Target Throw Vertical*	Pursuit Rotor at 40 RPM	Pursuit Rotor at 40 RPM		
Tire Run					

**Definers common across all groups.*

only group that does not consistently show this pattern of interrelationship is the group made up of older EMR girls. The cosines involving this group ranged from .356 to a high of .706.

Comparable Common Factor 3

As is indicated by the size of the cosines (see Table 4.9), the relationship among the groups in respect to Comparable Common Factor 3 is consistently substantial. All but two of the cosines are above .71, the lowest being .57, with the older EMR boys and the older EMR girls responsible for

Table 4.9

COSINES AMONG FACTOR AXES—COMPARABLE COMMON FACTOR 3

GROUPS	*Normal Boys*	*Normal Girls*	*GROUPS* *Young EMR Boys*	*Young EMR Girls*	*Older EMR Boys*
Normal Girls	.974				
Young EMR Boys	.796	.791			
Young EMR Girls	.834	.911	.712		
Older EMR Boys	.774	.651	.786	.730	
Older EMR Girls	.864	.755	.786	.570	.907

DEFINERS BY GROUPS IN DESCENDING ORDER OF FACTOR LOADINGS

Normal Boys	*Normal Girls*	*Young EMR Boys*	*Young EMR Girls*	*Older EMR Boys*	*Older EMR Girls*
Purdue Pegboard	Minnesota Manipulative*	Minnesota Manipulative*	Minnesota Manipulative*	Golfball Placement	Purdue Pegboard
Minnesota Manipulative*	Ring Stacking*	Ring Stacking*	Ring Stacking*	Ring Stacking*	Minnesota Manipulative*
Ring Stacking*	Purdue Pegboard	2-Plate Tapping	Pursuit Rotor at 40 RPM	Minnesota Manipulative*	Ring Stacking*
Golfball Placement	Golfball Placement			2-Plate Tapping	2-Plate Tapping
2-Plate Tapping	2-Plate Tapping			Tire Run	Golfball Placement
Tire Run	Pursuit Rotor at 40 RPM			Purdue Pegboard	Knee Extension
Pursuit Rotor at 40 RPM					

**Definers common across all groups.*

these low values. It is evident that this factor, namely, Fine Visual-Motor Coordination, is indeed similar across all six groups.

Comparable Common Factor 4

This factor, as was pointed out previously and as evidenced by the definers (see Table 4.10), is clearly a Fat or Dead Weight factor. The consistency of the definers across groups and the magnitude of the cosines among the groups indicate the high degree of commonality of this factor.

Table 4.10

COSINES AMONG FACTOR AXES—COMPARABLE COMMON FACTOR 4

GROUPS	*Normal Boys*	*Normal Girls*	*Young EMR Boys*	*Young EMR Girls*	*Older EMR Boys*
Normal Girls	.945				
Young EMR Boys	.791	.903			
Young EMR Girls	.859	.912	.960		
Older EMR Boys	938	.945	.824	.907	
Older EMR Girls	.916	.972	.881	.845	.940

DEFINERS BY GROUPS IN DESCENDING ORDER OF FACTOR LOADINGS

Normal Boys	*Normal Girls*	*Young EMR Boys*	*Young EMR Girls*	*Older EMR Boys*	*Older EMR Girls*
Abdominal Skinfold*	Subscapular Skinfold*	Bi-Iliac Breadth	Abdominal Skinfold*	Abdominal Skinfold*	Subscapular Skinfold*
Subscapular Skinfold*	Abdominal Skinfold*	Bi-Acromial Breadth	Triceps Skinfold*	Subscapular Skinfold*	Triceps Skinfold*
Triceps Skinfold*	Triceps Skinfold*	Triceps Skinfold*	Bi-Acromial Breadth	Triceps Skinfold*	Abdominal Skinfold*
Weight*	Weight*	Abdominal Skinfold*	Subscapular Skinfold*	Bi-Iliac Breadth	Bi-Iliac Breadth
	Bi-Iliac Breadth	Weight*	Bi-Iliac Breadth	Weight*	Weight*
	Bi-Acromial Breadth	Subscapular Skinfold*	Weight*		
	Scramble	Bicycle Ergometer Total	Bicycle Ergometer Total		
			Bicycle With Resistance		

**Definers common across all groups.*

All cosines are above .79 and 10 of the 15 cosines are higher than .90. Clearly, Fat or Dead Weight is a factor that accounts for a considerable part of the variance in motor performance of both normal and EMR children, young and older alike.

Comparable Common Factor 5

As may be noted in Table 4.11, Comparable Common Factor 5, being absent in the two older EMR groups, is not as clearly defined in the six subject groups as are the first four common factors. The definers indicate that this factor is largely organized around the abilities required in the railwalking tasks and, to a lesser extent, in the stork test. The similarities in respect to this factor are greatest between the normal boys and normal girls (.886) and between the normal girls and the young EMR girls (.848).

Table 4.11

COSINES AMONG FACTOR AXES—COMPARABLE COMMON FACTOR 5

GROUPS	*GROUPS* Normal Boys	Normal Girls	Young EMR Boys
Normal Girls	.886		
Young EMR Boys	.523	.496	
Young EMR Girls	.713	.848	.708

DEFINERS BY GROUPS IN DESCENDING ORDER OF FACTOR LOADINGS

Normal Boys	*Normal Girls*	*Young EMR Boys*	*Young EMR Girls*
Railwalk Forward	Railwalk Sideways	Railwalk Forward	Bass Test
Stork Test	Railwalk Forward	Railwalk Backward	Railwalk Sideways
Railwalk Backward	Railwalk Backward	Purdue Pegboard	Railwalk Backward
	Stork Test		Railwalk Forward
	Target Throw Vertical		Stork Test

Note: There are no definers for older EMR boys and girls.

Comparable Common Factor 6

This factor has previously been identified as one of Leg Power and Coordination. The nature and pattern of the definers shown in Table 4.12 support this observation, for they depend largely upon the effective use of the lower extremities in power-type activities. The cosines are moderate for the most part, ranging from the low .60's to the high .80's. It would seem safe to conclude that with the exception of the older EMR boys, there is considerable similarity among the groups on this factor. It should be noted

Table 4.12

COSINES AMONG FACTOR AXES—COMPARABLE COMMON FACTOR 6

	GROUPS			
GROUPS	*Normal Boys*	*Normal Girls*	*Young EMR Boys*	*Young EMR Girls*
Normal Girls	.685			
Young EMR Boys	.638	.759		
Young EMR Girls	.633	.860	.886	
Older EMR Girls	.589	.866	.946	.746

DEFINERS BY GROUPS IN DESCENDING ORDER OF FACTOR LOADINGS

Normal Boys	*Normal Girls*	*Young EMR Boys*	*Young EMR Girls*	*Older EMR Girls*
Scramble	35-Yard Dash	Scramble	150-Yard Dash	Sit-ups
35-Yard Dash	150-Yard Dash	35-Yard Dash	Scramble	Scramble
150-Yard Dash	Vertical Jump	150-Yard Dash	Mat Crawl	150-Yard Dash
	Standing Broad Jump	Mat Crawl	35-Yard Dash	Mat Crawl
	Scramble	Standing Broad Jump	Bicycle Without Resistance	Standing Broad Jump
	Mat Crawl	Tire Run	Railwalk Forward	Vertical Jump
		Bicycle With Resistance	Bicycle Ergometer Total	Tire Run
				35-Yard Dash

Note: There are no definers for older EMR boys.

that the cosines between groups are consistently the lowest in those instances where the normal boys are involved.

Comparable Specific Factors 1, 2, 3, and 4

Tables of cosines are not included for the comparable specific factors, since the number of definers on each factor is limited and the cosine values for the most part show only modest relationships among the groups on each factor. However, the definers are sufficiently consistent across groups to permit tentative identification of the factors; and while the definers are not common to all groups, the cosine values range for the most part from .50 to .75. In brief, the pattern of definers for the four comparable specific factors across the six subject groups would indicate that the following general abilities are characteristic of each factor:

Comparable Specific Factor 1	Muscular Endurance
Comparable Specific Factor 2	Flexibility (spinal extension)
Comparable Specific Factor 3	Static Balance
Comparable Specific Factor 4	Flexibility (spinal flexion)

Comments on the Findings

That the results obtained were not a reflection of using a single factor analytic procedure is evidenced by the marked agreement among the findings coming from the six factor analyses. The criteria that were set for identifying factors as comparable common factors were reasonably rigorous, namely, three or more variables with rotated factor loadings of .40 or more on at least four of the six derived solutions. To a large extent, this procedure ruled out the possibility of biasing the results because of the factoring technique used. Similarly, the criteria used for defining comparable specific factors were in no sense loose, namely, one or two variables with loadings higher than .40 on at least four of the six derived solutions.

The similarity in the factor structures among the groups, as noted by visual inspection, was verified by a procedure specially designed for the quantification of the similarities among factor structures. The similarity of comparable common factors was indeed substantial. These findings are consistent with results of the research of Clausen (1966) and Rarick (1968) previously cited.

The results obtained here on the EMR children do not lend themselves to precise comparison with the findings of other studies, partly because of the nonsimilarity in variables used and the sample of subjects employed in these studies, but also in respect to the more effective control in the present study of the confounding effect of chronological age. Clausen (1966) used primarily trainable mentally retarded children and the tests that were given were largely perceptual-motor in character. Obviously, the factors isolated would reflect the nature of the tasks, and hence his results had little similarity to the findings of this study. The recent research of Liemohn and Knapczyk (1974), using EMR boys and girls ages 64 months to 174 months, identified eight factors from a battery of some 35 gross and fine motor tasks. Again, their findings cannot be compared with the results obtained here because of the marked task differences in the two studies and the possible confounding effect of the subjects' wide age span in the former investigation.

The findings of the present study would seem to indicate that those basic abilities underlying the motor domain of EMR and normal boys and girls are indeed highly similar. While the factor structure of the older EMR children was somewhat less like that of the normal children than was the case of the younger EMR's, the differences were largely in the comparable specific factors.

Perhaps the finding of similarities in factor structures among the six groups of subjects should not be too surprising, for children anatomically are more alike than they are different. The lever systems and the muscle groups which activate these systems do not differ materially among children. If a task is not overly complex and if its requirements are understood, the task will, within limits, be done in much the same way by most children. For the most part, the end result is dependent upon refinements in the timing, application, and control of muscular force. Thus, the motoric differences between the normal and EMR children noted here were primarily differences in degree, not in the basic components underlying the motor domain of these children. While there is evidence that the factor structure may change as refinements in task performance occur (Fleishman and Hempel, 1954), there was little evidence of factor structure differences among the six subject groups used here, which were groups where there were marked differences in skill and motor performance levels.

Summary

This chapter presented the findings coming from factor analytic techniques applied to the intercorrelation matrices of the 47 physical growth and motor performance measures obtained on the two groups of normal children and the four groups of EMR children. The similarity of the factor structures among the six groups, particularly the six comparable common factors, was striking as evidenced by the similarity in the pattern of factor loadings for particular factors across groups. This similarity was evident not only by visual inspection, but also by the results of a procedure used to quantify relationships among common factors across different groups of subjects.

Chapter 5 / Motor Performance Typologies

The preceding chapter identified a factor structure of motor abilities of normal and EMR children that was strikingly consistent among the six groups of subjects under observation. Not only were the same factors common to all groups for the most part, but the similarities of the definers of a given factor were indeed substantial.

This chapter presents the findings coming from an extension of the results of the factor analyses utilizing the condensation method of object clustering (Tryon, 1967). This approach was used to develop person-clusters or typologies of motor performance of mixed groups of normal and young EMR boys and girls. In essence, this procedure provides a graphic profile of relatively homogeneous groups of subjects, homogeneous in respect to their performance levels on the basic components of motor performance as specified in the previous chapter. Thus, motor performance typologies were determined for each of four pairings of subject groups, namely, (1) normal boys–normal girls; (2) normal boys–young EMR boys; (3) normal girls–young EMR girls; and (4) young EMR boys–young EMR girls.

Methodological Considerations

The condensation method of person-clustering involves the grouping of persons who are similar in respect to a pattern of traits as evidenced by a profile similarity. This procedure is a means of determining the relationship among persons on a number of abilities, rather than correlating abilities within a group. The rationale for this approach is that given a broad array of data on a sample of persons, it is just as important to see how similar or how different these persons are on clusters of traits as it is to see how these characteristics themselves relate to each other.

The data for this analysis came from the previously described factor analyses for the four groups specified above. The development of the several person-clusters or typologies came from the definers of the five comparable common factors that accounted for the major proportion of the variance in motor performance of these four groups of children. The five comparable common factors which constituted the general framework for the person-clusters were (1) Strength-Power-Body Size, (2) Gross Limb-Eye Coordination, (3) Fine Visual-Motor Coordination, (4) Balance, and (5) Leg Power and Coordination. The definers, grouped according to factors and listed appropriately under the respective subject groups, appear in Table 5.1.

The procedure that was followed here in developing the person-clusters (object clusters) was the methodology developed by Tryon (1967), known as the condensation method. The initial step was to calculate standard scores for each subject on each definer in each of the five specified components of the motor domain. The standard scores of each subject on a given component were then summed and the sums of these scores converted to standard scores (mean of 50, *S.D.* of 10). Thus, each individual had five standard scores, one for each of the five components. These scores constituted an orthogonal Cartesian space of five dimensions.

The above approach, utilizing an equal weighting of definers, is recommended by Tryon and Bailey (1970). While predicted weights based on the correlations between the definers and the dimensions (factors) may be calculated, or factor loadings themselves may be used as weights, equal weighting for definers is easier to interpret and is perhaps more meaningful. This approach is supported by Dagenais and Marascuilo (1973) who reported no significant differences between the resultant weighted scores when raw scores were weighted by Guttman scores, factor loadings, or by the method of equal definer weighting.

The second step in person-clustering is to assign subjects temporarily into appropriate core *O*-types (subject types) using an arbitrary sectioning of the cluster score space. In the present investigation, a cluster score space of 243 sectors (3^5) was arbitrarily chosen, the number of sectors in this case being dependent upon the number of dimensions (five) and the number of categories (three) per dimension. While there is no set standard of defining the limits of each category, the cutoff points in this investigation were arbitrarily set at ± 1 *S.D.* On the *Z*-scale this gave the following three categories with

Table 5.1

DEFINERS USED IN THE MOTOR PERFORMANCE TYPOLOGIES GROUPED BY COMPARABLE COMMON FACTOR ACCORDING TO CONTRAST GROUPS

Comparable Common Factors	*Normal Boys Normal Girls*	*Normal Boys Young EMR Boys*	*Normal Girls Young EMR Girls*	*Young EMR Boys Young EMR Girls*
A. Strength-Power	Knee Flexion Knee Extension Elbow Flexion Elbow Extension Grip Strength Right Grip Strength Left	Knee Flexion Knee Extension Grip Strength Left Bicycle With Resistance	Knee Flexion Knee Extension Elbow Extension	Knee Flexion Knee Extension
B. Gross Limb-Eye Coordination	Target Throw Horizontal Target Throw Vertical Softball Throw	Target Throw Horizontal Target Throw Vertical Softball Throw	Target Throw Horizontal Target Throw Vertical Softball Throw	Target Throw Horizontal Target Throw Vertical Softball Throw
C. Fine Visual-Motor Coordination	Minnesota Manipulative Purdue Pegboard Golfball Placement Ring Stacking	Minnesota Manipulative 2-Plate Tapping Ring Stacking	Minnesota Manipulative Pursuit Rotor Ring Stacking	Minnesota Manipulative Ring Stacking
D. Balance	Railwalk Forward Railwalk Backward Stork Test	Railwalk Forward Railwalk Backward	Railwalk Forward Railwalk Backward Stork Test	Railwalk Forward Railwalk Backward
E. Leg Power and Coordination	35-Yard Dash 150-Yard Dash Scramble	35-Yard Dash 150-Yard Dash Scramble	35-Yard Dash 150-Yard Dash Scramble Mat Crawl	35-Yard Dash 150-Yard Dash Scramble Mat Crawl

their respective limits: High, above 60; Middle, 40 to 60; and Low, below 40. Thus, subjects with *Z*-scores in all five dimensions higher than 60 were temporarily assigned to the highest core *O*-type (*HHHHH*), whereas those with *Z*-scores in all five dimensions below 40 were temporarily assigned to the lowest core *O*-type (*LLLLL*). Those subjects with *Z*-scores on all five dimensions within the range of 40 to 60 were placed temporarily in the middle category (*MMMMM*). The other subjects were appropriately assigned to categories between the very highest and the lowest according to their respective *Z*-scores on the five dimensions. Clearly, most subjects would not fall within these three well-defined categories, since a given subject's *Z*-scores might place him high in one or two of the five dimensions and in the middle or low category in the others. Theoretically, the subjects in this investigation (if there were a sufficient number) could have been distributed among the 243 sectors on the initial casting.

A third step is to designate with one value the Euclidean distance *D* between the centroids of each core *O*-type. Based then on the researcher's decision regarding the final number of person types and/or the minimum number of persons per person-cluster, the core *O*-types are collapsed to the designated number by the successive combination of *O*-types with the smallest Euclidean distances.

The condensation method (the fourth step), an integral part of *O*-analysis, reduces the heterogeneity within the several *O*-types by retaining or reassigning subjects on the basis of the criterion root mean square (RMS). The criterion set here for inclusion within an *O*-type was arbitrarily set at a RMS of 10 or less. The RMS is the square root of the sum of the squared deviations of the individual's standard scores from those of the *O*-type to which he is compared, divided by the number of dimensions—five in this case. If the subject failed to meet this criterion with reference to any *O*-type, the subject was then identified as unique. The above procedure was followed through repeated iterations until there was no reassignment of subjects in two successive iterations.

Motor Performance Typologies: Normal and EMR Children

The aim of the procedure outlined above was to group together individuals from two diverse categories into person-clusters, individuals having similar motor performance profiles. Thus, by pooling the data from two diverse groups, the number and proportion of individuals falling within the bounds of the respective person-clusters could be determined. Four such determinations were made, using the following paired groups:

1. Normal Boys–Normal Girls
2. Normal Boys–Young EMR Boys
3. Normal Girls–Young EMR Girls
4. Young EMR Boys–Young EMR Girls

Normal Boys–Normal Girls

Nine person-clusters or typologies emerged from the analysis describing the motor performance profiles of 66 of the 71 boys and 69 of the 74 girls. Five of each sex had performance score profiles that were sufficiently unique to exclude them from any of the person-clusters. The profiles of the nine typologies (means and standard deviations) are shown in Figure 5.1. The difference in the profiles is clearly evident by visual inspection. Typology

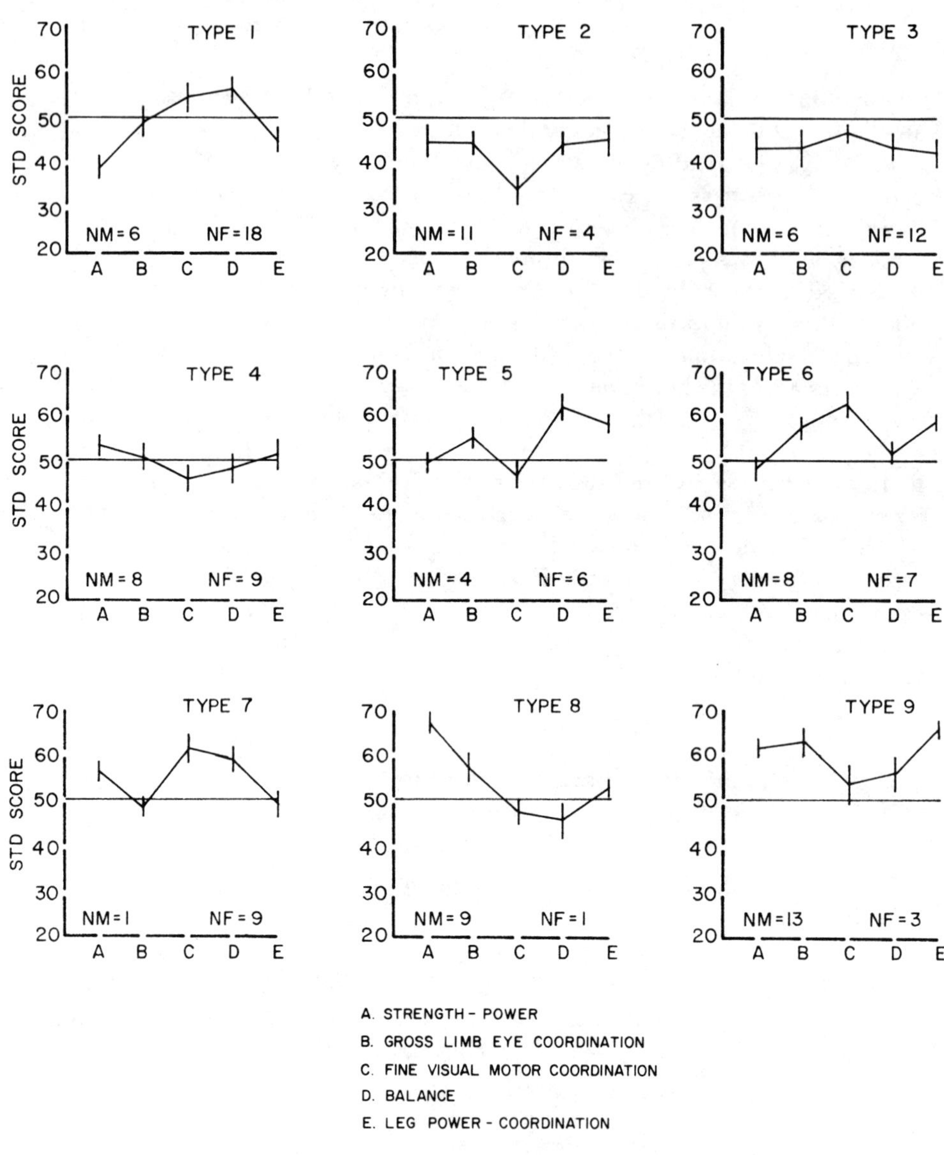

Fig. 5.1 Motor performance typologies of normal males and normal females

9, made up of 13 boys and 3 girls, has mean standard scores on all five components well above 50. Two person-clusters, namely, types 2 and 3, have mean standard scores with all components well below 50. These two types are made up of 11 boys and 4 girls, and 6 boys and 12 girls, respectively. Thus, the person-cluster with consistently the highest profiles is largely dominated by males, the two typologies with consistently the lowest profiles being approximately evenly divided between males and females. Types 8 and 9 are made up largely of males (22 boys and 4 girls) and have mean standard scores well above 50 on the factors Strength-Power, Gross Limb-Eye Coordination, and Leg Power and Coordination. These are basic components on which boys traditionally excel. On the other hand, types 1 and 7, predominantly made up of girls, show mean standard scores well above 50 on components of Fine Visual-Motor Coordination and Balance, abilities characteristically performed better by girls than boys.

Normal Boys–Young EMR Boys

Seventy of the 71 normal boys and 69 of the 71 young EMR boys met the criteria used for the assignment of subjects to the 11 person-clusters (see Figure 5.2). Types 10 and 11, made up collectively of 32 normal and 4 EMR boys, have mean standard scores well above 50 on all five components. Similarly, types 8, 10, and 11, with five times as many normal as EMR boys, have mean standard scores above 50 on all five components. These three types include 66 percent of the normal boys and 13 percent of the EMR boys. Types 1 and 5, with mean standard scores below 50 on all five components, include 22 EMR boys and no normal boys. In other types predominantly made up of EMR boys (types 2, 6, and 7), a large proportion of the standard scores were under 50. Thus, on those performance profiles which are indicative of poor overall motor performance, the EMR boys are relatively more numerous than the normal boys.

Normal Girls–Young EMR Girls

Profiles of the 10 person-clusters that emerged from the analysis of the data on the normal and the young EMR girls are shown in Figure 5.3. All of the normal girls and 61 of the 64 young EMR girls appear in these typologies. Type 10, which includes 15 normal girls and no EMR girls, has mean standard scores above 55 on all five components. The typologies with mean standard scores consistently below 50—types 1, 2, and 3—are made up of 22 EMR girls and include no normal girls. If, to the above, one then adds two types (4 and 5) that have only 1 of the 10 mean standard scores over 50, this adds 21 more EMR girls and 2 normal girls. Of the four person-clusters in which the mean standard scores on all five components are below 50, namely, types 1, 2, 3, and 5, the total is 51.5 percent of the EMR girls and only 2.7 percent of the normal girls. The profile analysis clearly demonstrates the marked inferiority of the EMR girls in these five basic components, an inferiority that is relatively greater sexwise than that noted for the EMR boys.

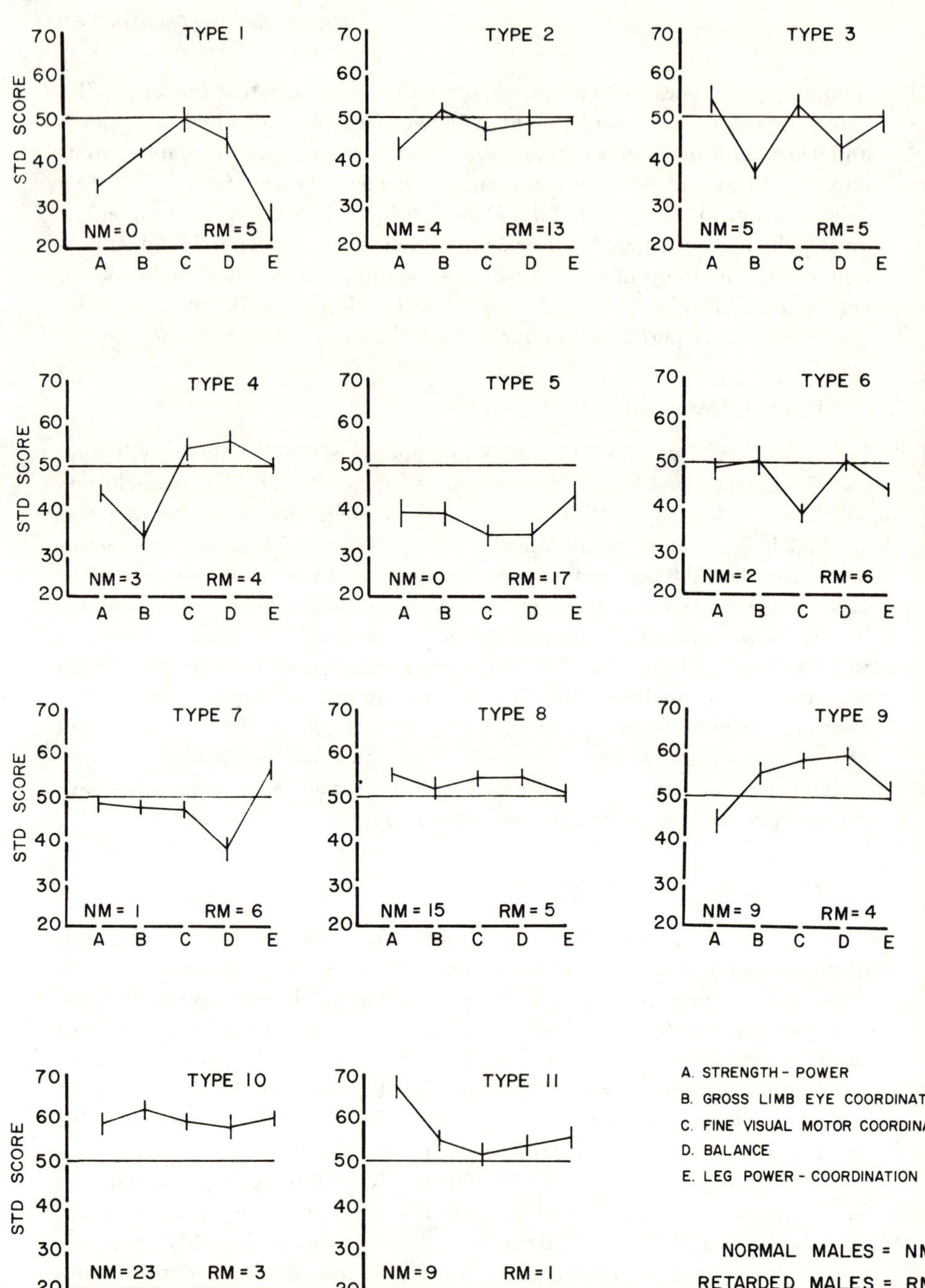

Fig. 5.2 Motor performance typologies of normal and retarded males

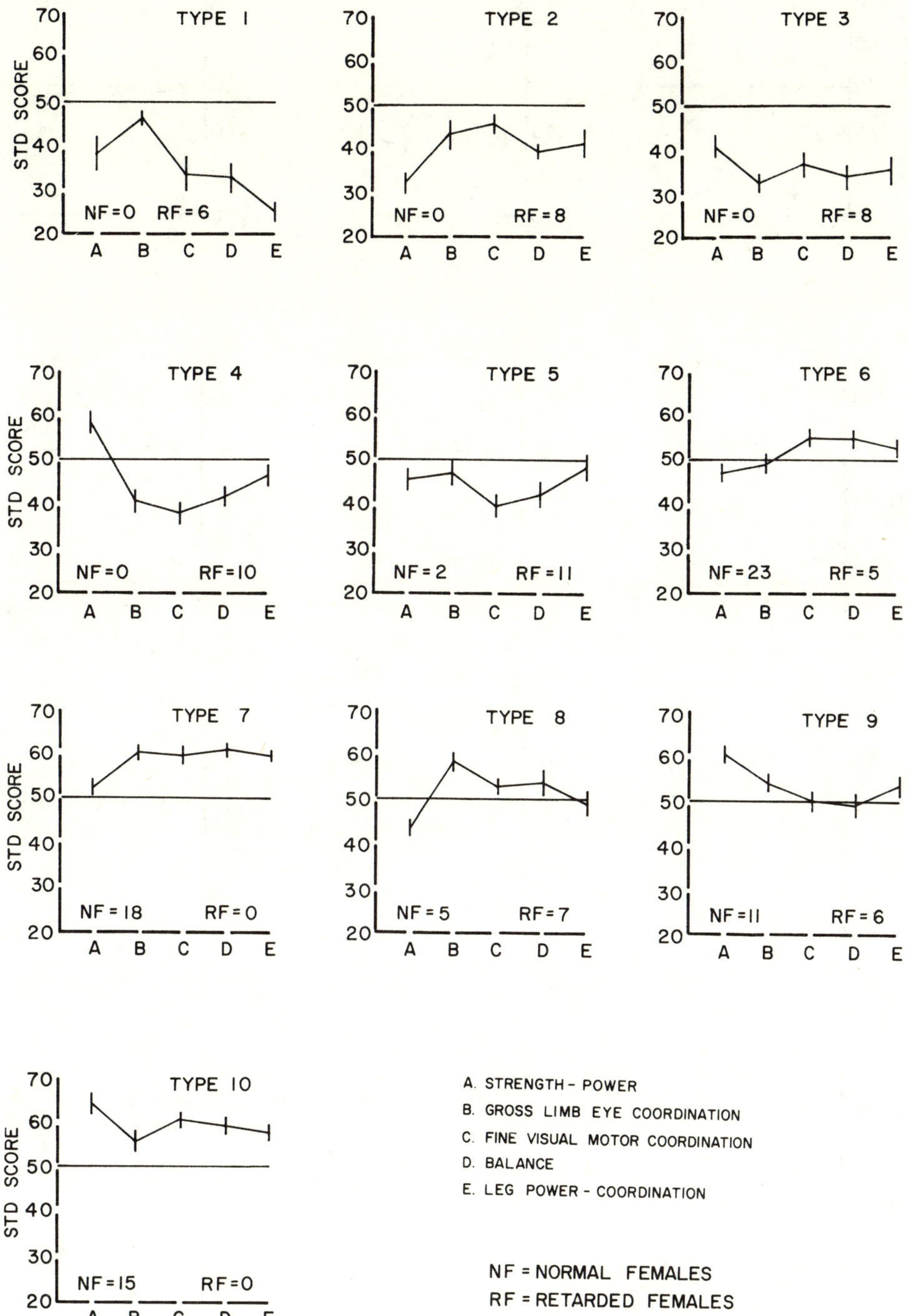

Fig. 5.3 Motor performance typologies of normal and retarded females

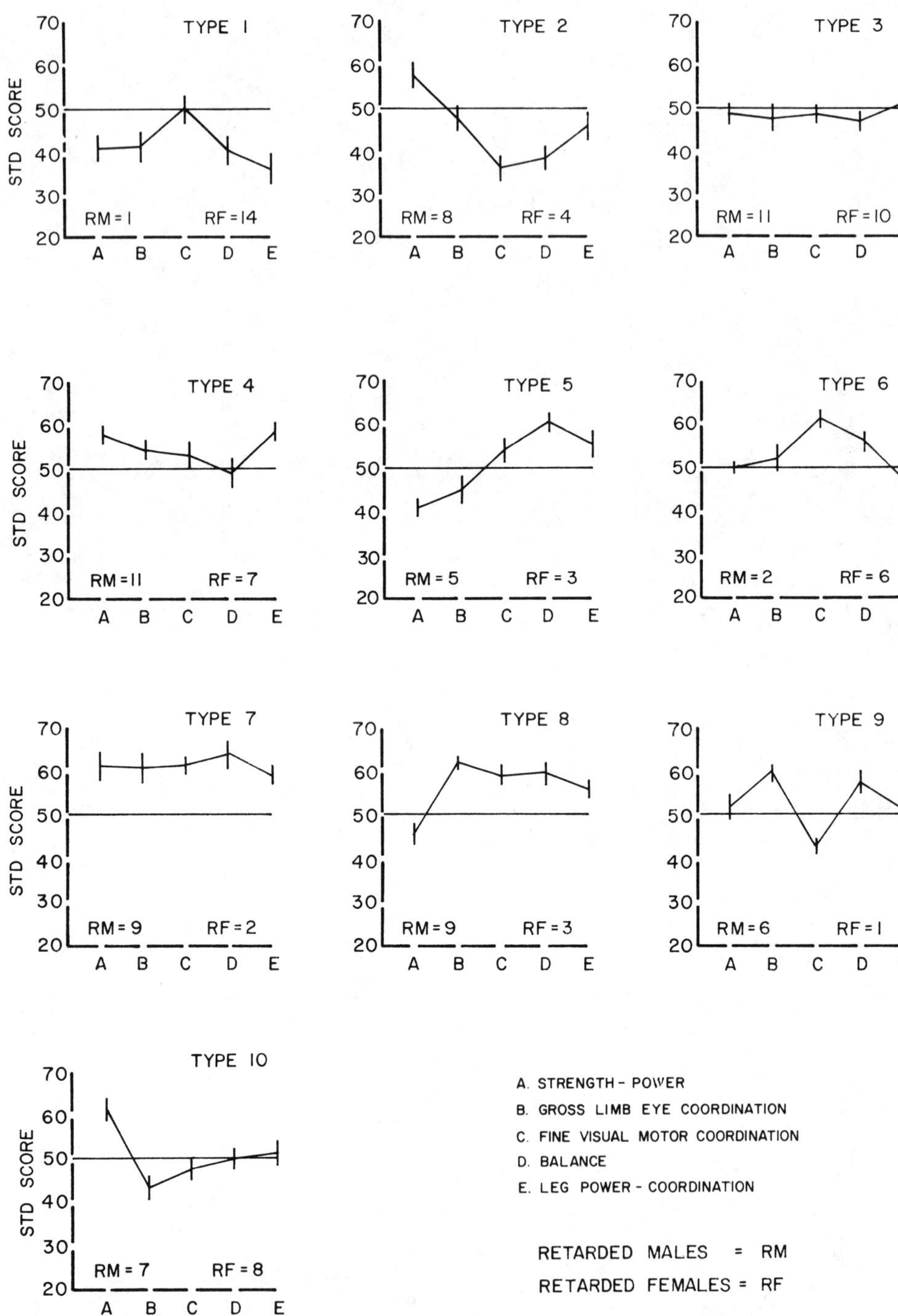

Fig. 5.4 Motor performance typologies of retarded males and retarded females

Young EMR Boys–Young EMR Girls

Profiles of the 10 typologies of the young EMR boys and girls with the distribution by sex in each person-cluster are shown in Figure 5.4. Type 7 is the only person-cluster with all mean standard scores above 50. It contains 9 EMR boys and 2 EMR girls. Types 4 and 8, with a preponderance of males, have mean standard scores above 50 on four of the five components. In contrast, type 1, with all mean standard scores of 50 or less, includes only 1 male and 14 females. Thus, as was the case with the normal subjects, there is a noticeable difference in the ratio of males to females in those clusters with relatively high mean values on the several components as contrasted with those having consistently low mean values.

Summary

Through use of the condensation method of object clustering, motor performance typologies were obtained for each of four pairings of subject groups: (1) normal boys–normal girls; (2) normal boys–young EMR boys; (3) normal girls–young EMR girls; and (4) young EMR boys–young EMR girls. In each instance, the typology was based on the respective definers of the five major components of motor performance. The number of types ranged from 9 to 11, the vast majority of subjects being included within the bounds of the several types. The types indicative of superior performance were dominated largely by males in comparisons made between the sexes, in the case of both the normal and retarded groups. There was similar domination by the normal males and normal females when comparisons within sex were made between normal and retarded subjects.

Chapter 6 | Discriminating Power of the Common Defining Variables

In making comparisons between well-defined subject groups such as males versus females or normals versus retardates, one may ask whether, on the basis of some performance or achievement criterion, the subjects properly belong in the groups in which they find themselves. This section addresses itself to this question, using motor performance variables as the criteria for making such determinations and limiting these determinations to the following four contrast groups: normal boys versus normal girls, normal boys versus young EMR boys, normal girls versus young EMR girls, and young EMR boys versus young EMR girls. Comparisons were not made using the older EMR boys and girls because of the lack of clear identification in both groups of all the comparable common factors, and because of the small number of definers in common with the other subject groups.

Procedural Steps

The appropriate procedure for the above determinations, and the one that was used here, is discriminant analysis. Essentially, discriminant function is a regression equation in which a dependent variable represents group membership. Each of the discriminant analyses used here involved only two groups. Thus, the appropriate analysis was a multiple regression analysis with the dependent variable having the values of 1 and 0. Using the motor performance measures (definers of the several comparable common factors) as independent variables and the vector of 1's and 0's as the dependent variable (group membership), the regression was solved in the usual manner. This resulted in *maximal discrimination* between the members of the comparison groups, the discrimination in these instances being based on motor performance scores only.

Discriminant analysis also provides the means of determining those variables or combinations of variables which are most significant in this kind of determination. It should be kept in mind that discriminant analysis provides a theoretical separation of subjects from contrast groups, the degree of separation being a function of the application of the weights generated in the discriminant equation to the appropriate raw scores and the probability limits set by the investigator.

The variables used in the four discriminant analyses included the definers of five of the six comparable common factors that were identified in an earlier chapter, namely, (1) Strength-Power-Body Size, (2) Gross Limb-Eye Coordination, (3) Fine Visual-Motor Coordination, (4) Balance, and (5) Leg Power and Coordination. Fat or Dead Weight, a factor of considerable consequence, was not retained since the concern here was to deal only with motor performance variables.

Comparisons Between Contrast Groups

Comparison 1. Normal Boys versus Normal Girls

The results of a 1×2 multivariate analysis of variance using 17 definers common to both the normal boys and the normal girls are shown in Table 6.1. The significant multivariate F value ($p < .0001$) shows the strong likelihood that there was a difference between the contrast groups in at least one of the variables. Following the method of Dunn (1961) for the 17 contrasts, a univariate F value greater than 9.09 is needed for a statistically significant difference. Under this criterion, the performance of the subject groups on this comparison differed on five variables. Three of them were definers of the Strength-Power-Body Size component, and in each case the direction of the difference favored the boys. The power of the throw was also greater for the boys, but paradoxically, the girls were superior to the boys on throwing accuracy in the vertical plane.

Application of discriminant analysis using the 17 variables common to the motor performance data of the normal boys and normal girls as assignment criteria showed that 141 of the 145 subjects were correctly categorized (see Table 6.2). In other words, the assignment of subjects to discrete categories on the basis of sex also correctly separated them motorically with over 97 percent accuracy of placement. Based on the criteria used, 68 of the 71 boys were characterized motorically as males and 73 of the 74 girls had the

Table 6.1

SUMMARY OF MULTIVARIATE AND UNIVARIATE ANALYSES USING A 1 × 2 DESIGN WITH 17 COMMON DEFINING VARIABLES FOR THE COMPARISON NORMAL BOYS VERSUS NORMAL GIRLS

F Ratio for Multivariate Test of Equality of Mean Vectors = 31.16[a] *df* = 17,127 *p* < .0001

Variable	*Comparable Factor*	*Hypothesis Mean Square*	*Univariate* F	p *Less Than*	*Coefficient*
Knee Extension	Strength-	335.42	4.23	.0415	−.0011
Elbow Flexion	Power-	29.04	11.79[b]	.0008	−.0033
Grip Strength Right	Body Size	75.78	12.07[b]	.0007	−.0032
Grip Strength Left		116.44	21.23[b]	.0001	−.0055
Target Throw Horizontal	Gross Limb-Eye Coordination	.18	1.32	.2523	−.0285
Target Throw Vertical		3.39	11.90[b]	.0008	−.0371
Softball Throw		6954.31	201.83[b]	.0001	.0063
Minnesota Manipulative	Fine Visual-	.92	.18	.6683	−.0013
Purdue Pegboard	Motor	10.03	4.34	.0388	.0022
Golfball Placement	Coordination	1.76	2.21	.1390	.0081
Ring Stacking		8.65	8.56	.0041	.0131
Railwalk Forward		34.24	1.32	.0644	.0009
Railwalk Backward	Balance	276.89	2.78	.0977	−.0004
Stork Test		678.37	8.18	.0049	.0001
35-Yard Dash	Leg Power	.54	3.48	.0644	−.0054
150-Yard Dash	and	14.49	2.05	.1543	.0017
Scramble	Coordination	.29	1.19	.2766	−.0063

[a]*Significant in excess of alpha = .05*
F *value required (17,127) = 1.77*
[b]*Significant in excess of alpha = .05*
t^2 *(Dunn) value required (17 contrasts) = 9.09*

Table 6.2

SUMMARY STATISTICS FOR THE DISCRIMINANT ANALYSIS BASED ON THE 17 COMMON DEFINING VARIABLES IN THE COMPARISON OF NORMAL BOYS VERSUS NORMAL GIRLS

Subject Group	*Sample Size*	*Mean Z*	*Variance Z*	*Standard Deviation Z*
Normal Boys	71	.1856	.0010	.0312
Normal Girls	74	.0699	.0007	.0256

C = Discriminant Standard Score = .1221

Number of Correct and Incorrect Placements of Subjects into Proper Sex Categories Based on Discriminant Analyses of the 17 Common Defining Variables

	Placements *Correct*	*Incorrect*	*Total*
Normal Boys	68	3	71
Normal Girls	73	1	74
Total	141	4	145

motor characteristic of females. Thus, the accuracy of the separation of the sexes using the 17 motor performance variables in a discriminant analysis is indeed remarkable.

The discriminatory capability of the 17 motor performance tests, when used in a stepwise manner to maximize this capability, is graphically shown in Figure 6.1. The initial variable entered is the one with the greatest univariate *F* value, in this instance the softball throw for velocity. As indicated in Figure 6.1, this variable alone will correctly identify a girl motorically as a girl 9 times in 10, and a boy as a boy 8 times in 10. With the addition of the second and third variables, the accuracy of placement rises to over 97 percent for the girls and 95 percent for the boys.

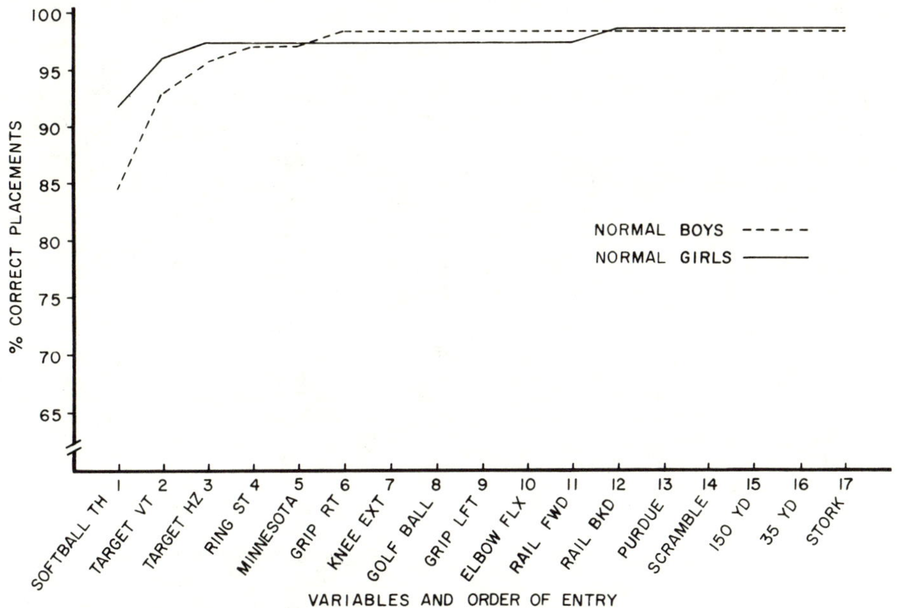

Fig. 6.1 Percentages of correct placements according to the order of entry of the 17 common defining variables resulting from a stepwise discriminant function analysis for the comparison of normal girls and normal boys

These findings indicate that on the basis of the motor performance information used here, it was possible within a very fine tolerance to almost totally separate the boys from girls, with the major separator being the throw for velocity and the best combination of three variables being the throw for velocity and the two throws for accuracy.

Comparison 2. Normal Boys versus Young EMR Boys

Fifteen variables within the five previously mentioned comparable common factors were common to both the normal boys and the young EMR boys. These variables, categorized according to comparable common factors,

Table 6.3

SUMMARY OF MULTIVARIATE AND UNIVARIATE ANALYSES USING A 1 × 2 DESIGN WITH 15 COMMON DEFINING VARIABLES FOR THE COMPARISON NORMAL BOYS VERSUS YOUNG EDUCABLE MENTALLY RETARDED BOYS

F Ratio for Multivariate Test of Equality of Mean Vectors = 12.26[a] *df* = 15,126 *p* < .0001

Variable	*Comparable Factor*	*Hypothesis Mean Square*	*Univariate* F	p *Less Than*	*Coefficient*
Knee Flexion	Strength-	1635.40	33.90[b]	.0001	−.0006
Knee Extension	Power-	1598.96	20.79[b]	.0001	.0001
Grip Strength Left	Body Size	759.95	107.20[b]	.0001	.0034
Bicycle With Resistance		686.84	86.34[b]	.0001	.0028
Target Throw Horizontal	Gross Limb-Eye	8.24	18.05[b]	.0001	−.0020
Target Throw Vertical	Coordination	5.52	13.11[b]	.0001	−.0038
Softball Throw		2827.11	50.33[b]	.0001	.0006
Minnesota Manipulative	Fine Visual-Motor	741.55	48.88[b]	.0001	−.0009
Ring Stacking	Coordination	254.49	76.38[b]	.0001	−.0041
2-Plate Tapping		392.23	21.51[b]	.0001	.0001
Railwalk Forward	Balance	4399.52	55.90[b]	.0001	.0006
Railwalk Backward		3500.18	31.24[b]	.0001	−.0003
35-Yard Dash	Leg Power	6.68	22.69[b]	.0001	.0065
150-Yard Dash	and	450.77	24.61[b]	.0001	.0003
Scramble	Coordination	9.59	16.67[b]	.0001	−.0006

[a]*Significant in excess of alpha = .05*
F *value required (15,126) = 1.80*
[b]*Significant in excess of alpha = .05*
t^2 *(Dunn) value required (15 contrasts) = 8.94*

are listed in Table 6.3, which provides a summary of the 1 × 2 multivariate analysis of variance employing these 15 definers. The multivariate *F* is highly significant ($p < .0001$). The significance of the foregoing is further evidenced by the fact that all 15 univariate *F* values exceed the criterion proposed by Dunn (1961). The direction of the difference in each case favors the performance of the normal boys.

With significant differences between the groups recognized for each of the 15 variables, the potential for a clear-cut discrimination between the two subject groups is high. Table 6.4 summarizes the discriminant capability for separation of the groups and it is indeed high.

Slightly under 90 percent (89.5 percent) of all subjects were correctly placed in their respective intellectual groups on the basis of their motor performance scores. All but four of the 71 intellectually normal boys were correctly placed, indicating that the composite motor performance scores of

Table 6.4

SUMMARY STATISTICS FOR THE DISCRIMINANT ANALYSIS BASED ON THE 15 COMMON DEFINING VARIABLES IN THE COMPARISON OF NORMAL BOYS VERSUS YOUNG EDUCABLE MENTALLY RETARDED BOYS

Subject Group	*Sample Size*	*Mean Z*	*Variance Z*	*Standard Deviation Z*
Normal Boys	71	.0680	.0002	.0126
Young EMR Boys	71	.0269	.0004	.0207

C = Discriminant Standard Score = .0525

Number of Correct and Incorrect Placements of Subjects into Normal and Disabled Categories Based on Discriminant Analyses of the 15 Common Defining Variables

	Placements		
	Correct	*Incorrect*	*Total*
Normal Boys	67	4	71
Young EMR Boys	60	11	71
Total	127	15	142

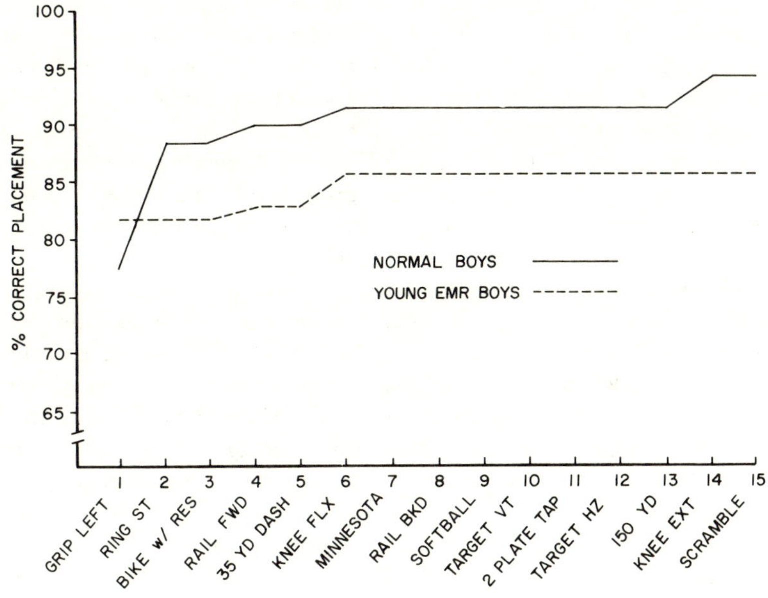

Fig. 6.2 Percentages of correct placements according to the order of entry of the 15 common defining variables resulting from a stepwise discriminant function analysis for the comparison of normal boys and young EMR boys

these subjects were more like those of their intellectually normal peers than like those of the retarded boys with whom they were compared. On the other hand, 11 of the EMR boys were motorically more like the normal boys than like their fellow retardates.

Figure 6.2 plots the maximum discriminatory power of the 15 common definers when plotted in a stepwise fashion. The cumulative discrimination with the successive addition of variables is shown at each of the 15 steps. Of the 15 variables, grip strength with the left hand had the greatest discriminating power. On the basis of this test alone, more than 75 percent of the educable retarded boys and over 80 percent of the intellectually normal boys were correctly identified. Maximum separation of the educable mentally retarded group was obtained after the inclusion of 6 of 15 variables. The percentage accuracy of placements, however, increased minimally from 81.6 percent after inclusion of the initial variable to 85.9 percent after inclusion of the sixth variable. On the other hand, improvement in accuracy of placements of the intellectually normal boys increased from 77.5 percent to 91.5 percent using 6 variables.

Comparison 3. Normal Girls versus Young EMR Girls

Table 6.5 gives the results of the multivariate and univariate analyses which were run on the 17 variables common to both sets of girls. The 17 variables, appropriately classified according to comparable common factors, are also shown in this table. The multivariate F value is significant beyond the .0001 level. When the criterion value for 17 contrasts (Dunn, 1961) is used, each of the univariate F's shows a significant difference in the performance distributions of the two groups, with the exception of elbow extension strength. In each instance, the difference is in the direction of superior performance for the normal girls.

The results of the discriminant analysis using all 17 common definers are shown in Table 6.6. The power of discrimination further supports the large numbers of univariate F values (note above) in that over 94 percent of all subjects were placed in their original subject groups when the 17 common definers served as the criteria for placement. Almost 90 percent of the EMR girls were correctly identified motorically as being members of the retarded group, whereas some 97 percent of the intellectually normal girls were correctly placed.

The percentage of correct motoric placements of normal and EMR girls and the order of entry of the 17 common definers through the use of discriminant function analysis are shown in Figure 6.3. There was approximately 90 percent correct placement of the normal girls and 80 percent correct placement of the EMR girls by use of the ring stacking test alone. Maximum discrimination in the normal girls required the use of seven tests, whereas only four were needed for the EMR girls. Among the seven definers

Table 6.5

SUMMARY OF MULTIVARIATE AND UNIVARIATE ANALYSES USING A 1 × 2 DESIGN WITH 17 COMMON DEFINING VARIABLES FOR THE COMPARISON NORMAL GIRLS VERSUS YOUNG EDUCABLE MENTALLY RETARDED GIRLS

F Ratio for Multivariate Test of Equality of Mean Vectors = 16.85[a] *df* = 17,120 $p < .0001$

Variable	*Comparable Factor*	*Hypothesis Mean Square*	*Univariate* F	p *Less Than*	*Coefficient*
Knee Flexion	Strength-	2782.38	64.39[b]	.0001	.0018
Knee Extension	Power-	4253.07	62.76[b]	.0001	−.0006
Elbow Extension	Body Size	12.09	1.85	.1766	−.0050
Target Throw Horizontal	Gross Limb-Eye	16.64	30.09[b]	.0001	.0016
Target Throw Vertical	Coordination	13.45	36.95[b]	.0001	.0020
Softball Throw		964.71	33.27[b]	.0001	−.0006
Minnesota Manipulative	Fine Visual-	898.57	84.93[b]	.0001	−.0017
Ring Stacking	Motor	392.04	130.25[b]	.0001	−.0042
Pursuit Rotor at 40 RPM	Coordination	74.64	53.54[b]	.0001	−.0023
Railwalk Forward	Balance	8722.53	115.54[b]	.0001	.0006
Railwalk Backward		13641.18	124.35[b]	.0001	.0007
Railwalk Sideways		5829.43	68.40[b]	.0001	−.0002
Stork Test		5622.65	67.09[b]	.0001	.0001
35-Yard Dash	Leg Power	23.53	58.28[b]	.0001	.0040
Mat Crawl	and	30.65	78.18[b]	.0001	.0026
Scramble	Coordination	40.25	57.61[b]	.0001	−.0091
150-Yard Dash		1446.39	64.10[b]	.0001	−.0001

[a]*Significant in excess of alpha = .05*
F *value required (17,120) = 1.79*
[b]*Significant in excess of alpha = .05*
t^2 *(Dunn) value required (17 contrasts) = 9.09*

Table 6.6

SUMMARY STATISTICS FOR THE DISCRIMINANT ANALYSIS BASED ON THE 17 COMMON DEFINING VARIABLES IN THE COMPARISON OF NORMAL GIRLS VERSUS YOUNG EDUCABLE MENTALLY RETARDED GIRLS

Subject Group	*Sample Size*	*Mean* Z	*Variance* Z	*Standard Deviation* Z
Normal Girls	74	−.0240	.0003	.0168
Young EMR Girls	64	−.0935	.0008	.0279

C = Discriminant Standard Score = .0645

Number of Correct and Incorrect Placements of Subjects into Normal and Disabled Categories Based on Discriminant Analyses of the 17 Common Defining Variables

	Placements		
	Correct	*Incorrect*	*Total*
Normal Girls	72	2	74
Young EMR Girls	58	6	64
Total	130	8	138

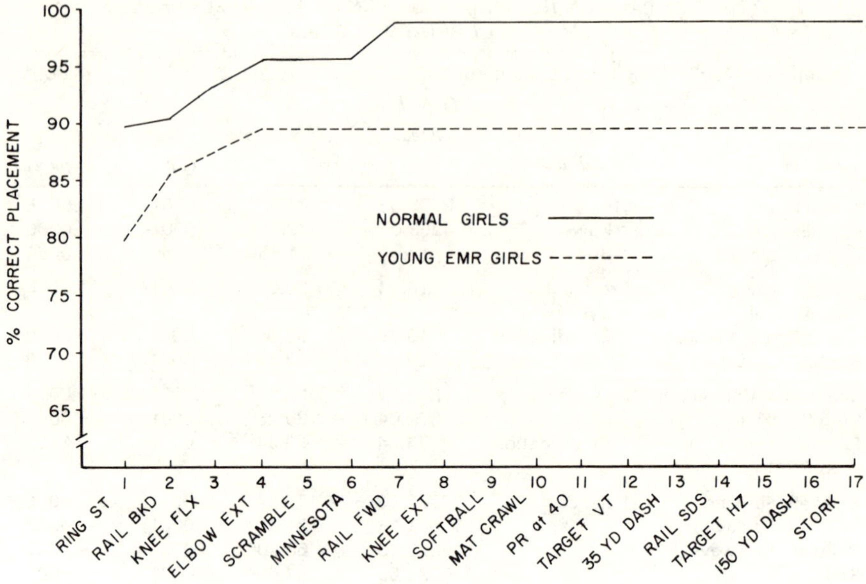

Fig. 6.3 Percentages of correct placements according to the order of entry of the 17 common defining variables resulting from a stepwise discriminant function analysis for the comparison of normal girls and young EMR girls

there were two tests of Fine Visual-Motor Coordination and two tests of Balance, two tests of Strength, and one measure of Leg Power and Coordination. It is interesting that no measure of Gross Limb-Eye Coordination had discriminating power, a dimension of motor behavior in which girls are notably weak.

Comparison 4. Young EMR Boys versus Young EMR Girls

The 13 common definers appropriately grouped by comparable common factors and the results of the multivariate and univariate analyses are shown in Table 6.7. The multivariate F is highly significant ($p < .0001$) and six of the 13 univariate F values are statistically significant according to the criteria of Dunn (1961). Four of the six involve common definers within the domain of Leg Power and Coordination, the other two being a gross limb-eye coordination task and a measure of balance.

The result of the discriminant analysis using the 13 common definers is shown in Table 6.8. There was approximately 83 percent accuracy of placement of subjects in their proper sex categories through use of the 13 common definers. In all, 11 of the 71 boys and 9 of the 64 girls were incorrectly placed.

Table 6.7

SUMMARY OF MULTIVARIATE AND UNIVARIATE ANALYSES USING A 1 × 2 DESIGN WITH 13 COMMON DEFINING VARIABLES FOR THE COMPARISON YOUNG EDUCABLE MENTALLY RETARDED GIRLS VERSUS YOUNG EDUCABLE MENTALLY RETARDED BOYS

F Ratio for Multivariate Test of Equality of Mean Vectors = 10.90[a] *df* = 13,121 $p < .0001$

Variable	*Comparable Factor*	*Hypothesis Mean Square*	*Univariate* F	p *Less Than*	*Coefficient*
Knee Flexion	Strength-Power-	421.28	7.29	.0079	.0005
Knee Extension	Body Size	63.96	.98	.3233	−.0004
Target Throw Horizontal	Gross Limb-Eye	.70	.98	.3241	−.0008
Target Throw Vertical	Coordination	.18	.36	.5479	−.0111
Softball Throw		3523.69	68.12[b]	.0001	−.0024
Minnesota Manipulative	Fine Visual-Motor	5.06	.23	.6282	.0009
Ring Stacking	Coordination	1.54	.28	.5978	.0030
Railwalk Forward	Balance	495.81	3.75	.0550	−.0003
Railwalk Backward		1765.82	14.36[b]	.0003	.0004
35-Yard Dash	Leg Power	8.98	16.18[b]	.0001	.0002
Mat Crawl	and	30.47	27.08[b]	.0001	−.0095
Scramble	Coordination	14.36	13.62[b]	.0001	−.0023
150-Yard Dash		426.84	12.28[b]	.0007	.0010

[a]*Significant in excess of alpha = .05*
F *value required (13,121) = 1.81*
[b]*Significant in excess of alpha = .05*
t^2 *(Dunn) value required (13 contrasts) = 8.58*

Table 6.8

SUMMARY STATISTICS FOR THE DISCRIMINANT ANALYSIS BASED ON THE 13 COMMON DEFINING VARIABLES IN THE COMPARISON OF YOUNG EDUCABLE MENTALLY RETARDED BOYS AND YOUNG EDUCABLE MENTALLY RETARDED GIRLS

Subject Group	*Sample Size*	*Mean Z*	*Variance Z*	*Standard Deviation Z*
Young EMR Boys	71	.0672	.0003	.0167
Young EMR Girls	64	.0324	.0002	.0155

C = Discriminant Standard Score = .0492

Number of Correct and Incorrect Placements of Subjects into Proper Sex Categories Based on Discriminant Analyses of the 13 Common Defining Variables

	Placements		
	Correct	*Incorrect*	*Total*
Young EMR Boys	60	11	71
Young EMR Girls	55	9	64
Total	115	20	135

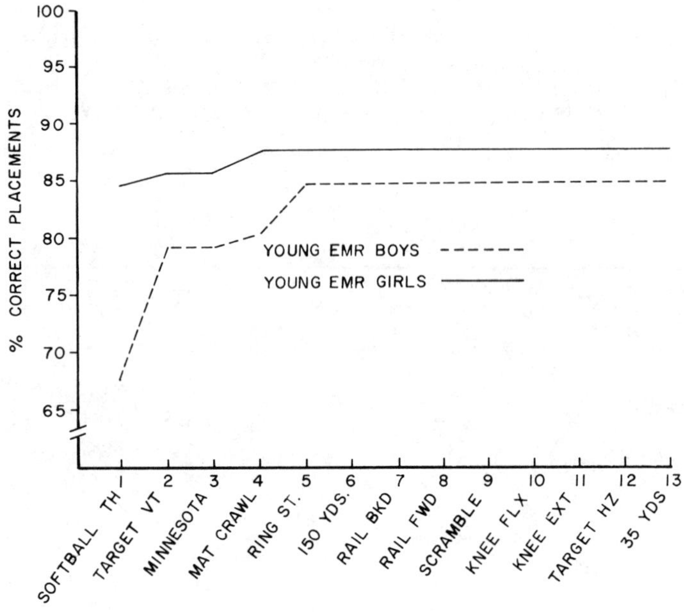

Fig. 6.4 Percentages of correct placements according to the order of entry of the 13 common defining variables resulting from a stepwise discriminant function analysis for the comparison of young EMR boys and young EMR girls

Figure 6.4 graphically portrays the results of the stepwise discriminant analysis. It is evident that in the case of the EMR girls, very little is added to the accuracy of separation after entering the first variable, namely, the softball throw for velocity. The accuracy of placement for the EMR girls using only the first definer is 84.3 percent, and it is raised only 3.2 percent when all 13 variables are used. In the case of the EMR boys, use of the first five definers is needed for good accuracy of placement (84.5 percent). These variables include two throwing tests, two fine visual-motor tasks, and a task that stresses leg power and coordination, namely, the mat crawl.

Summary of the Findings of the Multivariate and Univariate Analyses

The multivariate *F* values of all four of the comparisons cited in the previous section were all significant well beyond the .001 level. These differences were reflected in the univariate *F* values which disclosed significant differences when comparisons of respective common definers were made between groups of the same sex but of different levels of intelligence (normal boys versus EMR boys and normal girls versus EMR girls). For example, between-group comparisons of respective common definers were statistically significant ($p < .01$) for every variable, with the exception of elbow flexion strength in the comparison involving the girls. In each case, the superior performance was by the intellectually normal group. This is a clear indication that these EMR children as a group manifested poorer performance than children of normal intelligence in all five of the major motor components as defined by this investigation. Whether the degree of performance deficit in these children is similar for each of the major motor components or whether there are differential deficits in the five components cannot be answered by this analysis. One cannot, of course, rule out the possibility that lack of opportunity for participation in motor activities may be a factor equally as important as intelligence in accounting for the inferior performance of the EMR groups. This the present investigation was not equipped to study.

Summary of Discriminant Function Analysis

Power of Discrimination

Summarized results of the power of discrimination of the definers (used collectively) of the five major components of motor performance are given in Table 6.9. As is evident, the accuracy of assigning subjects from paired groups to their original classification (normal males, normal females, EMR males, or EMR females) using the motor definers as criteria for placement was indeed remarkably high, ranging from a low of 84.5 percent to a high of 96.6 percent accuracy. This indicates the clear-cut performance

Table 6.9

PERCENTAGE PLACEMENT OF SUBJECTS IN THEIR ORIGINAL ESTABLISHED CATEGORIES WHEN USING DEFINERS OF THE FIVE MAJOR COMPONENTS OF MOTOR PERFORMANCE

	Percentage Placement			
Comparisons	*Normal Boys*	*Normal Girls*	*Young EMR Boys*	*Young EMR Girls*
Normal Boys versus Normal Girls	98.5	98.6		
Young EMR Boys versus Young EMR Girls			84.5	87.5
Normal Boys versus Young EMR Boys	94.3		85.9	
Normal Girls versus Young EMR Girls		98.6		89.0

differences among the four groups in a rather dramatic way. In other words, males were separated from females almost as well by the motor performance criteria as by the criterion of sex and, similarly, the normal were distinguished from the retarded by the motor performance criteria.

Major Separating Variables

The discriminant analysis identified those variables common to the groups which were compared and those which had statistically significant discriminating powers in the four separate comparisons. The variables, in order of their discriminating power for each of the four comparisons, are as follows:

Normal Boys versus Normal Girls	*EMR Boys versus EMR Girls*	*Normal Boys versus EMR Boys*	*Normal Girls versus EMR Girls*
1. Softball Throw	Softball Throw	Grip Strength Left	Ring Stacking
2. Target Throw Vertical	Target Throw Vertical	Ring Stacking	Railwalk Backward
3. Target Throw Horizontal	Minnesota Manipulative	Bicycle With Resistance	Knee Flexion
4. Ring Stacking	Mat Crawl	Railwalk Forward	Elbow Extension
5. Minnesota Manipulative	Ring Stacking	35-Yard Dash	Scramble

For the comparisons between the boys and girls, four definers were common in both comparisons. The softball throw for velocity and the target throw vertical ranked one and two in discrimination power in each comparison. The variables that together contributed most to maximize motorically the separation between the sexes in both comparisons were definers of the components labeled Gross Limb-Eye Coordination and Fine Visual-Motor Coordination. Insofar as these groups are characteristics of other children of this age level, the evidence suggests that not only are there motoric variables which will, with high probability, separate children into their respective sexes, but the variables responsible for the separation are very much the same in retarded as in normal children.

For the comparisons within sex and between intellectual levels, a different result is seen. Although the first five variables differ in both comparisons with the exception of the ring stacking task, the proportional representation of comparable common factors that each combination of five variables defines is the same. Two variables define the common comparable factor labeled Strength-Power-Body Size, one is a Balance variable, one a Fine Visual-Motor Coordination variable, and the remaining variable is a definer of the common comparable factor Leg Power and Coordination.

This evidence suggests that to separate the educable mentally retarded from intellectually normal children on the basis of motor performance information, the best combination of five variables to maximize this separation should probably be variables that define the four components of the motor domain noted above. On the other hand, to maximize separation of boys from girls regardless of intellectual level, the best combination of five variables to select would be those variables that logically stress the components of Gross Limb-Eye Coordination and Fine Visual-Motor Coordination.

Chapter 7 / Implications of the Findings

Morphological and Motor Characteristics

As pointed out in Chapter 3, an investigation of the motor domain of mentally retarded children would be incomplete without giving consideration to the morphological characteristics of these children. Research has clearly established that institutionalized mentally retarded children are, on the average, markedly inferior to intellectually normal children in physical growth, and the more profound the mental retardation the greater is the growth deficit (Kugel and Mohr, 1963). However, there is considerable evidence which shows that not all classes of mentally subnormal children are retarded in physical growth, marked growth failure occurring primarily where there is evidence of chromosomal aberration, multiple congenital anomalies, or metabolic deficiency (Pozsonji and Lobb, 1967; Dutton, 1959).

There is no evidence to indicate that educable mentally retarded children as a group are metabolically deficient. It is not surprising, therefore, that the average stature of the retarded children in our sample was well within the normal range. However, both boys and girls were, on the average, heavy for their height. These findings parallel those obtained by Francis and Rarick (1959) on a sample of Madison and Milwaukee, Wisconsin, educable mentally retarded children in which it was found that while the heights and weights of these children were within the normal range, both the retarded boys and girls were heavy for their height. While the disparity was in neither case great, it is indicative of a trend on the part of these children toward obesity, particularly in view of the tendency for weight excess to increase with advancing age.

The above is perhaps brought into clearer focus when consideration is given to a comparison of body fat in normal and retarded children as assessed by skinfold measurements. The fact that both the retarded boys and girls in this investigation showed significantly greater skinfold thickness at all three measurement sites indicated that their relatively greater body weight was largely a reflection of excessive adipose tissue rather than lean body mass.

The evidence is now quite conclusive that obesity in metabolically normal children is largely a function of physical inactivity. This is borne out by the early research of Bruch (1940) and that of Johnson et al. (1956), in which it was found that the dietary habits of obese children and those of normal weight did not differ, but the daily physical activity of those who were obese was significantly less than that of the nonobese boys and girls. More recently, Parizkova (1963) has shown that there are dynamic fluctuations in body fat and muscle mass varying as a function of physical activity rather than calorie intake, and that weight curves usually obscure changes in body composition that result from a program of physical activity. There is now rather conclusive evidence that there are metabolic changes in fat tissue as a result of exercise which are in proportion to the intensity of the exercise. As Parizkova and Stankova (1967) and Parizkova (1966) have shown, muscular activity increases the body's ability to mobilize free fatty acids from the body's fat depots for utilization in the muscles in supporting the demands of exercise.

On the basis of the findings of the present investigation and in view of what is known about childhood obesity, it would seem clear that a major segment of this sample of retarded children had considerably more than the normal amount of body fat, a reflection of inadequate physical activity. Further support for this is the generally low level of motor proficiency exhibited by this sample of boys and girls, an indication of limited participation in physical activity. It would seem reasonable to believe that the poor motor performance of the retarded and the excessive quantity of body fat are interrelated to the extent that a vicious cycle of "poor performance-inactivity-accumulation of body fat" was set up.

Previous research on the gross motor performance of EMR children has shown that, as a group, these children lag two to four years behind the performance of normal children of the same chronological age (Francis and Rarick, 1959; Rarick et al., 1970). The present investigation has provided information on a broader range of motor skills than these earlier reports, but the findings here are essentially in agreement with them. Because of the limited sample sizes at each chronological age, sex and disability differences according to chronological age were not included in the analysis.

The magnitude of the retardation in strength of right and left grip in our sample of young EMR boys and girls is very much the same as that reported by Francis and Rarick (1959). The average grip strength of the normal children was much superior to that of the EMR children of equivalent age and compared favorably with that of the older EMR children, even though the latter as a group were more than three years the older.

While there are no normative data against which to compare the mean values of knee and elbow isokinetic strength, our sample of retarded children was well below the means of our sample of normal children of similar age on knee strength, but not on elbow strength. The similarity in mean performance of the retarded and normal in isokinetic strength of elbow flexion and elbow extension strength is difficult to explain in view of the marked superiority of the normal children in grip strength and knee strength. This may be an artifact in measurement, since one set of persons took the isokinetic strength measurements (using the Cybex) on the retarded subjects and a different set of two persons obtained the measurements on the normal subjects. Positioning of subjects is important in the use of the Cybex, and while every effort was made to standardize the testing operation, standardization of position for securing elbow strength is considerably more difficult than for knee strength. Hence, it is likely that real differences in strength may have been masked by variations in positioning of subjects on this test. It was evident from the variance analyses that the mentally retarded boys and girls were decidedly inferior to normal children in tests of muscular strength (elbow strength excepted), the performance of the girls being on the average relatively the poorer. The consistent superiority of the EMR boys to the EMR girls on measures of grip strength and knee strength suggests that the endogenous and exogenous factors that account for sex differences in the strength of the sexes operate similarly for retarded and normal children.

On tests that require explosive muscular force and utilize primarily phyletic movement patterns (such as running and jumping activities), the performance of the retarded children, while inferior to that of intellectually normal children, was not as poor as on tests that require considerable perseverance, particularly measures of muscular endurance (leg raise, trunk raise for time, and sit-ups). This is verified by the similarity in the mean values of the older retarded and the normal children on the former tests, but the markedly inferior performance of the retarded when the same comparison is used with the latter measures. It would seem that EMR children either do not have the muscular endurance of normal children *or* they are not as willing as normal children to accept the discomfort that accompanies tasks of this kind. This, of course, raises the question of test validity. Do such tests assess the retarded child's muscular endurance, his attention span or his willingness to endure physical discomfort?

The findings on flexibility were quite conclusive. It was evident that not only did the retarded children perform less well on all flexibility measures than normal children of the same age, but the flexibility scores of the older EMR children were, on the average, poorer than those of the normal children three years younger. The findings showed that the flexibility of the EMR boys was generally superior to that of the EMR girls, a sex difference not noted in the sample of normal children. The findings with this mentally retarded sample would lead one to hypothesize that range of motion is sex related. Such an hypothesis is in part supported by Fleishman (1964), who reported that in the adolescent years, boys on the average showed increased "extent flexibility" with advancing age, whereas girls exhibited the opposite trend.

The reason for the great difference in flexibility between the normal and the retarded children can be only conjecture at this point. It is generally recognized that maximum range of motion about a given joint depends largely upon the extent to which the muscles serving that structure are stretched by daily exercise involving the full range of motion. Clearly, a sedentary pattern of living, or one that involves limited physical activity, is not conducive to developing ligamental structures and muscles that permit full range of motion in those joints where freedom of movement is necessary. Based on the evidence presented here, it is apparent that a large proportion of these retarded children did not have the benefit of a program of physical activity which would develop a flexible body.

In the tests of fine visual-motor coordination, the extent of the performance deficit of the retarded children was slightly greater on the average than the deficit on the gross motor tasks. This general trend, while evident, was more apparent in the visual-motor tasks requiring manual coordination in transferring and placing objects, such as the Minnesota Manipulative, the Purdue pegboard, and the ring stacking tests, less evident in visual-motor tracking, the pursuit rotor. It is generally held that in the performance of tasks of manual dexterity, girls on the average perform better than boys in middle childhood. This tendency proved to be true with the normal children, but in the case of the retarded, the boys consistently outperformed the girls. This again points to the possibility of faulty assignment of children to special classes on the basis of present testing procedures, with more errors being made in the assignment of boys than girls. In all of the fine visual-motor tasks, while the deficit of the retarded children was substantial when matched with normals of the same age, the performance of the older retarded children was substantially better than that of the younger children. With advancing age these skills improve, and EMR children have the capability of acquiring manual skills at levels approaching those of normal children.

In all tests of balance, the retarded children as a group not only performed at a lower level than normal children of equivalent chronological age, but the scores of the older EMR children were, on the average, lower than the scores of the normal children three years younger. This follows the findings of other research comparing the balance performances of retardates and normal children (Francis and Rarick, 1959).

Following the trend previously noted, the performances of the retarded boys on all tests was superior to that of the retarded girls, the sex differences on most of the tests being greater in the retarded than in the normal.

The low but consistently positive correlations between I.Q. and the measures of balance and motor coordination are indicative of only a modest relationship between intellectual functioning and these aspects of motor behavior, but not at the level suggested by Ismail and Gruber (1967). Similarly, the correlations between I.Q. and the measures of fine visual-motor coordination were too low to be of predictive value. In retarded children as in intellectually normal children, intelligence as assessed was not highly correlated with either fine or gross motor performance.

Individual differences in performance on practically all of the motor tasks were substantially greater in this sample of EMR children than in the normal subjects who were tested. This is consistent with the findings of Clausen (1966) who reported larger standard deviations for his retarded than for his normal subjects in perceptual motor tests and tests of sensory perception. The broad range of individual differences in performances of EMR children included in this study is evidenced by the fact that on most tasks a few children performed at or above the 95th percentile of normal children and many were above the 50th percentile, although large numbers were below the 5th percentile. The findings here indicate that some EMR children had the capability of performing on a par with normal children. Few, if any, did perform on a par with normal children on all tasks; but by the same token, few normal children were superior in all skills, as is evidenced by the low-to-moderate relationships among motor test scores obtained on normal children.

In summarizing the motor performance differences between the EMR and the normal children, it should be pointed out that the present investigation provided data on a much wider range of gross and fine motor tests than previous studies. Where the tests were the same as those employed in earlier investigations, the findings reported here are generally consistent with previous research. It is clearly evident that on most motor tasks the majority of retarded boys and girls were exceeded by 80 to 90 percent of the normal children of the same age and sex. Worthy of note in the present investigation was the relatively greater retardation in the motor performance of the EMR girls. The reason for the relatively greater motor deficiency in EMR girls is not readily apparent. It may in part be a reflection of faulty classification of pupils, with greater inaccuracy in assigning males than females to special classes. Or it is possible that cultural factors and peer expectations operate differently among EMR boys and girls than among normal children. Both possibilities need to be studied.

Factor Structure

A major thrust of the present study was to determine the factor structure of motor abilities of EMR children. The wide range of variables included in this investigation and the nature of the sample make it unique in factor analytic studies of the motor domain of retarded children. Comparisons of the results of the factor analyses in this study with other factor analytic studies on the retarded, namely, the work of Clausen (1966) and Vandenberg (1964), are difficult because of the nature of the test items that were employed in their research. For example, Clausen used primarily sensorimotor tests, tests of sensory modalities, word association tests, and only a limited number of gross motor tasks. The work of Vandenberg, while including more gross motor tasks than that of Clausen, nevertheless tapped few of the basic abilities required in the broad range of physical activities characteristically used by children in our culture. Hence, the results of the present factor analysis will have to be viewed primarily in terms of the factor analyses that have been done on intellectually normal adolescents and young adults in which the tasks have been predominantly of the gross motor type (Fleishman, 1964; McCloy, 1956; Larson, 1941). The hypothesized factor structure which constituted the basis for the development of the tests used in the present study was based largely on the results of factor analytic studies of the gross motor domain of intellectually normal adolescents and young adults.

The factor structures which emerged from the data obtained on the two groups of normal children and the four groups of retarded children were in many respects remarkably similar. In no instance, however, did the factor structures of the six groups conform exactly to the hypothesized factor structure. It is clear that in this sample of normal and retarded children there were no such clearly defined factors as static muscular strength, dynamic muscular strength, or explosive muscular force as proposed by Fleishman (1964). These hypothesized components were all grouped into a single factor defined as a Strength-Power-Body Size factor in all six groups. A component of cardio-respiratory endurance did not emerge in any of the groups. This may have been a reflection of the use of an inappropriate test for these children or of the inability to motivate them to exercise to the point of fatigue. The variables selected for assessing this component either loaded on other factors (Strength-Power-Body Size or Leg Power and Coordination) or had loadings too low to be identified with a factor.

The hypothesized factors of static and dynamic balance could not be identified. In several of the groups, measures presumed to assess static and dynamic balance, respectively, loaded on a single factor. The tests of Fine Visual-Motor Coordination did consistently load on a single factor in all groups, as was the case for the measures of body fat.

It would seem that in this population of educable retarded and normal boys and girls, there was less specificity in motor skills than has been noted in factor analytic studies on older subjects. This is reasonable, for with advancing age humans are likely to spend more time and energy on those motor pursuits that they perform well and less time on those they do less well. Thus, with increasing age the basic components tend to become more clearly defined, and factors such as the Strength-Power-Body Size factor will be split up into several strength components, as well as components of power and body size.

In all six groups, Body Fat or Dead Weight emerged as a factor. This factor, while not accounting for a large proportion of the common variance, is nevertheless important in that it has a negative influence in tasks requiring the propulsion of the body mass. Factor analytic studies with young males have clearly indicated the negative role body fat plays in motor performance (Rarick, 1937; Fleishman, 1964).

The factor Fine Visual-Motor Coordination was extracted in all six groups and was readily identified because of the high and consistent loadings of the tests of fine visual-motor coordination. It is clear from the pattern of factor loadings on all six groups that there is a well-defined factor of fine visual-motor control in both normal and EMR boys and girls.

The hypothesized factors of static balance and dynamic balance did not emerge as such in all groups. As mentioned earlier, the tests designed to measure static and dynamic balance, respectively, frequently came out on the same factor. For example, the railwalking tests usually clustered on the same factor, but not necessarily on the factor that included the stabilometer and the bass test. It is interesting to note that Fleishman (1964) obtained two balance factors in his factor analytic study. Railwalking and tests similar to the Bass Test had high loadings on the same factor. The other balance factor he labeled "balance with visual cues," which is suggestive of the role that vision plays in balance.

The fact that the hypothesized factor flexibility did not emerge as a single factor was not surprising. Early research had pointed to a great deal of specificity in flexibility Hupprich (1950). Fleishman (1964) extracted two flexibility factors in his investigation; one he called "extent flexibility," the other "dynamic flexibility."

It should not be surprising that the factor structures of the six groups did not conform to the hypothesized factor structure, since the hypothesized factor structure, of necessity, had to be formulated on the basis of previous factor analytic work done on normal adolescents and normal young adults. What perhaps is surprising is the marked similarity in factor structures of the six groups as reflected by the substantial cosines among respective factors across all groups. True, the factor structures of the normal boys and normal girls were more alike than the factor structures of the normal and the retarded children. Yet, when one considers that in the light of the broad array of measures that was used there were four factors which accounted for well over half the common variance, namely, the factors of Strength-Power-Body Size, Body Fat, Fine Visual-Motor Coordination, and Gross Limb-Eye Coordination, a picture emerges that indicates quite clearly the way in which the motor abilities are structured in normal and EMR boys and girls and the similarities in these structures.

Implications for Curriculum Development

Society has rightly accepted the responsibility of providing educational opportunities for educable mentally retarded children. This has been done under the assumption that these children will profit from the educational experiences that have been made available to them. The difficulties associated with their education have been recognized, they have been provided with specially trained teachers and the pupil-teacher ratio is smaller than for normal children, thus permitting them more individualized instruction. The schools have acknowledged their responsibility by providing these children with experiences as nearly as possible like those offered to children of normal intelligence. The ultimate aim is to equip them with the skills and abilities needed to function satisfactorily in the mainstream of society. It is the position of the writers that the motor domain offers perhaps the best single avenue for helping the retarded child move toward this end. Up to the present time there has been no serious attempt to utilize this approach, in part because teachers qualified to assume this responsibility have not been available and in part because of the lack of adequate curriculum guides. Nor has there been a serious attempt to utilize the results of research in developing guidelines for curricula in physical education for mentally retarded children. In fact, curricula in physical education for intellectually normal children have for the most part been largely the result of tradition and experience.

To prepare recommendations for curriculum development, two basic types of information have been used. The first deals with those parameters of physical growth and motor development in which the EMR children differ most from intellectually normal children. This is clearly an important consideration, if the goal of education is to help these children develop as nearly like normal children as possible. The second considers the nature of the retarded as revealed by the factor structure of their motor abilities. This indicates the types of physical activity appropriate for them and the relative emphasis that should be given to each. The recommendations that follow are based on the research described in the preceding sections and are confined to educable mentally retarded boys and girls in the age range 6 through 13 years.

Individualization of Instruction

The broad range of individual differences in the motor tasks included in the present study provides clear evidence of the need for individualization of instruction in physical education for these children. While good educational practice has traditionally emphasized the need for individualizing instruction, the wider range of individual differences in motor performance of the retarded as compared to intellectually normal children leaves little doubt of the importance of adopting this procedure.

That individualizing instruction in physical education does result in improved motor performance of EMR children has been shown by the research of Rarick and Broadhead (1968), in which the motor performance of EMR children exposed to a 20-week individualized physical education program was significantly better than that of EMR children offered a group-oriented program for the same period of time. Those in the individualized program, while working basically on the same tasks as those in the group-oriented program, were working individually at their own level. This arrangement helped most of these children to avoid frustration and invidious comparisons, by providing a learning situation that was satisfying and motivating. Furthermore, it gave the teacher an opportunity to assign tasks geared to each child's ability level and enabled her to provide individual assistance when needed.

The relatively low pupil-teacher ratio makes individualization of instruction feasible, particularly when the teacher is provided with a teacher's aide. The research of Rarick and Broadhead (1968) clearly demonstrated that the special education teacher can provide competent instruction in physical education for these children when given an effective in-service training program and when provided with a qualified physical education supervisor.

Assessment of Motor Abilities

If physical education instruction for EMR children is to be educationally sound, it must give consideration to their motor needs, providing help where help is needed. In an earlier section of this report, the basic components that underlie the broad range of motor abilities of retarded and normal children was identified. An important function of factor analytic research is test construction. Test items that load high on a given factor can be used to assess this factor. For example, if the domain of motor performance of EMR children of a given age span can be described by nine factors, then a nine-item test battery (one test item for each factor) can be employed. Through the use of such a test, the teacher can identify within her own class those children who need help on a given basic component, and by individualizing the instruction she can select activities which draw upon those basic abilities in which help is needed. This does not mean that the entire instructional period should be devoted to these "remedial procedures," but rather that the teacher will have clearly in mind where each child needs help and can devote a portion of the instructional period to this end.

Physical Activity Needs of the Retarded as a Group

The preceding paragraphs have emphasized the need for individualization of instruction. Depending upon the nature and variability of the group, some of the instructional period will be devoted to group activities. The paragraphs that follow propose guidelines, based on the findings of this research, which it is believed will be helpful in planning general physical education experiences for EMR children. The recommendations in regard to allocation of program content that follow should be viewed solely as a general guide and obviously will vary with the needs of the children who are served.

Muscular Strength and Power. The program of physical education should devote a major part of its time (approximately 30 percent) to vigorous physical activities that place demands on the muscles of the trunk and limbs. Such activities as tumbling, gymnastics, self-testing activities that call upon reserves of muscular power, and all forms of locomotor activity, including hopping, jumping, skipping, leaping, and running, should have a prominent place in the program. Included also should be activities that require body support by the arms (overhead ladder and horizontal bar) and activities that require lifting, carrying, pushing, and pulling of reasonably heavy objects. Since marked individual differences in muscular strength and power are characteristic of educable mentally retarded boys and girls, and since this aspect of development is one in which they lag well behind normal children, it is important that a large proportion of their physical activity schedule be devoted to activities of this kind.

Gross Coordination of Limb and Body Movements. Approximately 10 to 20 percent of the variance in motor performance of EMR boys and girls is a function of individual differences in Gross Limb-Eye Coordination and Leg Power and Coordination. Since these two factors underlie the control of limb and body movements, children should be exposed to a broad range of activities that call upon (1) changes in the body's orientation in space, and (2) movements of the limbs in the projection and retrieval of objects. Thus, retarded children should be offered a variety of running activities; activities that stress quickness of bodily movement, such as rapid starts and sudden stops, directional changes while running, rapid crawling and turning on the mat, movement from the supine and prone position to the vertical and vice versa; and other kinds of movements requiring agility. In developing control of the limbs, the movement patterns of throwing, striking, catching, and kicking should be stressed. Since these movement patterns in the retarded child are frequently immature and uncoordinated, particular attention needs to be given to the quality of the movement patterns. Faulty patterns of movement can be corrected in EMR children just as they can in normal children, but only if the teacher is willing to provide the help. Approximately 20 percent of the instructional program should be devoted to activities that call upon these activities.

Balance. While balance did not emerge as a single independent factor, it was evident from the factor analyses that balance capabilities, while often contaminated with other abilities, are nevertheless important in accounting for individual differences in motor performance of EMR children. It is clear that retarded children, as is true of normal children, need a variety of activities rich in elements of balance. Approximately 5 to 10 percent of the program should be given over to activities of a balance type. Balance beam activities, hopping activities, gymnastic events of a balance type, and hand and foot balancing exercises that call upon many aspects of balance and body control, should have a prominent place in the curriculum.

Flexibility. As the factor analysis clearly showed, there is no general factor of flexibility. In view of the retarded child's poor performance on the tests of flexibility, it is evident that a significant proportion of the time allotment (5 to 10 percent) should be given to improving the retarded child's flexibility. Perhaps the most urgent need is to improve the range of motion in the spine and in the hip joint. Therefore, activities that stretch the flexors and the extensors of the spine and those of the hamstrings should receive the greatest attention.

Fine Visual-Motor Coordination. The factor of fine visual-motor coordination accounted for approximately 25 percent of the variance in motor performance of the older EMR children, less in the younger. While this aspect of development is normally not included within the domain of physical education, it is clear that the educational program should not ignore it. Not only did this component account for a considerable part of the common variance in motor performance, but the degree of retardation in fine motor skills was, on the average, great in both the EMR boys and girls. Hence, it is important that the educational program provide opportunities for a variety of experiences that require a range of manual skills such as painting, drawing, penmanship, assembly tasks, and use of hand tools.

Energy Expenditure. The findings reported here clearly show that a large segment of the EMR children are burdened with excess body fat. In view of their substandard level of motor performance, it would seem reasonable to believe that their level of energy expenditure is far less than it should be to support healthy physical growth. While the problem of childhood obesity among intellectually normal children has been with us for many years (Stuart, 1955), the problem is clearly of considerably greater magnitude in the mentally retarded. In the interest of assuring healthy growth, the level of energy expenditure of most of these children should be increased substantially. This means that the daily instructional physical education program for EMR children should encompass a time span of at least one hour, preferably divided into two sessions. The instructional program, while focusing on the acquisition of motor skills, must be sufficiently vigorous to call upon the child's energy reserves. In order to help the child meet his energy expenditure requirements, supervised after-school sports programs should also be provided.

It is obvious that not all EMR children have a tendency toward obesity. Hence, it behooves the school in its health appraisal program to identify the children with tendencies toward this problem, so that appropriate adjustments can be made in their program of physical activity. It should be kept in mind that skinfold measures are a better guide to body composition than are scales, providing a more effective picture of the relative distribution of lean body mass and body fat. If the child's metabolism is normal and if he is organically sound, a balanced daily regimen of physical activity and rest is the best guarantee of normal body weight, a healthy distribution of the tissue components, and an effectively functioning heart and circulatory system.

While the drive for physical activity in all healthy children is strong, it can be reversed if the physical activity experiences are not satisfying. This is usually what happens in the case of the unskilled child or the child who through physical or mental disabilities cannot keep pace with the peer group. It is the responsibility of the physical education instructional program to provide both normal and retarded children with the opportunity to develop their motor abilities and to improve their physical fitness. There must be sufficient time in the school day for this to be accomplished. Obviously, the retarded will need more time for this than intellectually normal children.

Integrated or Special Classes

The education of children in the I.Q. range of 50–75 has in recent years been handled primarily by special classes in the public schools. The rapid expansion of special class programs during the past 30 years has been accompanied by numerous investigations designed to determine the effectiveness of such programs, chiefly by comparing the educational outcomes of EMR children educated in regular classes and in special classes. Summaries of these investigations by Kirk (1964) and by Quay (1963) generally indicate that academic achievement is poorer in special classes and social adjustment is poorer in regular classes. The validity of these generalized conclusions is open to question in view of the methodological weakness of the studies, chiefly in respect to inappropriate or biased sampling. As Guskin and Spicker (1968) point out, by comparing EMR children in special classes with EMR children in regular classes, one is in essence comparing the less able with the more able EMR children.

Where careful matching was done for age, I.Q., socioeconomic status, previous school experience, and language background, EMR children in regular classes showed only slightly better than chance gains in overall classroom work and in reading over a 2-year period as compared to EMR children in special classes (Mullen and Itkin, 1961). Perhaps the most carefully controlled study to compare the academic performance of EMR children in regular and special classes was the investigation by Goldstein, Moss, and Jordan (1965) in which the sampling problem was avoided by the formation of new special education classes in districts where none had previously existed. Children were drawn randomly from the same population and assigned in an unbiased manner to special and to regular classes. In brief, the investigation showed that while the children in both groups (special class and regular class) made gains in measured I.Q., there was no significant difference between them. During the first 2 years, children in the regular class made the greater gains in reading skills, but this difference was not apparent by the end of the fourth year. No difference between the groups was noted in a specially developed test of basic information. The interaction of those in special classes with their neighborhood peers appeared more restrained than those in regular classes.

In effect, these investigations have essentially reinforced what we already know or should have known—that children profit from educational experiences to the extent that these experiences are adapted to their needs and capabilities. In the sense that special classes meet the educational needs of particular children, these classes will be effective. On the other hand, where regular classroom procedures can be adapted to the particular learning problems of EMR children, and under conditions where the social atmosphere of the classroom is healthy, EMR children will learn effectively. In other words, the learning arrangements must be adjusted to the child, whether he is in a special or a regular class; and where this is done, the setting appears to be of little consequence.

In the past few years the trend has been toward normalization—moving the child back into the mainstream of education where possible. The concept is basically sound, but it is not without its problems. The premise upon which such a procedure rests is greater individualization of instruction, improved diagnostic procedures, and referral for special assistance when indicated. The concept that retarded children and intellectually normal children should learn to live together, both in work and in play, is indeed sound. This mandates that each child must learn to accept his own strengths and weaknesses and those of his peers—not a simple task. Obviously, there are instances where the gaps in ability are so great that the situation becomes unmanageable. This requires special attention, a teaching-learning situation removed from the environment of the regular classroom. The essential point is that the child be encouraged to function in as normal an environment as possible, as long as it is a pleasant and profitable learning situation. This means that the school must do its best to see that such an environment is provided, one that is sufficiently flexible, secure, and stimulating to permit learning to occur.

What does this mean for physical education? The generally held belief that mentally retarded children are more nearly normal in motoric functions than in conceptual development has been in part supported by the data reported here. Nevertheless, the retardation is substantial, on the average, the retarded males being approximately 1 standard deviation below the mean of normal males of equivalent chronological age and the retarded females approximately $1\frac{1}{2}$ standard deviations below their normal female counterparts. The differences noted here were more dramatically shown through the use of discriminant analysis and by the formulation of person-clusters. It is equally clear that a sizable number of EMR's perform at or above the level of many intellectually normal children on some motor tasks. Given the proper instruction, perhaps as many as 50 percent of these children will in time perform at the level of the majority of intellectually normal children.

The rationale for integration of EMR children with normal children in the physical education instructional program is no different from that of integration in any other aspect of the curriculum. If the child is able to cope with the situation emotionally and can make progress in his motor development, integration would seem to be the answer.

That integration of EMR children with intellectually normal children is feasible is evidenced by the research of Stein (1965) which showed that at the conclusion of a year of integrated physical education instruction, approximately half of the scores of the EMR boys (grades 7 and 8) were higher than the mean values of the AAHPER Youth Fitness Test. The results provide support for the belief held by many that motor performance differences between normal and EMR boys are in no small degree a reflection of differences in opportunity for supervised physical activity.

It should be kept in mind, however, that inadequacies in the motor realm are readily apparent to those in the peer group, perhaps more so than in areas of cognitive development. Thus, unless the situation is carefully handled, an attitude of disapproval of the group, expressed or sensed, will assuredly convince the learner of his inadequacies in yet another dimension of his already ineffective behavior. In cases where task failure is obvious, integration in the usual class activities is clearly not recommended. The wise teacher in the integrated program can provide for individualization of instruction in an unobtrusive way, for many intellectually normal children also have motoric problems—problems that are unfortunately ignored by many teachers. If the class size is reasonable and if trained teacher's aides are provided, there would seem to be no reason why individual help could not be given to those with motor problems, regardless of their intellectual level.

Where the above is not feasible, there is now documented evidence to indicate that special education teachers can provide competent instruction in physical education, if given the help of knowledgeable supervision (Rarick and Broadhead, 1968). There is no defensible reason why competent motoric education in the schools should not be provided for both intellectually normal and educationally handicapped children.

Bibliography, Part I

1. Barry, J., and T. K. Cureton. "Factorial Analysis of Physique and Performance in Prepubescent Boys." *Research Quarterly* 32 (1961), 283–300.
2. Bruch, Hilda. "Obesity in Childhood: IV. Energy Expenditure in Obese Children." *American Journal of Diseases of Children* 60 (1940), 1082–1109.
3. Canadian Association for Health, Physical Education and Recreation. *The Physical Work Capacity of Canadian Children.* Toronto, 1968.
4. Clarke, A. D. B. *Proceedings of the London Conference on the Scientific Study of Mental Deficiency* 1 (1962), 89.
5. Clarke, D. H., and F. M. Henry. "Neuromotor Specificity and Increased Speed from Strength Development." *Research Quarterly* 32 (1961), 315–25.
6. Clausen, Johs. *Ability Structure and Subgroups in Mental Retardation.* London: Macmillan and Co., Ltd., 1966.
7. Coleman, J. W. "The Differential Measurement of the Speed Factor in Large Muscle Activities." *Research Quarterly* 8 (1937), 123–30.
8. Cumbee, F. Z. "A Factorial Analysis of Motor Coordination." *Research Quarterly* 25 (1954), 412–28.
9. Dagenais, F., and L. A. Marascuilo. "The Effect of Factor Scores, Guttman Scores, and Sample Sum Scores on the Size of *F* Ratios in an Analysis of Variance Design." *Multivariate Behavioral Research* 8 (1973), 491–502.
10. Dingman, Harvey F., and Arthur B. Silverstein. "Intelligence, Motor Disabilities, and Reaction Time in the Mentally Retarded." *Perceptual and Motor Skills* 19 (1964), 791–94.
11. Dunn, O. J. "Multiple Comparisons Among Means." *Journal of the American Statistical Association* 56 (1961), 52–64.
12. Dutton, G. "The Size of Mentally Defective Boys." *Archives of Diseases of Children* 34 (1959), 331–43.
13. Ellis, Norman R., and William Sloan. "Relationship Between Intelligence and Simple Reaction Time in Mental Defectives." *Perceptual and Motor Skills* 7 (1957), 65–67.

14. Fleishman, Edwin A. *The Structure and Measurement of Physical Fitness.* Englewood Cliffs, N. J.: Prentice-Hall, Inc., 1964.

15. Fleishman, E. A., and W. E. Hempel. "Changes in Factor Structure of a Complex Psychomotor Test as a Function of Practice." *Psychometrika* 19 (1954), 239–52.

16. Francis, R. J., and G. L. Rarick. "Motor Characteristics of the Mentally Retarded." *American Journal of Mental Deficiency* 63 (1959), 792–811.

17. Glass, G. V., and P. A. Taylor. "Factor Analytic Methodology." *Review of Educational Research* XXXVI (1966), 566–87.

18. Goldstein, H., J. W. Moss, and L. J. Jordan. *The Efficiency of Special Class Training on the Development of Mentally Retarded Children.* Cooperative Research Project No. 619. Washington, D.C.: U.S. Office of Education, 1965.

19. Gordon, W. *Proceedings of the London Conference on the Scientific Study of Mental Deficiency* 2 (1962), 587.

20. Guskin, S. L., and H. H. Spicker. "Educational Research in Mental Retardation." In Norman Ellis (Ed.), *International Review of Research in Mental Retardation.* New York: Academic Press, 1968.

21. Harmon, H. H. *Modern Factor Analysis* (2nd ed.). Chicago: University of Chicago Press, 1967.

22. Harris, C. W. "On Factors and Factor Scores." *Psychometrika* 32 (1967), 363–79.

23. Harris, C. W., and H. F. Kaiser. "Oblique Factor Analytic Solutions by Orthogonal Transformations." *Psychometrika* 29 (1964), 347–62.

24. Harris, M., and C. W. Harris. "A Factor Analytic Interpretation Strategy." *Educational and Psychological Measurement* 31 (1971), 589–606.

25. Henry, F. M., W. S. Lotter, and L. E. Smith. "Factorial Structure of Individual Differences in Limb Speed, Reaction, and Strength." *Research Quarterly* 33 (1962), 70–84.

26. Holman, P. "The Relationship Between General Mental Development and Manual Dexterity." *British Journal of Psychiatry* 23 (1933), 279.

27. Hotelling, H. "Analysis of a Complex of Statistical Variables into Principal Components." *Journal of Educational Psychology* 24 (1933), 417–41, 498–520.

28. Hupprich, Florence L., and Peter O. Sigerseth. "The Specificity of Flexibility in Girls." *Research Quarterly* 21 (1950), 25–33.

29. Ismail, A. H., and C. C. Cowell. "Factor Analysis of Motor Aptitude of Preadolescent Males." *Research Quarterly* 32 (1961), 507–13.

30. Ismail, A. H., and J. J. Gruber. *Integrated Development: Motor Aptitude and Intellectual Performances.* Columbus, Ohio: Charles E. Merrill Books, Inc., 1967.

31. Johnson, M. L., B. S. Burke, and J. Mayer, "Relative Importance of Inactivity and Overeating in Energy Balance of Obese High School Girls." *American Journal of Clinical Nutrition* 4 (1956), 37–44.

32. Kaiser, H. F. "The Varimax Criterion for Analytic Rotation in Factor Analysis." *Psychometrika* 23 (1958), 187–200.

33. Kaiser, H. F. "Psychometric Approaches to Factor Analysis." *Invitational Conference on Testing Problems.* Princeton, N. J.: Educational Testing Service, 1964, 37–45.

34. Kaiser, H. F., and J. Caffrey. "Alpha Factor Analysis." *Psychometrika* 30 (1965), 1–14.

35. Kaiser, H. F., S. Hunka, and J. D. Bianchini. "Relating Factors Between Studies Based on Different Individuals." *Multivariate Behavioral Research* 6 (1971), 409–22.

36. Kirby, Janet K. "Motor Learning and Performance in Mentally Retarded Children as Related to Age and Sex." Unpublished Master's Thesis, University of California, Berkeley, 1969.

37. Kirk, S. A. "Research in Education." In H. A. Stevens and R. Heber (Eds.), *Mental Retardation: A Review of Research.* Chicago: University of Chicago Press, 1964, 57–99.

38. Kugel, R. B. and J. Mohr. "Mental Retardation and Physical Growth." *American Journal of Mental Deficiency* 68 (1963), 41.

39. Larson, L. A. "A Factor Analysis of Motor Ability Variables and Tests for College Men." *Research Quarterly* 12 (1941), 499–517.

40. Liemohn, W. P., and D. R. Knapczyk. "Factor Analysis of Gross and Fine Motor Ability in Developmentally Disabled Children." *Research Quarterly* 45 (1974), 424–32.

41. Lombard, Olive M. "Breadth of Bone and Muscle by Age and Sex in Childhood." *Child Development* 21 (1950), 229–39.

42. Malpass, L. F. *Responses of Retarded and Normal Children to Selected Clinical Measures,* Section 1. Carbondale, Ill.: Southern Illinois University Press, 1959.

43. McCloy, C. H. "A Factor Analysis of Tests of Endurance." *Research Quarterly* 27 (1956), 213–16.

44. Mullen, F. A., and W. Itkin. *Achievement and Adjustment of Educable Mentally Handicapped Children.* Cooperative Research Project S.A.E. 6529. Chicago: Board of Education, 1961.

45. Parizkova, Jana. "Impact of Age, Diet, and Exercise on Man's Body Composition." *Annals of the New York Academy of Sciences* 110 (1963), 661–74.

46. Parizkova, Jana. "Nutrition and its Relation to Body Composition in Exercise." *Proceedings Nutrition Society* 25 (1966), 93–99.

47. Parizkova, Jana, and L. Stankova. "Release of Free Fatty Acids From Adipose Tissue in Vitro after Adrenalin in Relation to the Total Body Fat in Rats of Different Age and Different Physical Activity." *Nutrition Dieta* 9 (1967), 43–55.

48. Peterson, K. L., P. Reuschlein, and V. Seefeldt. "Factor Analyses of Motor Performance for Kindergarten, First and Second Grade Children: A Tentative Solution." Unpublished paper, Department of Physical Education, Michigan State University, East Lansing, Michigan, 1974.

49. Pozsonji, J., and H. Lobb. "Growth in Mentally Retarded Children." *Journal of Pediatrics* 71 (1967), 865–68.

50. Pryor, Helen B., and H. E. Thelander. "Growth Deviations in Handicapped Children." *Clinical Pediatrics* 6 (1967), 501–12.

51. Quay, L. C. "Academic Skills." In N. R. Ellis (Ed.), *Handbook of Mental Deficiency.* New York: McGraw-Hill Book Co., 1963, 664–90.

52. Rabin, Herbert M. "The Relationship of Age, Intelligence and Sex to Motor Proficiency in Mental Defectives." *American Journal of Mental Deficiency* 62 (1957), 507–16.

53. Rao, C. R. "Estimation and Tests of Significance in Factor Analysis." *Psychometrika* 20 (1955), 93–111.

54. Rarick, G. L. "An Analysis of the Speed Factor in Simple Athletic Activities." *Research Quarterly* 8 (1937), 89–105.

55. Rarick, G. L. "The Factor Structure of Motor Abilities of Educable Mentally Retarded Children." In G. A. Jervis (Ed.), *Expanding Concepts in Mental Retardation.* Springfield, Ill.: Charles C Thomas, 1968, 238–46.

56. Rarick, G. L., and G. D. Broadhead. *Effects of Individualized Versus Group Instruction on Selected Parameters of the Development of Educable Mentally Retarded and Minimally Brain Injured Children.* Madison, Wis.: University of Wisconsin (Department of Physical Education), 1968.

57. Rarick, G. L., V. D. Seefeldt, and Ionel F. Rapaport. *Physical Growth and Development in Down's Syndrome. An Eight Year Longitudinal Study.* Madison, Wis.: University of Wisconsin (Department of Physical Education), 1966.

58. Rarick, G. L., J. H. Widdop, and G. D. Broadhead. "The Physical Fitness and Motor Performance of Educable Mentally Retarded Children." *Exceptional Children* 36 (1970), 509–19.

59. Reynolds, E. L. "Differential Tissue Growth in the Leg During Childhood." *Child Development* 15 (1944), 181–205.

60. Roberts, G. E., and B. E. Clayton. "Some Findings Arising Out of a Survey of Mentally Retarded Children. Part II: Physical Growth and Development." *Developmental Medicine and Child Neurology* 11 (1969), 584–94.

61. Sjostrand, T. "Changes in Respiratory Organs of Workmen at an Ore Smelting Works." *Acta Medica Scandinavica* Supp. 196 (1947), 687–99.

62. Sloan, W. "Motor Proficiency and Intelligence." *American Journal of Mental Deficiency* 55 (1951), 394–406.

63. Stein, Julian U. "Physical Fitness of Mentally Retarded Boys Relative to National Age Norms." *Rehabilitation Literature* (Special Report) 26 (1965), 205.

64. Stuart, Harold C. "Obesity in Childhood." *Quarterly Review of Pediatrics* 10 (1955), 131–45.

65. Stuart, H. C., and E. H. Sobel. "The Thickness of the Skin and Subcutaneous Tissue by Age and Sex in Childhood." *Journal of Pediatrics* 28 (1946), 637–47.

66. Tredgold, A. F., R. F. Tredgold, and K. Soddy. *A Textbook of Mental Deficiency.* Baltimore: Williams and Wilkins, 1956.

67. Tryon, R. C. "Person-Clusters on Intellectual Abilities and on MMPI Attributes." *Multivariate Behavioral Research* 1 (1967), 5–35.

68. Tryon, R. C., and D. E. Bailey. *Cluster Analysis.* New York: McGraw-Hill Book Co., 1970.

69. Vandenberg, S. G. "Factor Analytic Studies of the Lincoln Oseretsky Test of Motor Proficiency." *Perceptual and Motor Skills* 19 (1964), 23–41.

70. Wendler, A. J. "A Critical Analysis of Test Elements Used in Physical Education." *Research Quarterly* 9 (1938), 64–76.

71. Widdop, James H. "The Motor Performance of Educable Mentally Retarded Children With Particular Reference to the Identification of Factors Associated With Individual Differences in Performance." Unpublished Doctoral Dissertation, Madison, Wis.: University of Wisconsin, 1967.

Part II / THE EFFECTS OF INDIVIDUALIZED VERSUS GROUP ORIENTED PHYSICAL EDUCATION PROGRAMS ON SELECTED PARAMETERS OF THE DEVELOPMENT OF EDUCABLE MENTALLY RETARDED, AND MINIMALLY BRAIN-INJURED CHILDREN

Chapter 8 / The Nature of the Experiment

Introduction

A concept which has made only a limited impact on professional educators is that educationally handicapped children may profit from well-designed school programs of physical education. But in some quarters there is a growing belief that many of the physical, intellectual, sensory, social, and emotional needs of these children can be met through carefully planned and well-executed physical activity programs. Clinical reports to this effect are numerous, but experimental evidence which supports this view is not impressive. Most research has involved very small samples of children over short periods of time and under conditions with limited experimental control. Thus, there is little substantive information available regarding the possible influence which physical activity programs have on these children. The very nature of the handicap and the child's attitude toward his limitations suggest that the setting in which instruction takes place may well be critical in promoting optimum development.

This investigation has examined the effects of specially planned physical activity programs upon the motor, strength, intellectual, social, and emotional development of educable mentally retarded children and minimally brain-injured (MBI) children of elementary school age. Since most educators believe that physical education should be a part of the school curriculum for all children, this is clearly a question of some importance. Yet a study by Rarick, Widdop, and Broadhead (1967b) showed that almost half the educable mentally retarded children in the public schools of the United States had no physical education. In Britain, too, an unsatisfactory position prevails with few educationally handicapped children receiving the range and quality of the curriculum in physical education afforded to their peers. Indeed, this may be a feature of the educational system of many countries, and it is not surprising, therefore, that the level of motor performance is low in children who are rarely given the opportunities provided for others. The subaverage skill in motor tasks, reported by several investigators (AAHPER, 1968; Francis and Rarick, 1959; Hayden, 1964; Rarick, Widdop, and Broadhead, 1967a, 1970; Sloan, 1951; Stein, 1963; Widdop, 1967), should not be accepted as irreversible. The opportunity to attain satisfaction and a sense of accomplishment through achievement in the motor domain is a right of all children.

Several reasons (excuses) have been proposed to explain the lack of school physical education for educationally handicapped children. First, since special education classes are usually established primarily because most of the children do not make satisfactory progress in the fundamental school processes and skills, the emphasis has been upon academic work. Even a move toward stressing social and vocational skill has brought limited changes in the traditional special school curriculum. Second, children placed in classes for the minimally brain-injured are frequently denied physical education because many authorities in special education appear to believe, like Cruickshank and his colleagues (1961), that gross movements should be inhibited, to be replaced by a very stereotyped, tightly structured school routine. Likewise, many physically handicapped children do not have such opportunities either because it is assumed that there is little that they can achieve or for reasons of safety. A third reason is the shortage of physical education teachers who are sensitive to these children's needs and are qualified to teach them. Whatever the reasons, the fact is that physical education lessons are not a part of the curriculum for many children in special education, and only approximately a quarter of all educable retardates (the majority group in special education) have an hour or more of physical activity per week. Such a position is quite contrary to the aims of education and special education noted in numerous texts (Bilborough and Jones, 1963; Cameron and Pleasance, 1963; Cruickshank, Bentzen, Ratzeburg, and Tannhauser, 1961; Dunn, 1963).

Interesting reports by Corder (1966), Nunley (1965), Oliver (1958, 1960), and Solomon and Pangle (1966, 1967) have indicated that positive changes in behavior may be elicited by the addition of physical activity lessons to the daily school curriculum for minimally brain-injured children and for trainable and educable mentally retarded children. The present study was designed to develop the tenets previously described, under conditions which might reasonably be expected to prevail in the setting of ordinary schools.

Scope of the Study

The research was a cooperative venture between the University of Wisconsin and the Galena Park, Pasadena, and Deer Park Independent School Districts, Harris County, Texas.

The aim was to determine the role of different types of physical education programs in modifying the motor, strength, intellectual, social, and emotional development of educable mentally retarded children and minimally brain-injured children in the age range 6 to 13 years. All the children in special classes for the EMR and for the MBI in the elementary schools of these three contiguous districts participated in the experiment. Ultimately, this involved 275 EMR children and 206 MBI children. Intact classes of retardates and of brain-injured children were divided into two chronological age groups; and then from each group of age/educational disability classes, random procedures assigned whole classes to one of four experimental treatments. Two of the treatments entailed physical education programs, each with a different orientation, and two involved no special physical education instruction. Of the latter two treatments, one was an art education program to control for the Hawthorne effect, and the other served as a control (the usual classroom instructional program).

Such a research plan was used to control for possible confounding treatment effects. First, there was the probability that special treatment in and of itself might elicit changes in behavior of some, but not all, of the children. Were this to occur, such changes would be additional to the maturational changes anticipated for all the children in a study lasting approximately 6 months and would indicate the existence of the Hawthorne phenomenon. Second, it was possible that the three specially planned instructional programs might be differentially effective in being associated with changed behavior. Thus, the study could describe the extent to which physical education on the one hand, and art education on the other, elicited changes in particular aspects of development. For the three special groups of classes, the processes of maturation and the likely Hawthorne influence were common components of their special programs. The nature of the physical education and art education programs provided a component which was different. Third, there was the possibility that one type of physical education program might be more effective than the other in influencing the developmental processes. Control for the likelihood that the children might be differently affected, according to their chronological age, sex, and category of educational disability, was also included in the research design.

Two distinct programs of physical education were designed: one where the children always worked alone and the other where the children always worked with a partner or as a member of a team or group. The rationale for the use of the individualized approach rested upon the belief, held by some, that educationally disabled children need to have the security of working individually at their own level, where the distractive influences of their peers are at a minimum and the tensions and frustrations brought on by invidious comparisons and competition for peer status are practically nonexistent. Conversely, others believe that some of the traumatic effects of group interaction in motor skill development for those children are not great and that the social values resulting from group play far outweigh the possible negative influences on skill learning.

The physical education and art education programs were taught by the classroom teachers for approximately 35 minutes each day for 20 weeks of school. Several standardized tests, selected to assess the five parameters of development previously mentioned, were completed by the children prior to, and at the conclusion of, the experimental programs. Careful in-service training of the classroom teachers preceded the testing and teaching phases of the experiment.

Since a primary purpose of school physical education programs is to enable children to become reasonably proficient in the motor activities of our culture and at the same time develop desirable patterns of social behavior, an investigation of the influence of programs with two distinct types of orientation seemed to be worthwhile. The opportunity also to examine the relative influence of the art education program on these boys and girls gave an added value to the research.

Chapter 9 / Experimental Design and Procedural Steps

Research Design

Overview

As pointed out in the preceding chapter, three of the four experimental treatments involved specially planned programs of work which were different from the usual school routine. A comparison could therefore be made between those treatments having a special program and those having no special program whatsoever. Of the special treatments, two involved physical education and the other was an art program which involved no gross motor activity, thus allowing a comparison between two essentially different types of school lessons. The two physical education programs involved a different social organization of the class, one being directed toward the individual and the other toward the group. The children in all three experimental programs were fully aware that the lessons were special, but they were unaware that the central focus of the project was on physical education per se. It was a difference in the nature, and not the quality, of the treatment which was planned; and the research procedures outlined seemed to attack the problem of the Hawthorne effect in a realistic manner so that the results reported later might make a useful contribution to a knowledge of how groups of educationally disabled children can profit from their schooling. The children in the fourth treatment group followed the usual instructional program, receiving no special treatment, and thus served as the experimental control.

In summary, the research sought answers to the following three questions: First, what were the changes in the measures of motor, strength, intellectual, social, and emotional development of children who followed the three special experimental programs (two physical education and one art) as compared to those who pursued their usual classroom instructional programs? Second, could differences in measures of these five aspects of development be noted between children who followed the special physical education programs and those in the art program? And third, were any differences noted in the above aspects of behavioral development of the children in the individualized physical education program as compared to those children in the group-oriented physical education program? In answering these questions, due consideration was given to the educational disability, chronological age, and sex of the children.

Subjects

The subjects for the study were enrolled in special classes for educable mentally retarded children and minimally brain-injured children in the elementary schools of the adjacently located Galena Park, Pasadena, and Deer Park Independent School Districts, Harris County, Texas. Every child so identified and placed in such classes, and who was medically able, took part in the investigation. The policies and procedures governing the identification and placement of these children were those of the Texas Education Agency (1965), although these policies could be adjusted somewhat to meet the needs of local conditions. Texas school law stipulated that to be eligible for placement in a class for the educable mentally retarded, a child must have an I.Q. in the approximate range 50–70 and must be judged capable of benefiting from a curriculum specifically designed to develop social and vocational skills. The minimally brain-injured children, on the other hand, were to be of normal intelligence or above, but with difficulties in learning such that a regular school program was not appropriate for them. Such learning difficulties had to be attributable to "an organic defect caused by a neurological condition." Prior to a child's placement in a class, the school district was required to obtain evidence from a physician indicating positive findings from a neurological evaluation.

A total of 49 classes of children was involved in the project: 25 classes of educable mentally retarded children and 24 classes of minimally brain-injured children. The distribution of classes, by education disability and age, for each school district is shown in Table 9.1. Over 500 children took part in the study, although some attrition occurred as children moved into or away from the project classes during the experiment. There was no apparent reason to suggest that attrition occurred because of a factor related to the conduct of the project. Since the study was concerned with developmental changes observed during a period of 6 months, only data from children who

Table 9.1

NUMBER OF CLASSES BY DISABILITY AND AGE LEVEL, ACCORDING TO SCHOOL DISTRICT

	EMR Children		*MBI Children*	
	Younger	*Older*	*Younger*	*Older*
Galena Park	5	5	3	4
Deer Park	3	1	3	2
Pasadena	4	7	6	6

completed both the pre- and post-tests were used. The personnel of the school districts interpreted the regulations for the placement of the children quite strictly, for the majority of MBI children had I.Q.'s within ± 1 standard deviation of the mean (measured by the Stanford-Binet or WISC Tests). The majority of the EMR children also had I.Q.'s within the regulation range. Minor departures can be explained by current diagnostic procedures, which

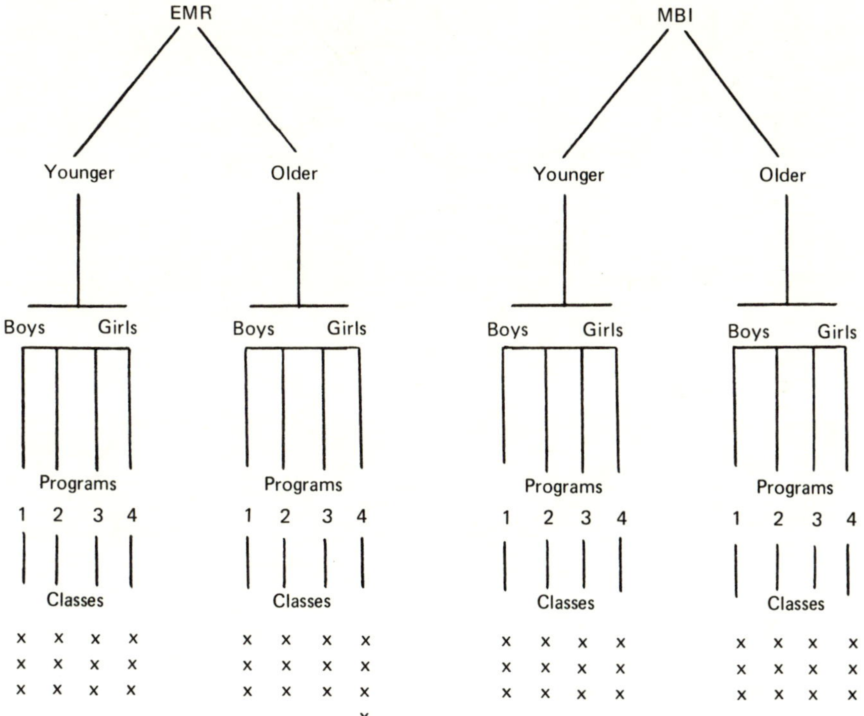

Fig. 9.1 The research design: educational disability × age × sex × program treatment (with number of classes); program 1: individualized physical education program; program 2: group-oriented physical education program; program 3: art program; program 4: the usual instructional program.

include an assessment of facets of behavior in addition to the measure of intelligence (Heber, 1959).

Classes were grouped according to educational disability (EMR and MBI) and chronological age (younger and older). The younger children were ages 6 to 9 years, and the older children were ages 10 to 13 years. From each of the four groups—younger EMR, older EMR, younger MBI, older MBI—the 49 classes were assigned randomly to the four experimental treatments or programs, as shown in Figure 9.1. The geographical locations of the school districts and the locations of the elementary schools where EMR and/or MBI classes were housed appear in Figure 9.2.

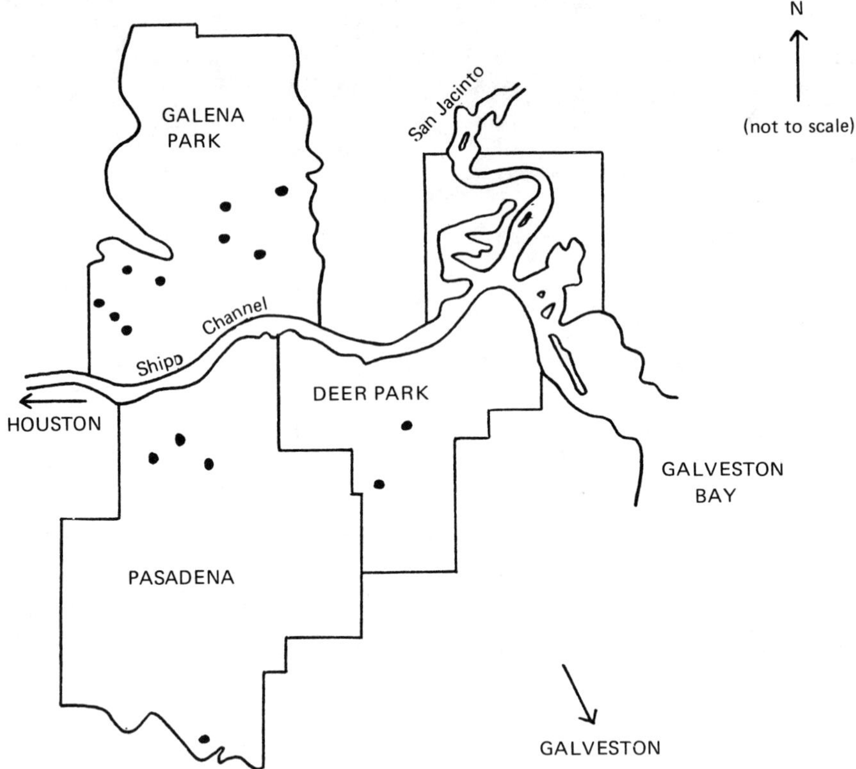

Fig. 9.2 Location of the school districts with sites of schools with participating classes.

Treatment of the Data

In the four factor experimental design, three factors—educational disability, age, and sex—each had two levels. One factor—program—had four levels. The number of children categorized by treatment (program), disability, age level, and sex is shown in Table 9.2.

Table 9.2

THE NUMBER OF CHILDREN WHO COMPLETED THE PROGRAMS

Treatment Group (Program)	*Younger EMR children*		*Older EMR children*	
	Boys	*Girls*	*Boys*	*Girls*
1	20	13	17	23
2	21	15	24	10
3	20	11	22	13
4	16	7	22	21
	77	46	85	67
TOTALS	123		152	

Treatment Group (Program)	*Younger MBI children*		*Older MBI children*	
	Boys	*Girls*	*Boys*	*Girls*
1	16	6	23	5
2	22	3	22	8
3	18	6	18	10
4	23	2	17	7
	79	17	80	30
TOTALS	96		110	

TOTAL EMR = 275; TOTAL MBI = 206; TOTAL COMPLETING PROGRAM = 481.

PROGRAM 1: Individualized Physical Education Program; PROGRAM 2: Group-Oriented Physical Education Program; PROGRAM 3: Art Program; PROGRAM 4: Usual Instructional Program.

Data from both pre- and post-tests were collected from 32 test items and were grouped into the appropriate parameter of development (motor, strength, intellectual, social, or emotional). Intact classes of children were randomly assigned to the four treatments or programs; hence, for each dependent variable, class means, subdivided by sex, were used in a multivariate analysis of covariance. Sampling errors were adjusted so that the statistical significance of the differences between the adjusted means could be determined.

A computer program,* entitled "Multivariance: Univariate and Multivariate Analysis of Variance and Covariance," was used on a C.D.C. 3600 machine at the University of Wisconsin Computing Center.

For each hypothesis tested, the procedure calculated an overall *F* value

*The program was originally developed in the Statistical Laboratory of the Department of Education at the University of Chicago and was later modified by Mr. Jeremy D. Finn, State University of New York at Buffalo. It was adapted for users at the University of Wisconsin by Mr. James Bavry of the Research and Development Center for Cognitive Learning of the Department of Educational Psychology.

for the vector of variables and also provided univariate *F* values for each dependent variable in the vector. The 5 percent level of statistical significance was used to determine tenability of the null hypotheses. Fifteen hypotheses were initially tested for each of four parameters of development. Because it was necessary to administer different personality questionnaires to the younger and older children, a separate analysis was used in treating the data on emotional behavior. Thus, for this parameter, there was a three factor design, with separate but identical analyses being used for each of the two age levels. Those hypotheses for which overall significant *F* values had been obtained were reexamined, first, so that the adjusted means could be obtained for each item in each vector, thus allowing the direction of a reported difference to be described (for example, where significance occurred for a two-level factor), and second, where significance occurred for the four-level factor (program), so that the calculation of the planned comparisons could be made, using the within cells error term. Since this research attempted to answer three major questions, it was appropriate to use this method of planned, orthogonal comparisons, as suggested by Hays (1963). This procedure is outlined in Table 9.3.

Table 9.3

ASSIGNED WEIGHTS FOR THREE PLANNED COMPARISONS

	Experimental Programs			
Comparison	*Individual Physical Education*	*Group Physical Education*	*Art*	*Usual*
1	+1	+1	+1	−3
2	+1	+1	−2	−0
3	+1	−1	−0	−0

The Assessment of Development

Overview

Among other influences, the success of the research project depended upon the quality of the experimental programs and the sophistication of the instruments of evaluation. The selection of tests to meet the requirements of validity and feasibility of administration was a major problem. The number of subjects involved and the range of parameters of development to be assessed made it impossible to ignore the issue of feasibility. The age, intellectual level, and achievement status of the children precluded the use of many tests, for there are few tests designed specifically for children with limited verbal and performance skills. The number of children—in excess of 500—and the need to test during a limited duration of time eliminated long tests requiring the presence of trained and experienced school psychologists. Since classroom teachers were to be involved in testing, problems of organization were anticipated; hence, the tests used were chosen to cause a minimum of disturbance within class. All motor performance tests were conducted out-of-doors. Other testing took place inside the school buildings, ensuring that the environment for testing was similar for all the children.

Motor Performance Tests

This aspect of development was assessed by a version of the seven-item Physical Fitness Test Battery of the American Association for Health, Physical Education, and Recreation (AAHPER, 1961). The modified version (AAHPER, 1968), which entailed a change in three of the original tests, was found appropriate for use with EMR children and was used successfully in a nationwide study of the motor performance of such children (Rarick, Widdop, and Broadhead, 1967a). The seven items purport to measure basic components of physical fitness, such as muscular strength, speed of movement, agility, coordination, and endurance. While some would argue that these tests are crude measures of these components, nevertheless they do include many of the basic skills and abilities required for successful participation in the physical activities of childhood and youth. The following is a brief description of each of the seven items, as administered in the present study.

FLEXED ARM HANG. A horizontal bar was adjusted to the height of the subject. Where necessary, a portable doorway gym bar was used. The subject was instructed to take an overhand grasp (palms facing away from the body) and was assisted to a position where the body was raised completely from the floor, the chin was above but not touching the bar, and the elbows were flexed. A stopwatch was used to record, to the nearest 1/10 of a second, the length of time the subject held the position. Only one correct trial was given.

SIT-UPS. The subject assumed a supine position with the legs extended and the feet approximately shoulder width apart. The fingers were interlaced and the hands placed at the back of the neck. A partner held down the subject's ankles, the heels being in contact with the floor at all times. The subject then sat up, turned the trunk to the left, and touched the right elbow to the left knee. After returning the trunk to the back-lying position, the subject again sat up, turned the trunk to the right, and touched the left elbow to the right knee. The exercise was repeated, alternating sides. One point was given for each complete correct movement of touching the elbow to the knee. The number of sit-ups the subject executed in 1 minute constituted the score. One trial only was given.

Shuttle Run. Two parallel lines were marked on the floor, 30 feet apart. Two blocks of wood, 2 inches by 2 inches by 4 inches, were placed a few inches apart behind one of the lines. The pupils started from behind the other line. On the signal, "Are you ready? Go!" the pupil ran to the blocks, picked up one, and returned to the starting line where he placed the block. He then ran to pick up the other block, which he carried back across (past) the starting line. Two trials were given, with the better elapsed time counting as the score. Timing was to the nearest 1/10 of a second.

Standing Broad Jump. The subject stood with the feet several inches apart, very close to, but not touching, the take-off line, and was directed to jump as far as possible, using a two-foot take-off and two-foot landing. Each pupil was allowed three trials, with the best trial, measured in inches from the take-off line to the heel or part of the body that touched the floor nearest to the line, serving as the score. The measurement was made in inches to the nearest 1/2 inch.

50-Yard Dash. Two pupils were tested at the same time. Both took the position behind the starting line. The signal, "Are you ready? Go!" was given, the last word accompanied by a downward sweep of the starter's arm to give a visual signal to the timer, who stood at the finishing line. The score was the elapsed time between the starter's signal and the instant the pupil crossed the finishing line. One trial was given, and the time was recorded to the nearest 1/10 of a second.

Softball Throw. The pupil was directed to throw a 12-inch softball from a designated point behind a restraining line. Three throws were allowed, and the longest throw was measured from the throwing point to the landing point. Only overhand throws were allowed, and the distance was measured to the nearest 6 inches.

300-Yard Run. On the signal, "Are you ready? Go!" the pupil ran the 300-yard distance which was marked out. Walking was permitted but discouraged. The time in minutes and seconds was taken to the nearest 1/10 of a second. Two or more pupils ran at the same time, but each was individually timed.

Motor performance tests of the kind used here have reportedly been shown to have substantial test-retest reliability when used with normal boys and girls. Acceptable reliabilities have also been reported when track-and-field type tests have been used with retarded children. For example, Francis and Rarick (1959) reported most test-retest reliabilities in the range of .85 to .95 when using a variety of gross motor tests purporting to measure such components of gross motor behavior as strength, running speed, agility, jumping, and throwing performances. More recently, Rarick and Dobbins (1972) obtained substantial test-retest reliabilities with EMR boys and girls on a wide assortment of gross motor tests. Of the tests identical to or similar to the ones used here, the test-retest reliabilities were in the high .80's and the .90's. There is no reason to believe that the children's performances in this investigation would be less reliable.

The writers hold that the measures of motor performance used here assess important dimensions of the gross motor behavior of children that are needed for successful participation in the physical activities of the child's world. Such measures have been widely accepted as appropriate tests of the basic components of motor performance of children (Espenschade, 1940; McCloy, 1932; Hunsicker and Reiff, 1965). Hence, it seems reasonable to claim validity for these tests on logical grounds.

All tests were conducted according to the instructions published in the AAHPER Test Manual (1968). The tests were administered to groups of classes at a central location. The problems of transportation and distance were such that for testing purposes classes were grouped according to school district. At each testing station were at least one teacher and one or more senior high school boys to assist with the testing. The procedures for testing and recording had been previously reviewed with the teachers and the boys at in-service meetings, and all were fully familiar with the requirements of the tests that they were to administer.

Strength Testing

Grip Strength. A Naragansett hand dynamometer was used to measure the grip strength of the right and left hands. The instrument was inserted into the palm of the hand of the standing subject, with the dial facing the palm so that there was no possibility of the dial being touched by the fingers. The subject held the instrument toward the ground and was instructed to make a short maximal squeeze in a downward direction, making sure that neither the instrument nor the subject's arm contacted the body.

Pull and Thrust. In the pull and thrust measures, the instrument was inserted into a metal frame attachment specially designed for measuring pulling and thrusting strength. The standing subject gripped the handles of the push-pull attachment, holding the instrument opposite, but not touching, the chest. The elbows were elevated so that the forearms were in a horizontal position. According to the test being performed, the subject was encouraged to pull or thrust. Two trials were given on the pull and two on the thrust test, the best on each serving as the score.

Face validity was claimed for the four dynamometric grip strength measures. Working with mentally retarded boys and girls ages 8 through adolescence, Francis and Rarick (1959) reported satisfactory reliability coefficients for each of the four measures, all being above $r = 0.86$ and most above $r = 0.91$.

All the testing was carried out by one of the investigators and a trained co-worker who was experienced in the test procedure and in working with retarded and brain-injured children.

Intellectual Development

Bender Motor Gestalt Test. This test was used to assess the nonverbal intelligence of the children. It was constructed by Koppitz (1966) and is described in great detail in the comprehensive text. Nine figures and drawings are presented one by one to the subject, who attempts to copy them on a sheet of paper. In the scoring system, each figure copy is assessed for accuracy. Deviations and distortions are reported by Koppitz to reflect immaturity or perceptual difficulties, as well as to indicate emotional characteristics and attitudes.

Peabody Picture Vocabulary Test. Designed by Dunn (1965), this test purports to assess a subject's verbal intelligence without requiring a written response. The test consists of a series of bold line drawings of items familiar to most children, grouped in fours (called a plate) with each plate being shown visually with a request for a specific verbal response, such as, "Show me . . . Can you . . . ," from the subject. The four drawings of each plate denote words of demonstrated equal difficulty, with the plates becoming progressively more demanding.

Although the Bender Test is widely used as a measure of nonverbal intelligence, few studies have examined its reliability. Koppitz (1966) cited a study in which 30 protocols were examined for interscorer objectivity among five scorers. Pearson product-moment correlations ranging from $r = 0.88$ to $r = 0.96$ were obtained. In a study which used young children from the low and middle socioeconomic groups of the community, interscorer correlations also reported by Koppitz ranged from $r = 0.56$ to $r = 0.66$. Since the period between the two sets of tests had been 4 months, and hence this period could reflect maturational changes in visual-motor perception, these results were thought to be satisfactory. Also cited by Koppitz (1966) was a study which reported a close relationship between the performance of 90 young children on the Bender Test and their performance on the nonverbal aspects of the

WISC, thus providing support for use of the Bender Test as a measure of nonverbal intelligence.

The Peabody Picture Vocabulary Test has been the subject of several reliability studies. Initially, Dunn (1965) reported product-moment correlations ranging from $r = 0.67$ to $r = 0.84$ for alternate forms of the test which had been given to children over a wide age range. Research on the PPVT has also been conducted with retarded subjects, and coefficients of equivalence were reported by Budoff and Purseglove (1963) to be $r = 0.85$ for institutionalized teenage retardates. Other reports of acceptable reliability estimates have been published by Dunn and his colleagues for educable and trainable retardates and for cerebral-palsied children. Dunn claimed that the test had content validity, but he also reports studies which show evidence of the statistical validity of the test.

Both the Bender and Peabody Tests were administered by the classroom teachers to each child individually and according to the instructions set out by Koppitz (1966) and by Dunn (1965). In-service meetings, held prior to the first set of testing, were completed with the aid of the chief school psychologist for the Galena Park Independent School District. The scoring of the Peabody Test was carried out by the investigators, and the interpretation of the Bender Test protocols was completed by a psychologist at the University of Houston who was experienced in scoring according to the Koppitz procedures. Protocols were scored blind.

Social Development

A sociometric test was administered to each child at the beginning and at the conclusion of the project. Children provided information indicating which of their classmates they preferred to have on a team for physical education and which they preferred to sit next to in class or to work with in class, as well as identifying those classmates they preferred not to have in each of the three everyday situations. This enabled measures to be obtained on the social acceptance of each child. The sociometric procedure was employed to evaluate the children's feelings toward each other, and the data were used to produce indices of acceptance and rejection, similar to those suggested by Gronlund (1959). Adjustments were made to take account of differential class sizes. Following the work of Oliver (1960), the three "choice" scores were pooled to form an acceptance score, and similar procedures provided rejection scores.

The Cowell Test (1958) was originally designed to be used with secondary school boys. In it the classroom teacher indicates the extent to which each of 10 positive statements is descriptive of the subject. Form B of the test, which involves 10 negative statements, was not used in this study. Each time, it was the student's behavior in group situations which was being assessed.

For example, one of the behaviors to which the teacher responded was the extent to which the subject was frank, talkative, and sociable and did not stand on ceremony. Another concerned the subject's tendency to be self-composed, seldom showing signs of embarrassment. The teacher recorded on a 4-point scale whether the subject showed a particular behavior markedly, somewhat, only slightly, or not at all.

The very nature of the way children react to one another poses reliability problems in sociometry. It was found by Bronfenbrenner (1944) that the stability of results over a period of time increased with the age of the subjects. Gronlund (1959) suggested that over a period of months, the children who are chosen tend to remain so, and the same holds for those who are seldom chosen. A most elaborate study by Bonney (1943) showed that for a group of second-grade children, a high degree of stability of sociometric status occurred. Insofar as the six questions asked for preferences or choices, the validity of the test was self-evident.

It has been noted earlier that the age and level of intellectual ability of many of the children precluded the use of all but a small number of tests. The main reasons for using the Cowell Index as a measure of social development were that the test seemed appropriate and it had previously been used successfully in a nationwide study of the environmental factors associated with the motor performance and physical fitness of educable retardates (Rarick, Widdop, and Broadhead, 1967b). There is no evidence in the literature of the reliability and validity of this test with educationally disabled children, and the results presented in this study must at best be tentative.

The sociometric test was administered individually and privately to the children. In each case, the positive (choosing) form of the three questions was asked before the negative (rejecting) form of the same questions. Every effort was made by the classroom teacher to provide an atmosphere of confidentiality which was deemed necessary for honest answers. The pupils were made aware that they had an unlimited number of choices and/or rejections from their own class. For the Cowell Test, the classroom teacher completed a copy of form A of the test for each child in the class. Tests were scored by the investigators.

Emotional Development

Personality Questionnaires. The Early School Personality Questionnaire (Coan and Cattell, 1966) was used with the younger children, and the Children's Personality Questionnaire (Porter and Cattell, 1959, 1963) was employed with the older children. Both inventories are well known and have been developed by factor analytic techniques, being designed to assess the major dimensions of human personality. Each dimension or factor is defined by two poles or extremes, one being represented by low scores, the other by high scores. With the exception of the intelligence factor, high or low scores are not necessarily "good" or "bad" traits, although some characteristics may be more widely socially acceptable than others! The Children's Personality Questionnaire has been used successfully with educable retardates by Porter, Collins, and McIver (1965).

THE EMOTIONAL INDICATORS. The Bender Test, used in part as an emotional indicator, was described earlier in this chapter. However, its use there was as a measure of nonverbal intelligence. Research cited by Koppitz (1966) has shown that the test is valuable in identifying children with emotional problems and discriminating between well-adjusted and poorly adjusted children. The manner in which the drawings were produced by a child was thought to be related to factors of personality and attitude. Deviations and distortions were held by Koppitz to be examples of immature visual-motor perception. Included in the list of indicators were dashes where circles should have been drawn, drawings which were too large or too small, and drawings which showed much overwork and reinforcement of lines.

At the time of this writing, no reliability data appear to have been published for the Early School Personality Questionnaire. The authors of the Children's Personality Questionnaire have reported several types of reliability coefficients for each factor. Test-retest and split half coefficients, reported by Porter and Cattell (1959), were satisfactory.

For the Bender Test, details of reliability have been given earlier in the chapter. Insofar as the total protocol reliabilities have been satisfactory, it was assumed that the deviations and distortions were likely to be repeated. Face validity is claimed for the emotional indicators, subject to the experience of the protocol interpreter. Koppitz (1966) has presented evidence that children with known emotional problems tend also to have immature visual-motor perception and register poor developmental scores.

All the tests were administered by the classroom teachers, with the testing being done individually or in small groups, according to the procedures suggested. Teachers were free to decide the best climate for testing, and hence no particular testing regimen was followed. All personality inventories were scored according to the instructions contained in the test manual and by a person at the University of Wisconsin experienced in scoring these tests. Details of the test administration and scoring of the emotional indicators of the Bender Test have been described earlier.

Additional Information

The date of birth and I.Q. of each subject were recorded from the school files. In most cases, the tests used were the WISC or the Stanford-Binet. The height of each child was recorded to the nearest 1/2 inch and the weight recorded to the nearest pound, both at the beginning and conclusion of the project. The school nursing staff was responsible for taking the measurements.

In-Service Training of Class Teachers

Prior to the beginning of the experiment, before any testing or any teaching had started, several in-service meetings were held to inform and instruct the classroom teachers in the testing and teaching procedures that were to be followed. It was well known that few elementary schools in the country were staffed with fully qualified physical education or art teachers. This was also true of the schools in the three school districts, and hence the opportunity for children in special education to participate in these activities had been extremely limited. The plan called for the special experimental programs to be taught by the classroom teachers. One significant advantage of this was that rapport already existed between the teacher and the children in the class. Many teachers were excited at the possibilities afforded by the research, but few were experienced in handling the physical education or art activities; therefore, the in-service training was supplemented by the additional support of a supervisor who worked closely with the teachers.

A complete overview of the project was presented at the in-service meetings so that a full understanding of the research, its aims, and its methods would exist in each school district. As described earlier, all the teachers received detailed information concerning the administration of the motor performance, psychological, and behavioral tests. Other meetings were held, attended only by the teachers connected with a particular special program. At such meetings, the discussion concerned the teaching program and ways of presenting the material to the children. Each teacher was given a teaching manual which included details of the aims and objectives of the particular program, together with ways of demonstration and observation, source materials, and a guide to the progression which might be possible during the first half of the experiment. Numerous additional meetings with individual teachers or with groups of teachers occurred throughout the project, and supplementary source materials were provided. All the teachers received remuneration for the time spent at the evening in-service meetings.

Throughout the period of the experiment one of the investigators, acting as supervisor, traveled from school to school visiting classes, observing the teachers teach, observing the children in the ways they reacted to the presentation of the teaching materials, discussing the work with the teachers, and teaching part or whole lessons. The teaching was done to allow the teachers to see their own classes at work and to demonstrate to the teachers how the teaching should proceed and how teaching material could be handled and developed in different ways. A schedule was drawn up which made it possible to observe each teacher at least twice in every three weeks. Changes were made in this schedule from time to time, for example, when problems occurred with the equipment or the quality of the teaching. Obviously, the teachers were not equally adept at teaching this unfamiliar work; thus, extra effort was needed to ensure that all the teaching was effective and proceeding along lines which were consistent with the aims of the project and with good teaching technique.

It is important to point out that the school principals and district administrative staff fully supported the teachers and the investigators at all times.

The Special Experimental Programs

Overview and Program Rationale

The design of satisfactory special programs was of obvious importance to the success of the project. Thus, it was necessary to construct programs which were so distinct that each could reasonably be expected to elicit effects which differed according to the parameter of development being examined. Similarly, it was appropriate that the children in the special programs knew that they were involved in something special, just as the other subjects were unaware that they too were involved in the project.

Many children start school having a rich background of movement experiences, while some have had only limited opportunities to develop this aspect of their lives and perform the basic motor skill patterns that are expected of them very inadequately in school. Motor development is dependent upon experiences so numerous that all possible movement patterns should be given to children in organized physical education lessons.

The rationale for the use of the individualized approach rested upon the belief, held by some, that mentally retarded children and brain-injured children need to have the security of working individually at their own level, where the disturbing and sometimes distractive influences of their peers is at a minimum, and where the tensions and frustrations of invidious comparisons and competition for status are practically nonexistent. Others believe that the traumatic effects of group interaction in motor skill development for these children are not great, and that the social values resulting from group play far outweigh any possible negative influences on skill learning. Thus, there was also logical support for the group-oriented physical education program. Since a primary purpose of a physical education program is to help children become reasonably proficient in the motor activities of our culture, while at the same time they develop desirable patterns of social behavior, an investigation of the influence of special programs with these two distinct types of orientation seemed to be desirable.

The art program was designed specifically to control for the possible existence of the Hawthorne effect, discussed in detail by Roethlisberger and Dickson (1939) and by Cook (1962). Just as the two physical education programs involved gross motor activity, so the art program was devoid of the use of the big muscle groups. The basic aims of all the special programs were similar, and equal attention was devoted to the planning and supervision of each program.

The types of teaching materials presented to the children were geared to their ages, aptitudes, and abilities. Few would question that physical activity and art provide children with goals which are relatively easily seen. Although the conditions under which these children could most effectively acquire desirable behaviors have not yet been comprehensively identified, it was recognized that the setting in which the learning took place was highly important and the role of the teachers in providing successful, rather than failing, experiences was understood.

At no time during the conduct of the experimental programs were any test items included. Hence, children did not practice the tests, nor was instruction given which might have contaminated the results.

The Individualized Physical Education Program

The program was designed primarily to satisfy the basic need of children for movement, by providing an enjoyable range of movement experiences, some familiar to them, others requiring the adaptation of established movement patterns into new and unfamiliar movements. The orientation was to individualize the instruction, building on the child's present motoric capabilities, challenging him with movement experiences commensurate with his capabilities but nevertheless sufficiently demanding to require his full attention. The teaching of basic everyday motor skills, always stressing good postural habits, was also an important aim.

For approximately 35 minutes each day, for 20 school weeks, the classes had specially planned physical education lessons. All work took place with the child working individually at his own level of ability, but still within the limitations of the task at hand. Thus, both the social organization of the group of children and the manner in which the tasks were accomplished by each child indicated and validated the individualized nature of the program. Movement patterns were used by themselves—for example, with a variety of jumping activities—and together in sequence work involving the joining of movements of different patterns, as in a run, jump, land, roll, and balance. Through the application of the concepts of time, space, force, and flow, a wide range of movements was experienced by each child. The central focus was upon improving the child's proficiency in the basic movement patterns, progressing systematically from the simple to the more complex. All the activity was graded to each child's level.

Sequence work was seen as a progression of the earlier work. Although the basic ingredient of the program was to make certain that the children were physically active, it was stressed that they should understand and be able to communicate much of what was involved. The challenge was that the lessons presented should be purposeful not only for the body but also for the mind; therefore, the concomitant learnings associated with the programs were carefully planned and not allowed to occur haphazardly. In all types of work, for each of the three special programs, the vocabulary of the teacher was very important, not only in achieving action on the part of the children but in challenging them intellectually, too.

To help the class teachers, activities were planned in blocks of work which could be undertaken within a given period of time. Two examples of the work appear in Appendix C. There was great flexibility in the way, and the extent to which the timetable was adhered to, and the frequent discussions between teacher and supervisor often helped to direct future work.

An attempt was made to have the physical education lessons follow some observable form, rather than be merely a conglomeration of unrelated activities. Since these were classroom teachers, interested but not practiced in teaching physical education, it was suggested that, in general, lessons should be in three parts: introductory, main, and closing activities. That the lessons commenced without delay was of extreme importance, and many teachers gave instructions for the introductory activity before the class left the room—for example, "When you reach the field (area), find your own space and show me how many different ways you can . . . ." The lessons started with the children moving, rather than the teacher explaining.

In many cases, introductory activities were new, to be developed later in the main section of the lesson, or were a repetition or further practice of an activity previously learned. The main section of the lesson, also the longest in time, was usually devoted to developing previously learned activities in new situations. The closing section of the lesson, which lasted only a few moments, was frequently used for an activity which was well known and liked by the class. The outlines of work were guides only, for the teachers were free to choose which activities to include in relation to the age, ability, behavioral traits, and previous reactions of the class. It was important to include something new and also to repeat something familiar during the lesson. Frequent use was made of small apparatus such as rubber balls of several sizes, mats, ropes, hoops, and bean bags. When this occurred, each child had his own piece of equipment, never sharing with another child.

Most lessons took place out-of-doors, since the climate of the Gulf Coast area of south Texas allowed this. But exceptions did occur from time to time, and each school had a large auditorium, gymnasium, or multipurpose room which proved quite adequate.

During the first week of the program, walking and running activities were stressed so that with the introduction of differences in speed, direction, and pattern, a wide variety of movements could be performed. Later, the idea of style was introduced, and then work on running and jumping commenced, with the emphasis upon differences in the type of jump. Running and jumping movements were often repeated, and a wide range of activities was experienced by each child, though not the same activities, necessarily, in quality or style or inventiveness. Landing was taught as a specific skill, and then it was developed through the introduction of other movements, either before or after the landing. Thus, elementary sequence work was developed, where several movements were joined together into one activity which had a beginning and an ending. Clearly, this type of experience was good in serving the great range of abilities which was found in each class. Repetition of the same movements was considered to be just as important as the pursuit of a wide variety of different movements.

Individual mats were provided for each child, and a range of rocking and rolling movements was used by the children. These movements became part of the sequence work. Though small apparatus had been used sparingly in the early parts of the program, it was possible to use the apparatus as a main focus of attention. Special emphasis was given to work with large and small balls, and the specific skills of throwing and catching were taught and practiced. Other pieces of equipment were used increasingly during these middle stages of the program.

The Christmas holiday divided the teaching period into two nearly equal parts. Prior to the holiday, a great deal of work involved a repetition of activities or types of work which were felt to have been most liked by the class and which appeared to the teachers to have been the most worthwhile.

Two types of work followed the holiday. One was of a recapitulatory nature, with walking and running movements being developed, for example, stressing the use of speed, space, style, and direction. Also, ball-handling skills, bouncing, catching, throwing, and rolling were developed, both with respect to variety of movement and the ability of each child to perform well. An increasing portion of the work entailed weight-bearing activities and the transference of weight from body part to body part.

During the last weeks of the program, specific skills such as the handstand, handwalk, cartwheel, crab, and headstand were introduced to all the classes. But the main emphasis was upon the most difficult work, difficult for both the teachers and the children. A selection of tasks for sequence work had been included in the teacher's guide, but the teachers encouraged all the children to explore and experiment with this type of work, combining movements of their own choosing into sequences. The important need to repeat and improve sequences was stressed, with the teachers reiterating, "Try to repeat your sequence so that you can show and tell the class what you were doing."

The Group-Oriented Physical Education Program

The general aims of the group-oriented physical education program were the same as those described for the individualized physical education program.

For approximately 35 minutes each day, for the 20 school weeks of the project, the classes had specially planned physical education lessons. Within each classroom group, all the work took place with each child working with a partner, or as a member of a group. Thus, every child in this special program always worked in cooperation with or in competition with the other members of the class. The partner activities, team activities, and class games involved basically the same movement experiences as in the individualized program, and the use of the concepts of time, space, force, and flow was continually stressed, always in relation to a partner or a group. The composition of the groups and the pairing of the children changed very frequently with the changes sometimes being child initiated and sometimes brought about by the teachers. For example, a small boy was purposely matched with a tall, strong boy in a partner activity; but in such a situation, the qualities of height and strength were not part of the activity. Instead, the boys were involved in an activity where cooperation was the main focus. Similarly, in activities where boys and girls were partners or in groups together, the task was carefully chosen so that the children could cooperate.

Within each type of group activity, the work began at a very simple level and progressed in its complexity as the program advanced. Such progression took account of the skill level of the children and the amount of organization that was involved for the teacher to manage and for the children to understand. In this way, it was possible to provide the children with a very large number of activities which were challenging, geared to their level of ability, and appropriate for their chronological age. For both experimental physical education programs, the types of activities to be presented to the children were included in a teaching manual, and the contents of these manuals were frequently discussed by the teachers and the supervisor of the teaching program.

Some examples of the three types of activities comprising this special program appear in Appendix D. The notion that activities were planned in blocks of work, which acted as a frame of reference and a guide for the class teachers, was adopted for this special program.

At the beginning of the program, the work was quite elementary in all the class activities, in partner activities, and relays. Simple activities were taught so that the teachers and the classes could become familiar with organizing these different types of work. At the same time, a repertoire of activities was being built around which further repetition, practice, and development could take place. As for the individualized physical education program, most of the group-oriented teaching took place out-of-doors in the pleasant Texas climate.

During the second and third weeks of the program, the main aim was to introduce new activities, but some previously learned activities were repeated and developed, sometimes with the addition of small equipment. It should be recalled that a child never had sole use of any piece of equipment, be it a ball, a hoop, a mat, or a rope. A piece of equipment was always used by a minimum of two children.

With a repertoire of activities being built up, the establishment of good lesson form was a main objective; therefore, in addition to a main section of the lesson, there were introductory and closing activities. This arrangement allowed the incorporation of many new activities, of the types which appear in many physical education texts—games and activities which so many children in our schools experience and enjoy.

As the program progressed, equipment was used more frequently, and for some lessons the equipment became the main focus. The equipment proved to be a helpful motivating force in this program.

One aspect of the work which was apparent throughout and was stressed during the second half of the program was the standard of performance of each child. By aiming at improving the quality of the movements and extending an understanding of the activities, the staff thought the benefits to the children would be increased. Hence, it became possible for some of the teachers to increase the pace of the lessons and to switch activities more efficiently, thus making the challenges greater for the children. It was quite obvious that the rules of each activity were important, and they became increasingly important as the program developed. This meant that because of the greater understanding achieved by the children and the greater experience of the teachers, the quality of the work improved significantly and a great amount of physical activity and social interchange occurred for each child.

The Art Program

The major aim of the art program was to satisfy the need for creative activities by providing the children with a wide variety of successfully performed experiences which would help them to develop a feeling for color, shape, texture, size, and perspective. While encouraging good work habits, the program aimed at teaching the basic manipulative skills which would result in the improved performance of the children. The contribution of art to the education of the whole child was a main aim.

As for each of the special experimental programs, the subjects in the art program had their specially planned and guided art education lessons for approximately 35 minutes each day for the 20 weeks. The children worked at a variety of tasks. Much of the work took the form of projects, and these included clay modeling, letter designs, drawings, finger painting, the construction of mobiles, and potato painting. There was a good variety of working media available—for example, paper plates and cups, straws, doilies, string, yarn, powder paint, brushes, glue, pencils, crayons, clay, paper clips and fasteners, pipe cleaners, construction and drawing paper, newsprint, stiffboard, staplers, plastic tape, toothpicks, dried beans and peas, pasta, and vegetables and fruit. Each teacher was given abundant supplies of these materials but also was encouraged to use other materials. All work took place indoors.

In general, the teaching material was of four types: painting, pasting, paper cutting, and construction work. It was considered that there was a clear progression from painting to construction work, the assignments becoming increasingly demanding and requiring greater background and experience on the part of the children. Not only was there progression between each section, but within each section the tasks and experiences were not all of equal complexity.

The teachers were issued booklets which indicated the aims and methods of the programs and included many examples of specific tasks which could be provided for the children. This information was supplemented during the middle stages of the program. A few examples from each of the four sections of work are included in Appendix E. It was thought important to provide the teachers with all this quite specific information, as none of them was a qualified art teacher. Nevertheless, it would be quite wrong to believe that the work proved stereotyped and limited to the suggestions provided for the teachers. Not only were other projects and ideas used at the teachers' own initiative, but the children were also encouraged to invent and explore with materials and ideas.

As before, the activities were organized in blocks of work. This arrangement was used only as a guide, but it was much needed at the beginning of the program. For the first weeks, all work consisted of painting and pasting, since these activities required the least background from the teachers and fewer skills from the children. As the work progressed, much of the time was devoted to paper cutting, with lesser amounts given to painting and pasting. The weeks close to Halloween, Thanksgiving, and Christmas suggested a variety of suitable and enjoyable topics to be developed and led easily to the construction work. The skills required of the children for these activities were considerable, but because the work could be adjusted by the teachers to the child's level of ability and creativity, each pupil could be successful in the work. The children were not only painting and constructing, but they were also learning how to discuss the shapes, decorations, designs, and colors that were being developed.

In this program, as with the physical education programs, teachers made use of the children and their work for demonstration. It was acknowledged that the motivating force of child demonstration was a powerful one, and the ability of the teachers to use this technique was stressed. Thus, children often observed while one or more of the class showed something different, something well done, or something which showed an improvement; discussion took place so that not only could the children share their ideas but they could learn to accept their own work for its own worth. A teacher's question, "What do you notice about the direction of the blue lines on Gerry's drawing?" helped to test the children's powers of observation and elicited various responses. In summary, in attempts to describe the special experimental programs, the value of the work was seen as being infinitely more than a series of unrelated activities merely being presented in some predetermined order. The programs were primarily educative, designed to influence the development of the children; the secondary, albeit vital, trait was the teaching medium, either physical education or art education.

The Usual Classroom Instructional Program

The classes in this program, though involved in both sets of tests, were not aware that they were participating in a research project. They followed their usual instructional program, receiving no special treatment or any specially planned physical education lessons. The cooperation of the teachers of this group of children was considerable, since they could see what changes were being tried by some of their colleagues. But discussion of the research among colleagues did not occur; a careful but unobtrusive observation by the teachers of the special programs, school principals, and the program supervisor ensured this.

Chapter 10 / The Effects of the Special Programs

Introduction

The primary purpose of the investigation was to determine the role of specially planned physical activity programs in modifying selected aspects of the development of educable mentally retarded children and minimally brain-injured children of elementary school age.

The experiment was designed to answer three questions. First, what were the differential effects on the motor, strength, intellectual, social, and emotional development of children who followed the three special experimental programs (two physical education and one art) as compared to those who pursued their usual classroom instructional program? Second, were differences noted in any of the above aspects of the development of the children who were included in the special physical education programs, compared with those in the special art program? And third, what differences were there in the motor, strength, intellectual, social, and emotional development of the children in the individualized physical education program as compared to those in the group-oriented physical education program? The research design took full account of possible treatment effects according to educational disability, chronological age, and sex of the children.

Thus, for the motor, strength, intellectual, and social parameters of development, a four factor experimental design provided for an analysis of the main and interaction effects of sex, age (younger and older), educational disability, and program.

Because the younger and older children were given different personality inventories, a separate analysis for emotional development was used for the children ages 6 to 9 years and for those ages 10 to 13 years. In each case, the three factor design assessed the effects of sex, educational disability, and program. The hypotheses tested have been listed in Tables 10.1 and 10.2. A 5 percent level of statistical significance was set for the rejection of each of the 74 null hypotheses tested. Tables 10.3 and 10.4 show that only 12 were found untenable, 3 being first order interactions and 1 a second order interaction effect.

The remainder of this chapter presents a detailed review of the results of the multivariate analyses, with specific reference to the 12 rejected null hypotheses. There is a full discussion of the differential effects of the four programs upon those parameters of development where statistically significant results were noted. Significant analyses are shown in tabular form, and Figures have been included to indicate the specific items which appear from the univariate analyses to have been most influential in the multivariate

Table 10.1

NULL HYPOTHESES TESTED: THE EMOTIONAL PARAMETER OF DEVELOPMENT

1.	Main Effect:	Program
2.	Main Effect:	Disability
3.	Main Effect:	Sex
4.	Interaction Effect:	Sex × Program
5.	Interaction Effect:	Disability × Program
6.	Interaction Effect:	Disability × Sex
7.	Interaction Effect:	Disability × Sex × Program

Table 10.2

NULL HYPOTHESES TESTED: THE MOTOR, STRENGTH, INTELLECTUAL, AND SOCIAL PARAMETERS OF DEVELOPMENT

1.	Main Effect:	Program
2.	Main Effect:	Age
3.	Main Effect:	Disability
4.	Main Effect:	Sex
5.	Interaction Effect:	Disability × Age
6.	Interaction Effect:	Disability × Sex
7.	Interaction Effect:	Disability × Program
8.	Interaction Effect:	Age × Sex
9.	Interaction Effect:	Age × Program
10.	Interaction Effect:	Sex × Program
11.	Interaction Effect:	Disability × Age × Sex
12.	Interaction Effect:	Disability × Age × Program
13.	Interaction Effect:	Disability × Sex × Program
14.	Interaction Effect:	Age × Sex × Program
15.	Interaction Effect:	Disability × Age × Sex × Program

Table 10.3

THE RESULTS OF THE HYPOTHESIS TESTING: THE MOTOR, STRENGTH, INTELLECTUAL, AND SOCIAL PARAMETERS OF DEVELOPMENT

Effect	*Motor Performance*	*Strength Development*	*Intellectual Development*	*Social Development*
		Probability Less Than		
Program	0.0001*	0.7179	0.0182*	0.3915
Disability	0.0022*	0.0698	0.0024*	0.2005
Age	0.3424	0.1197	0.0029*	0.0887
Sex	0.3035	0.7292	0.2222	0.4247
Disability × Age	0.3864	0.1411	0.1173	0.5941
Disability × Sex	0.2864	0.2419	0.7890	0.3411
Disability × Program	0.0653	0.7122	0.5362	0.9401
Age × Sex	0.5135	0.0810	0.2698	0.3446
Age × Program	0.0248*	0.5403	0.5294	0.7559
Sex × Program	0.1068	0.3628	0.3451	0.8434
Disability × Age × Sex	0.9014	0.5281	0.9498	0.8719
Disability × Age × Program	0.0654	0.1941	0.1690	0.7050
Disability × Sex × Program	0.9531	0.9420	0.7906	0.7611
Age × Sex × Program	0.5337	0.7265	0.9274	0.8438
Disability × Age × Sex × Program	0.6455	0.2545	0.2173	0.9744

**Null hypothesis rejected at the 5 percent level.*

Table 10.4

THE RESULTS OF THE HYPOTHESIS TESTING: THE EMOTIONAL PARAMETER OF DEVELOPMENT

Effect	*Younger Children*	*Older Children*
	Probability Less Than	
Program	0.0043*	0.3924
Disability	0.0247*	0.1468
Sex	0.0380*	0.3443
Sex × Program	0.3257	0.8677
Disability × Program	0.0439*	0.0364*
Disability × Sex	0.5886	0.4326
Disability × Sex × Program	0.0334*	0.2969

**Null hypothesis rejected at the 5 percent level.*

tests. It is important to stress that the differences represented in the Figures are between the adjusted cell means from the analyses of covariance.

Strength and Social Development

It is apparent from Table 10.3 that no differential main or interaction effects resulted from the hypothesis testing for either the strength test items or the measures of social development.

There were four variables comprising the strength development parameter, namely, grip strength for right and left hands, and the double-handed pull and thrust measurements. In addition, height and weight were obtained on each subject. Perhaps it is important to point out that no specific work of a strengthening nature occurred in any of the experimental programs. Thus, while gains in strength might have been expected to occur over a 6-month period as a function of maturation, no measurable changes were noted which would imply that any one treatment program was superior to any other in affecting this trait.

Nor were any of the 15 null hypotheses rejected which determined the effects of the experimental programs on the children's social development as assessed either in general or as a function of educational disability, chronological age, or sex. Since these measures of social development were objective and supplemented by other observations of a subjective nature, the failure to reject any of the hypotheses was somewhat surprising. This was because the program supervisor, the directors of special services of the school districts, and most of the teachers of the special program classes had volunteered the observation that many children previously rejected by their classmates were later much better accepted by the class. It had been observed that some children appeared to have "come out of their shells" and showed increased confidence during the program.

The test items were the Cowell Social Behavior Trend Index (Cowell, 1958), which is largely a measure of outgoing or extroverted behavior, and assessments of peer acceptance or rejection, obtained by sociometric techniques. It was anticipated that the involvement of children in programs that were directed to their capabilities, rather than to their limitations, should result in the development of positive, extroverted behavior. Additionally, it was expected that the children in the group-oriented physical education program would have demonstrated changes in measured behavior because of the particular program design. None of this was shown in the results. The notion that the social development of children in special education should be improved through this medium remains valid, and it is believed that further exploration of this premise should prove valuable.

Modifications in Motor Performance

Overview

It was previously mentioned that a modified version of the AAHPER Test Battery (AAHPER, 1968) was used to assess the motor performance of all the children in the study. Using pre- and post-test scores, multivariate analysis of covariance was used to test the 15 hypotheses listed in Table 10.3. Three of these were rejected at the 5 percent level of significance. No second or third order interaction effect was significant. The three rejected null hypotheses were for the main effect of program, the main effect of disability, and the interaction effect of age and program.

Main Effect of Program

As previously pointed out, three special programs and one involving no special treatment were used. The nature of the four programs has been fully described. All four programs were educational, being appropriate to the needs, abilities, and interests of the children. Both physical education and art education programs are often described as being chiefly recreational. The aims of the specially planned programs in this research were wider in scope. It was vital for the children to increase their understanding of what was being done as well as to improve their level in the various skills. It should, perhaps, be pointed out again that the test items themselves were never part of any of the instructional programs, thus avoiding the pitfall that has clouded the findings of some of the earlier research on exceptional children. In this study, the interest was in examining the role of educational programs in eliciting changes in several aspects of development, and the procedures just alluded to were considered totally unacceptable and were not repeated here.

The results of the multivariate analysis of covariance which tested the main effect of the program on motor performance are included in Table 10.5. The hypothesis that there were no differential effects attributable to the programs was rejected ($F = 5.7401$; $p < 0.0001$). Although the performance change in the 300-yard run did not yield a statistically significant univariate F value, the contribution of the other six variables in the vector can be seen.

Table 10.5

MOTOR PERFORMANCE: MAIN EFFECT OF PROGRAM
FOR MULTIVARIATE TEST OF EQUALITY OF MEAN VECTORS

F = 5.7401* p less than 0.0001 df = 21 and 41.2517

Variable	*Between Mean Square*	*Univariate* F	p *Less Than*
1. Arm Hang	137.8034	11.5934	0.0001
2. Sit-ups	236.1245	31.8839	0.0001
3. Shuttle Run	3.4775	3.1991	0.0304
4. Standing Broad Jump	286.7837	23.9260	0.0001
5. 50-Yard Dash	2.0725	11.6984	0.0001
6. Softball Throw	300.4803	20.9408	0.0001
7. 300-Yard Run	8157.0355	0.9924	0.4033

df *for Hypothesis = 3,* df *for Error = 55, 7 covariates had been eliminated.*
**Null hypothesis rejected at the 5 percent level.*

In order to determine if the effects of the programs did, in fact, differ, three planned orthogonal comparisons were made. The first was a multivariate comparison of the mean motor performance of the three special programs with the mean performance of the classes which had no special program. Table 10.6 indicates that the null hypothesis was tenable ($F =$

Table 10.6

PLANNED COMPARISON FOR MOTOR PERFORMANCE TESTS: MAIN EFFECT OF PROGRAM—HYPOTHESIS ONE

That no differences exist between the motor performance of those children having Special Programs and those having no Special Program.

FOR MULTIVARIATE TEST OF EQUALITY OF MEAN VECTORS

F = 1.8039   *p* less than 0.1078   *df* = 7 and 49.0000

Variable	*Between Mean Square*	*Univariate* F	p *Less Than*
1. Arm Hang	0.7836	0.0659	0.7984
2. Sit-ups	31.7530	4.2876	0.0431
3. Shuttle Run	2.8894	2.6581	0.1088
4. Standing Broad Jump	34.2425	2.8568	0.0967
5. 50-Yard Dash	0.0667	0.3764	0.5421
6. Softball Throw	19.7007	1.3730	0.2464
7. 300-Yard Run	25966.3939	3.1591	0.0811

df *for Hypothesis* = *1,* df *for Error* = *55, 7 covariates had been eliminated.*

1.8039; $p < 0.1078$). In other words, children offered the special physical education and art programs showed no greater overall changes in motor performance than those in the control group. Only for the sit-ups was there a significant univariate F value.

The second null hypothesis, comparing the mean motor performance of those in the physical education programs with that of the children in the art program, was rejected ($F = 13.6005$; $p < 0.0001$). Six of the seven variables of the vector contributed significantly to the F value (see Table 10.7), with the contribution of the 300-yard run being minimal. The direction of the difference was determined by an examination of the relative positions of the adjusted means, which are shown graphically in Figure 10.1. It is clear that after adjustments were made for pre-test differences, the physical education classes demonstrated a superior position to the art classes. Of particular note was the softball throw for distance, a test which was consistently discriminatory, where differences in performance were most marked. While data on the 50-yard dash are not illustrated, reference to Table 10.7 shows the significant effect of this variable on the multivariate F.

It was important to know whether differences in motor performance existed between the classes involved in the individualized physical education program and those included in the group-oriented program. From Table

Table 10.7

PLANNED COMPARISON FOR MOTOR PERFORMANCE TESTS: MAIN EFFECT OF PROGRAM—HYPOTHESIS TWO

That no differences exist between the motor performance of those children having Physical Education Programs and those having the Art Program.

FOR MULTIVARIATE TEST OF EQUALITY OF MEAN VECTORS

F = 13.6005* p less than 0.0001 df = 7 and 49.0000

Variable	*Between Mean Square*	*Univariate* F	p *Less Than*
1. Arm Hang	126.2370	10.6204	0.0020
2. Sit-ups	362.1002	48.8944	0.0001
3. Shuttle Run	4.7130	4.3358	0.0420
4. Standing Broad Jump	382.8774	31.9329	0.0001
5. 50-Yard Dash	3.6121	20.3886	0.0001
6. Softball Throw	648.9616	45.2269	0.0001
7. 300-Yard Run	22.0453	0.0027	0.9589

df *for Hypothesis* = *1,* df *for Error* = *55, 7 covariates had been eliminated.*
**Null hypothesis rejected at the 5 percent level.*

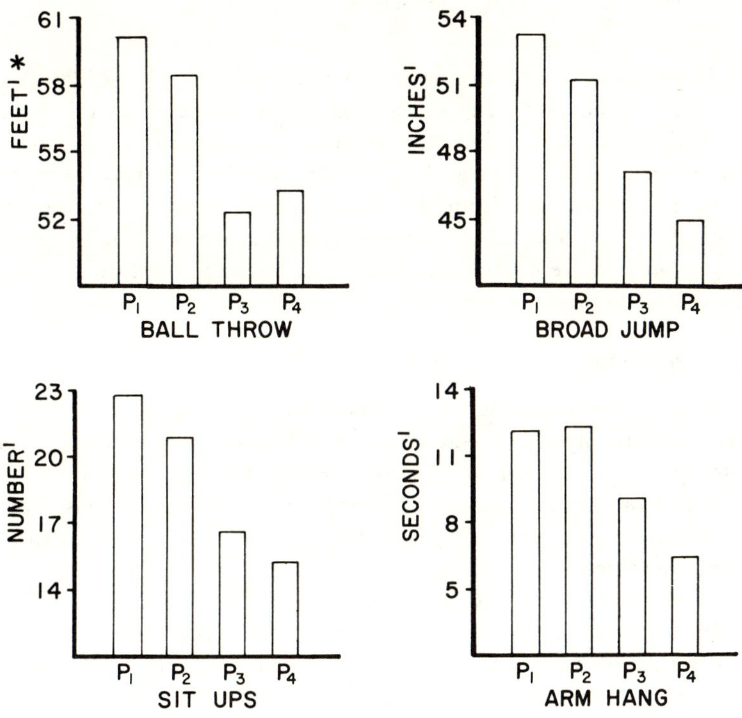

Fig. 10.1 Motor performance: main effect of program for the softball throw, standing broad jump, sit-ups, and arm hang. Program 1: individualized program; program 2: group-oriented program; program 3: art program; program 4: control or usual program.

Table 10.8

PLANNED COMPARISON FOR MOTOR PERFORMANCE TESTS: MAIN EFFECT OF PROGRAM—HYPOTHESIS THREE

That no differences exist between the motor performance of those children having the Individualized Physical Education Program and those having the Group-Oriented Physical Education Program.

FOR MULTIVARIATE TEST OF EQUALITY OF MEAN VECTORS

F = 13.2257* p less than 0.0001 df = 7 and 49.0000

Variable	*Between Mean Square*	*Univariate* F	p *Less Than*
1. Arm Hang	340.8233	28.6736	0.0001
2. Sit-ups	353.7761	47.7704	0.0001
3. Shuttle Run	3.9292	3.6147	0.0626
4. Standing Broad Jump	462.6839	38.6011	0.0001
5. 50-Yard Dash	2.8525	16.1009	0.0002
6. Softball Throw	253.6721	17.6787	0.0001
7. 300-Yard Run	6.6760	0.0008	0.9774

df *for Hypothesis* = *1,* df *for Error* = *55, 7 covariates had been eliminated.*
**Null hypothesis rejected at the 5 percent level.*

10.8, it is apparent that there were clear differences ($F = 13.2257$; $p < 0.0001$). Five of the seven test items had a significant effect on the multivariate F value. To determine the direction of the differences, the adjusted means were examined, and it is clear from Figure 10.1 that for three of the four items illustrated, the individualized program showed superiority. It appeared, therefore, that the individualized physical education program elicited greater relative changes in motor performance than did the group-oriented physical education program.

Interaction Effect of Age × Program

The results of the multivariate analysis, shown in Table 10.9, point to a statistically significant interaction between age and program for the motor performance test battery as a whole. In other words, the treatments affected motor performance differently at the two age levels. For two of the seven items, the arm hang and the softball throw, the univariate F values were significant.

The interpretation of the interaction effect was carried out by the previously described planned comparisons and by examining the relative positions of the adjusted means for each of the four treatments by age level. Details of these comparisons are included in Tables 10.10, 10.11, and 10.12, and are shown in Figures 10.2 and 10.3. The four illustrated test items were selected because they repeatedly demonstrated that, in a rejection of the null hypothesis, they were contributing to differences in group performance. It can be seen from Table 10.10 that the null hypothesis for the first planned

Table 10.9

MOTOR PERFORMANCE: INTERACTION EFFECT OF AGE × PROGRAM FOR MULTIVARIATE TEST OF EQUALITY OF MEAN VECTORS

$F = 1.7912$* p less than 0.0248 $df = 21$ and 141.2517

Variable	*Between Mean Square*	*Univariate* F	p *Less Than*
1. Arm Hang	51.9664	4.3720	0.0079
2. Sit-ups	16.5629	2.2365	0.0943
3. Shuttle Run	0.4751	0.4371	0.7274
4. Standing Broad Jump	18.6789	1.5584	0.2099
5. 50-Yard Dash	0.2651	1.4965	0.2257
6. Softball Throw	40.6417	2.8324	0.0466
7. 300-Yard Run	9933.4612	1.2085	0.3153

df *for Hypothesis = 3,* df *for Error = 55, 7 covariates had been eliminated.*
**Null hypothesis rejected at the 5 percent level.*

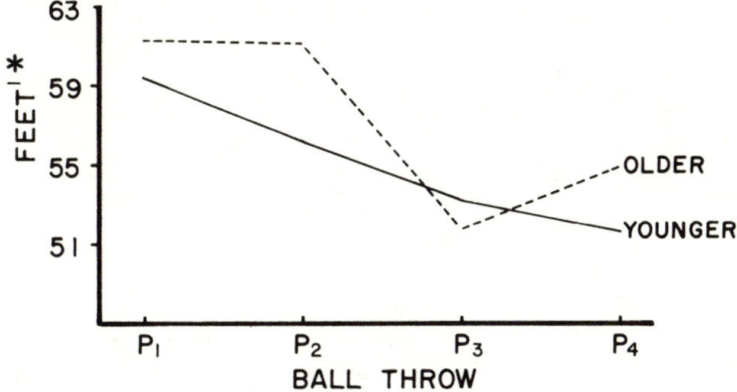

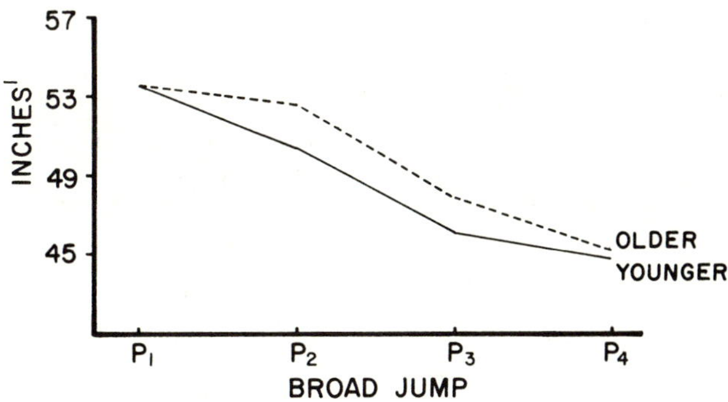

*Cell means adjusted for covariates

Fig. 10.2 Motor performance: interaction effect of age × program, for the Softball throw and standing broad jump. Program 1: individualized program; program 2: group-oriented program; program 3: art program; program 4: control or usual program.

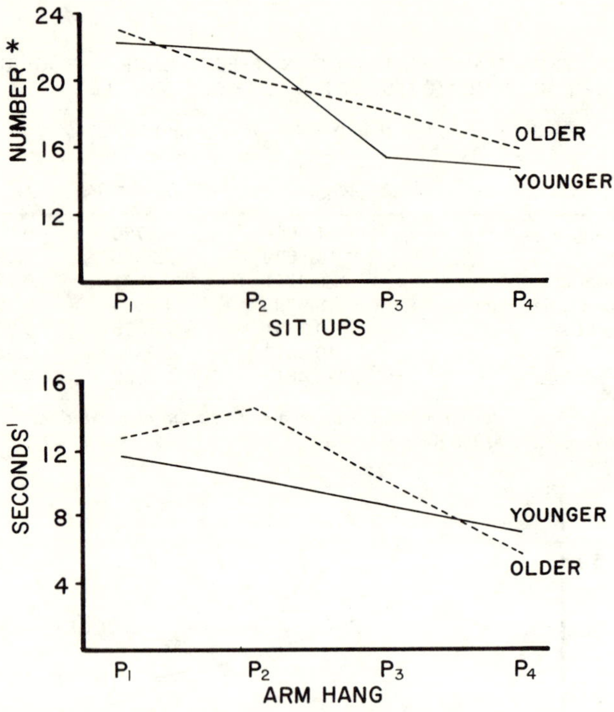

*Cell means adjusted for covariates

Fig. 10.3 Motor performance: interaction effect of age × program, for the sit-ups and arm hang. Program 1: individualized program; program 2: group-oriented program; program 3: art program; program 4: control or usual program.

Table 10.10

PLANNED COMPARISON FOR MOTOR PERFORMANCE TESTS: INTERACTION EFFECT OF AGE × PROGRAM—HYPOTHESIS ONE

That no differences by age exist between the motor performance of those children having Special Programs and those having no Special Program.

FOR MULTIVARIATE TEST OF EQUALITY OF MEAN VECTORS

$F = 1.0098$ p less than 0.4362 $df = 7$ and 49.0000

Variable	*Between Mean Square*	*Univariate* F	p *Less Than*
1. Arm Hang	19.7103	1.6582	0.2033
2. Sit-ups	4.2589	0.5751	0.4515
3. Shuttle Run	0.9750	0.8970	0.3478
4. Standing Broad Jump	20.1556	1.6816	0.2002
5. 50-Yard Dash	0.3780	2.1338	0.1498
6. Softball Throw	42.5543	2.9657	0.0907
7. 300-Yard Run	3100.4774	0.3772	0.5417

df *for Hypothesis = 1,* df *for Error = 55, 7 covariates had been eliminated.*

comparison was tenable ($F = 1.0098$; $p < 0.4362$). In other words, the special treatments had no differential effects on the measured motor performance of children of the two age levels, compared with children in the control groups. The contribution of the univariate test for the softball throw, $p < 0.0907$, was the largest of any test item in the vector, and it is mentioned because it appeared to discriminate levels of performance when other analyses or comparisons were being made.

In examining whether there were differences by age in the motor performance test scores of those in the two physical education programs compared with those in classes in the art program, the null hypothesis was rejected at the 5 percent level (see Table 10.11). The multivariate F value was 2.3961, $p < 0.0344$. This showed that the treatment effects differed as a function of age level. In general, the effect was greater on the older than on the younger children. As is shown in Figures 10.2 and 10.3, the superiority of the two physical education programs over the art program in affecting

Table 10.11

PLANNED COMPARISON FOR MOTOR PERFORMANCE TESTS: INTERACTION EFFECT OF AGE × PROGRAM—HYPOTHESIS TWO

That no differences by age exist between the motor performance of those children having Physical Education Programs and those having the Art Program.

FOR MULTIVARIATE TEST OF EQUALITY OF MEAN VECTORS

F = 2.3961* *p* less than 0.0344 *df* = 7 and 49.0000

Variable	*Between Mean Square*	*Univariate* F	p *Less Than*
1. Arm Hang	3.9432	0.3317	0.5670
2. Sit-ups	41.9406	5.6632	0.0209
3. Shuttle Run	0.0286	0.0263	0.8718
4. Standing Broad Jump	3.4453	0.2874	0.5941
5. 50-Yard Dash	0.4144	2.3392	0.1319
6. Softball Throw	65.5848	4.5707	0.0370
7. 300-Yard Run	20450.3103	2.4880	0.1205

df *for Hypothesis* = *1,* df *for Error* = *55, 7 covariates had been eliminated.*
**Null hypothesis rejected at the 5 percent level.*

motor performance is clearly apparent in each of the four tests, but the effect of age on program was not consistent across test items. Generally, the differential progress achieved by the older children was the greater, with this being most clearly shown for the sit-ups and softball throw.

The results of the planned comparison to determine whether the effects of the two physical education programs on the motor performance of the children differed by age level are shown in Table 10.12. The multivariate test ($F = 1.6198$; $p < 0.1521$) showed no significant interaction effect of program by age. In other words, the differential effects of the programs on

Table 10.12

PLANNED COMPARISON FOR MOTOR PERFORMANCE TESTS: INTERACTION EFFECT OF AGE × PROGRAM—HYPOTHESIS THREE

That no differences by age exist between the motor performance of those children having the Individualized Physical Education Program and those having the Group-Oriented Physical Education Program.

FOR MULTIVARIATE TEST OF EQUALITY OF MEAN VECTORS

$F = 1.6198$ p less than 0.1521 $df = 7$ and 49.0000

Variable	*Between Mean Square*	*Univariate* F	p *Less Than*
1. Arm Hang	102.4624	8.6202	0.0049
2. Sit-ups	0.7969	0.1076	0.7442
3. Shuttle Run	0.7533	0.6930	0.4088
4. Standing Broad Jump	30.3841	2.5349	0.1171
5. 50-Yard Dash	0.0138	0.0777	0.7815
6. Softball Throw	0.9376	0.0653	0.7993
7. 300-Yard Run	2427.4128	0.2953	0.5891

df *for Hypothesis = 1,* df *for Error = 55, 7 covariates had been eliminated.*

the motor performance of the children were similar at both age levels. Only on the arm hang was there a significant interaction, this being greater in the older than in the younger children.

Main Effect of Disability

The inclusion of minimally brain-injured children in this investigation added a dimension not present in earlier studies. In fact, there is very little data on the level of performance of these children on gross motor tasks or on the role which physical education lessons involving gross motor performance play in their development. Hence, the examination of the change in the motor performance of the minimally brain-injured children as contrasted to that of the educable mentally retarded children was of considerable interest.

The results of the multivariate analysis for the main effect of educational disability on the motor performance of these children are given in Table 10.13. It is seen that the hypothesis was rejected at the 5 percent level ($F = 3.8363$; $p < 0.0022$). Thus, for this parameter of development, the educable mentally retarded children and the minimally brain-injured children differed in their overall performance. As is indicated by the univariate F values, the strongest contribution to this difference is from the softball throw ($p < 0.0002$). The standing broad jump and the 50-yard dash also contribute significantly. The magnitude and direction of these differences are graphically shown in Figure 10.4. On three of the selected four test items, the minimally brain-injured children improved their performance to a greater degree than the educable mentally retarded children. As may be noted, the

Table 10.13

MOTOR PERFORMANCE: MAIN EFFECT OF DISABILITY FOR MULTIVARIATE TEST OF EQUALITY OF MEAN VECTORS

$F = 3.8363^*$ p less than 0.0022 $df = 7$ and 49.0000

Variable	*Between Mean Square*	*Univariate* F	p *Less Than*
1. Arm Hang	0.2330	0.0196	0.8892
2. Sit-ups	15.5160	2.0951	0.1535
3. Shuttle Run	3.4150	3.1416	0.0819
4. Standing Broad Jump	71.2234	5.9421	0.0181
5. 50-Yard Dash	1.0018	5.6544	0.0210
6. Softball Throw	251.0211	17.4939	0.0002
7. 300-Yard Run	7731.2315	0.9406	0.3364

df *for Hypothesis = 1,* df *for Error = 55, 7 covariates had been eliminated.*
**Null hypothesis rejected at the 5 percent level.*

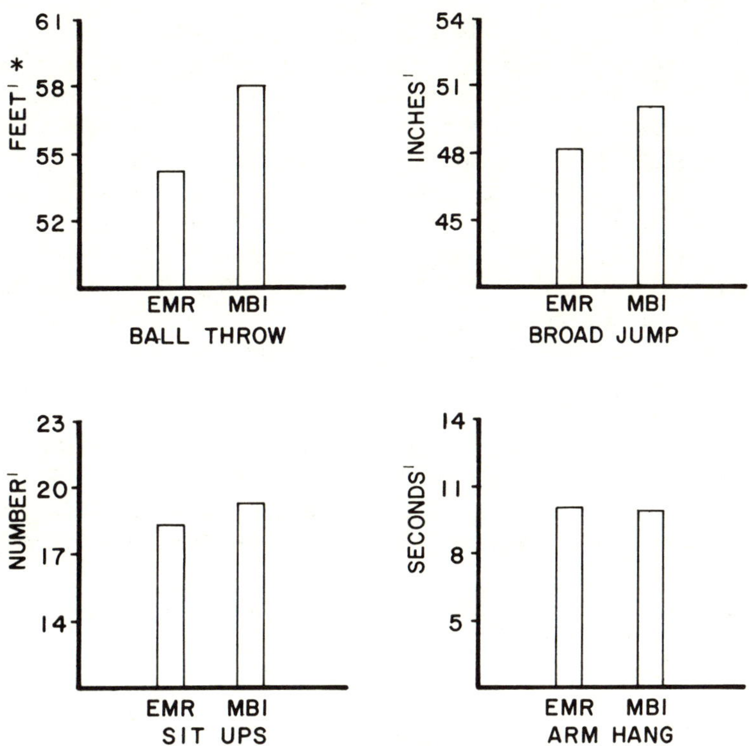

Fig. 10.4 Motor performance: main effect of disability for the softball throw, standing broad jump, sit-ups, and arm hang.

results on the arm hang are very similar, with the retardates showing slightly better performance.

Further Observations on the Findings

Although seven motor performance test items were used to provide information on this parameter of development, a review of the univariate *F* values in the many analyses reveals that four test items usually strongly influenced the rejection of the null hypotheses. These four test items were the arm hang, the sit-ups, the standing broad jump, and the softball throw.

From 15 original hypotheses tested, three were found untenable: the main effect of program, the interaction effect of age and program, and the main effect of disability. The results of the multivariate and univariate analyses and the planned comparisons would seem to warrant several observations:

1. The main effect of the experimental physical education programs was to bring about greater improvement in motor performance in the classes which followed the individualized program than in those included in the group-oriented program. It was also evident that the physical education programs produced greater positive changes in these variables than did the art program. While the mean performance gains of those in the classes in the three specially planned experimental programs, taken collectively, did not differ materially from the gains of those involved in their usual classroom instruction program, this could be attributed to the dampening effect of those in the art program.

2. As was evident from the significant interaction effect of age on program, the general improvement in motor performance of the older children was greater than that of the younger.

3. In examining the main effect of the educational disability of the children, it was clear that even after adjustments had been made for differences in the pre-test scores, the performance changes of the minimally brain-injured children were superior to those of the educable mentally retarded children.

The role of chronological age as a main effect in the research was not clearly demonstrated for the motor performance parameter of development. However, from the results of the interaction effects, it appeared that the older children, ages 10 to 13 years, demonstrated a greater improvement in performance than the children ages 6 to 9 years, but that this result was dependent upon the effects of the programs.

Figures 10.5, 10.6, 10.7, and 10.8 show the pre- and post-test scores of the children on each of the four previously mentioned test items. For each test, sharp increases were shown in almost every case in the classes in the specially planned programs, whereas in almost half of the cases there was a decrease in the motor performance of the children who were denied these opportunities. For example, a decrease in performance on the arm hang can be noted in seven of the eight illustrations (Figure 10.5), and in five of the eight cases on the standing broad jump (Figure 10.6). A particularly noticeable drop in performance was apparent on the arm hang of the older male retardates in the usual classroom instructional program. Those children ranked first on the pre-test scores but last on the post-tests.

An examination of the overall changes in performance on all the motor tests showed that the pattern for the classes in the special art program differed from that for the classes in the other two special programs. On the standing broad jump, the performance of those classes regressed in two of the eight comparisons (Figure 10.6); and it decreased also in one of the eight for the softball throw (Figure 10.7) and in one of the eight for the sit-ups (Figure 10.8). This is contrasted with the pattern for the two physical education programs, where a decrease was noted on only one occasion, the younger brain-injured girls on the arm hang, while sharp increases were mostly shown.

The comparative increases shown by the two groups of classes in the physical education programs can best be noted by referring to Figure 10.8, which indicates the pre- and post-test means for the sit-ups. While marked gains are shown by the classes in the physical education programs, regardless of the educational disability, age, or sex of the groups, in five of the eight comparisons the greater gains are those of the children in the individualized program. This feature is readily apparent also for the standing broad jump (Figure 10.6), but less so for the arm hang and the softball throw (Figures 10.5 and 10.7, respectively).

The extent to which performance increases could be attributed to differences in the category of educational disability of the children was indicated previously as favoring the minimally brain-injured children. This can be noted particularly from Figure 10.8, which shows the pre- and post-test mean scores for the sit-ups. Although improved performance on this event was quite consistent, the steeper slopes of the lines favor the brain-injured children. In addition, the brain-injured children who pursued their usual classroom instructional program were more likely to have retained or improved their level of performance and, therefore, were less likely to regress than were the educable retardates. This same observation is supported by observation of Figures 10.5, 10.6, and 10.7.

The following summarizes the results of all the analyses:

1. Improved motor performance was, on the average, characteristic of those in classes involved in all the special experimental programs but was not so typical of the performance of the groups of children who were denied the special programs.

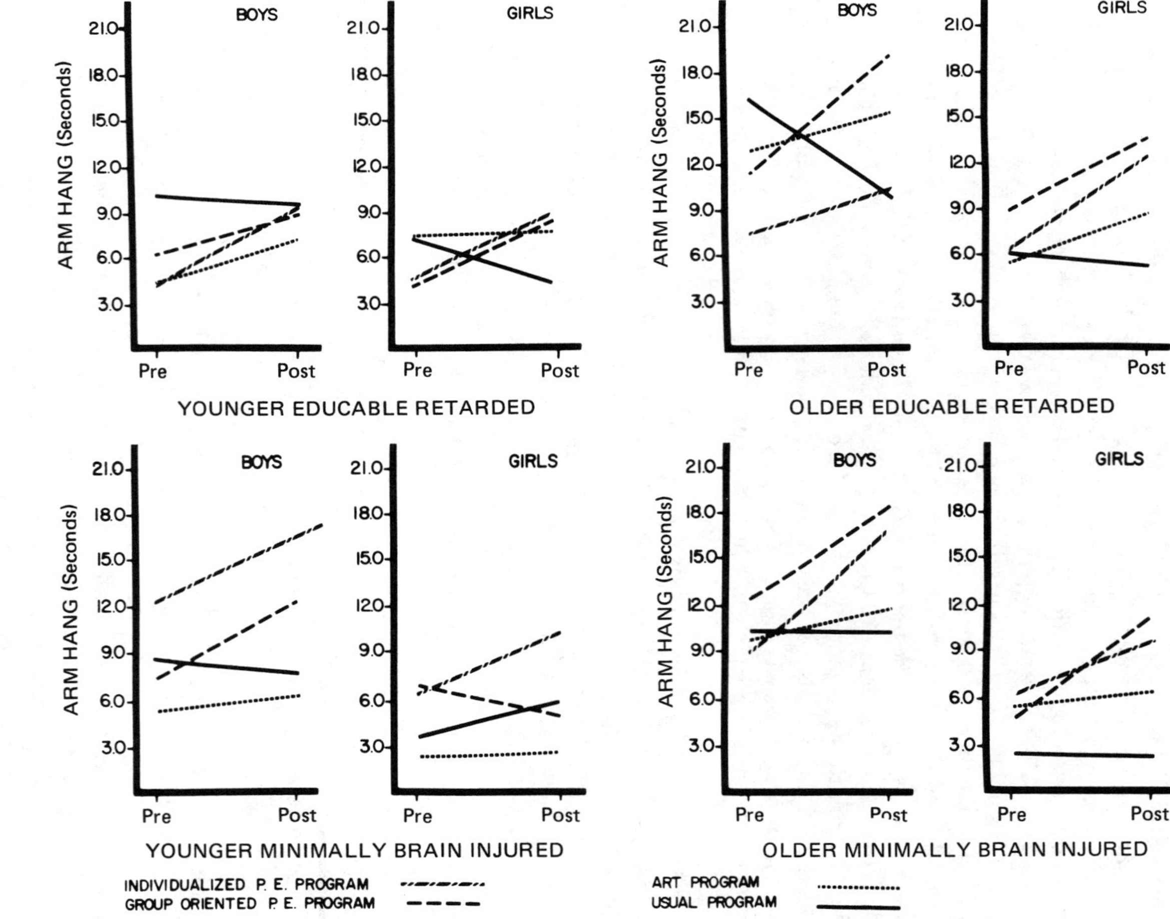

Fig. 10.5 Mean pre- and post-test arm hang scores, by treatment according to disability, age, and sex.

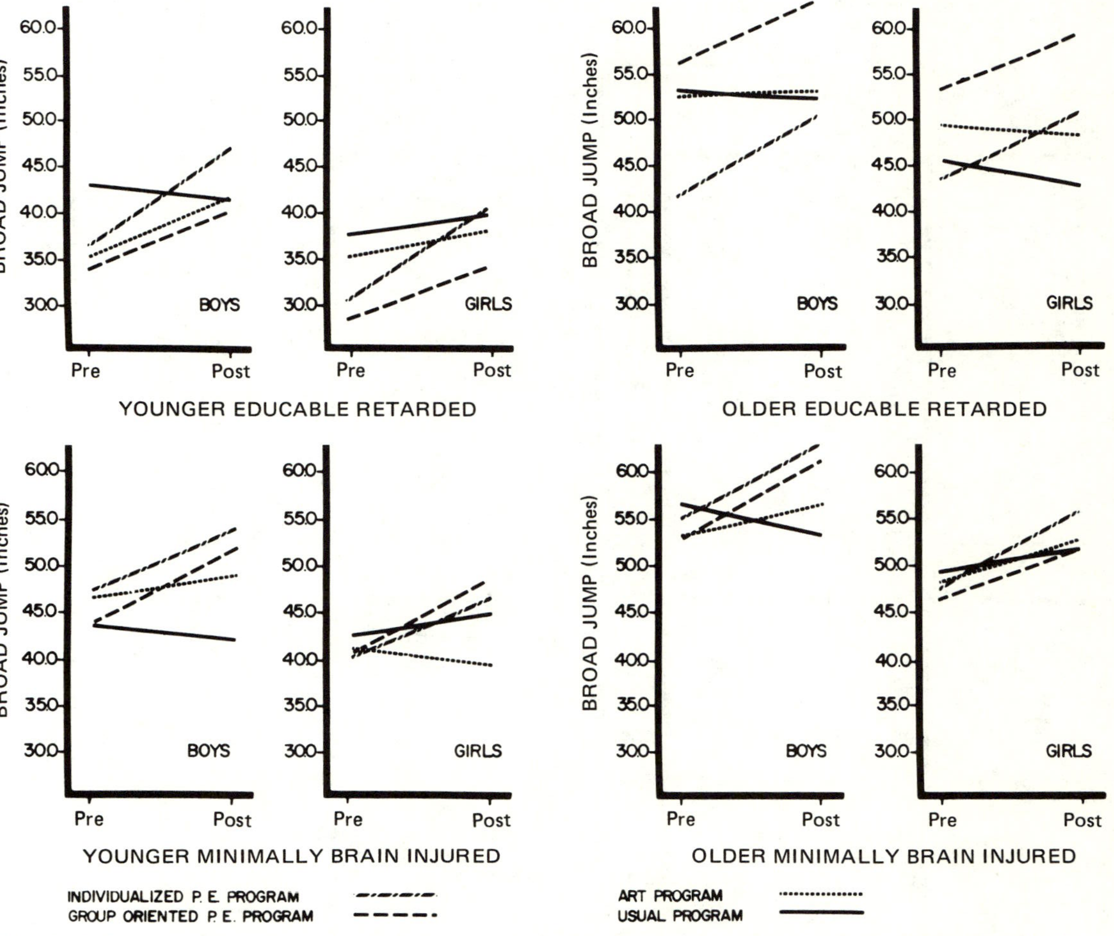

Fig. 10.6 Mean pre- and post-test standing broad jump scores, by treatment according to disability, age, and sex.

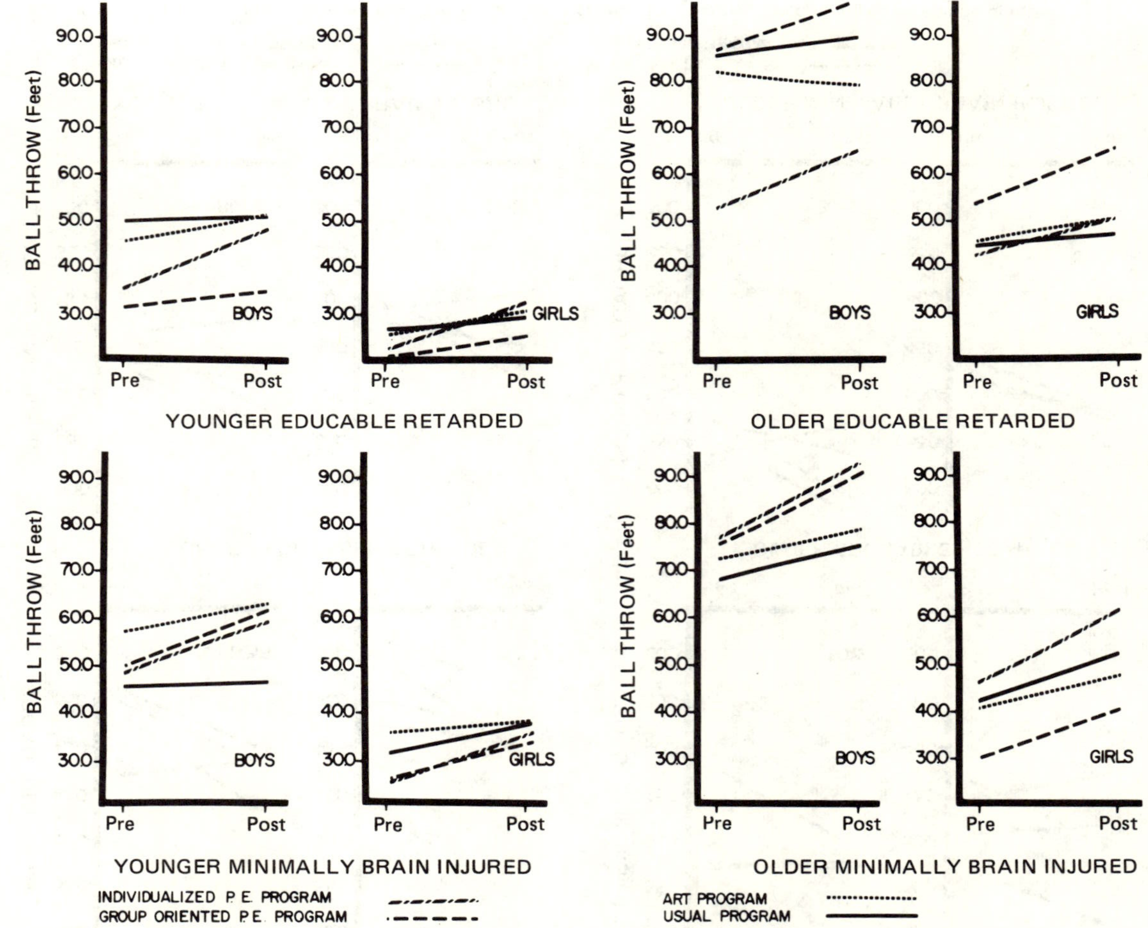

Fig. 10.7 Mean pre- and post-test softball throw scores, by treatment according to disability, age, and sex.

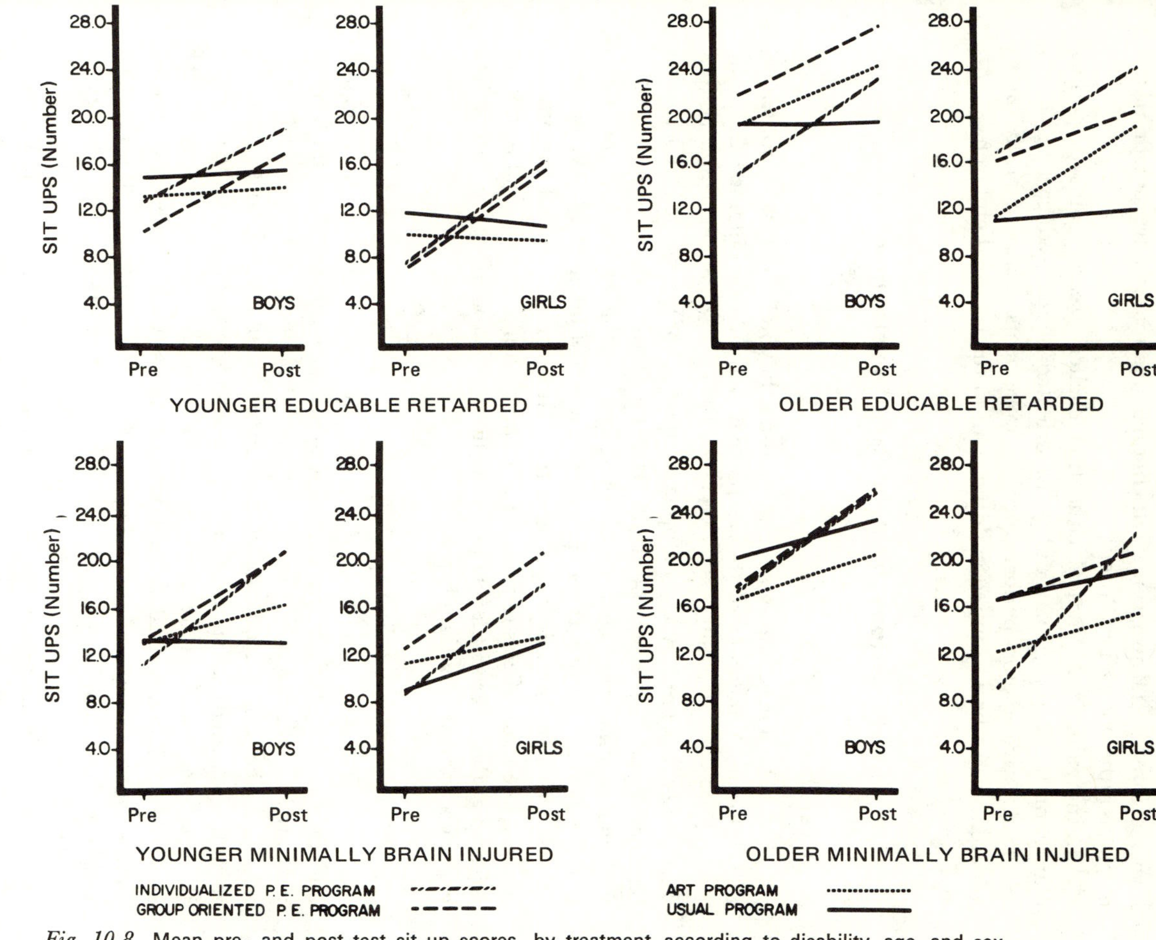

Fig. 10.8 Mean pre- and post-test sit-up scores, by treatment according to disability, age, and sex.

2. The improvements in motor performance favored those in the classes involved in physical education rather than art, but the performance changes of those in the art groups exceeded the changes of those who were not involved in a special program. This finding was more characteristic of the older than the younger children.

3. Individualized physical education elicited greater gains in performance, on the average, than did group-oriented physical education.

4. Relative motor performance improvements were generally more apparent in the brain-injured children than in the retarded children.

Modifications in Intellectual Development

Overview

Two measures were used to assess the intellectual development of the children. A measure of the verbal component was obtained from the Peabody Picture Vocabulary Test (Dunn, 1965). The Bender Motor Gestalt Test protocol, scored by the Koppitz method (1966), provided information on the nonverbal component. Data from these two tests were subjected to multivariate analysis of covariance, making it possible to examine the effects of the experimental programs on these measures of intellectual development as a function of disability, age, and sex. Three of the 15 null hypotheses, namely, the main effects of program, disability, and chronological age, were rejected at the 5 percent level of significance (see Table 10.3). No interaction effect was statistically significant.

Main Effect of Program

Research studies by Oliver (1958) and Lowe (1966) in England, and by Corder (1966) in the United States, had indicated that the level of measured intelligence was raised after special physical activity lessons were added to the school curricula of educationally subnormal boys (educable mentally retarded). Despite differences which were apparent in the design of these studies, and despite problems and limitations of the research, the reported results were similar. Such findings might well have been supported by the work of Solomon and Pangle (1966, 1967) except for the reported inappropriate conditions under which the post-testing of intelligence occurred.

In the present research, the main effect of program is clearly indicated in Table 10.14, which gives the results of the multivariate test. It is apparent that differences attributable to chance are remote ($F = 2.6719$; $p < 0.0182$). The same table shows that the Peabody Picture Vocabulary Test was largely responsible for the overall significant F value, with $p < 0.0027$.

Table 10.14

INTELLECTUAL DEVELOPMENT: MAIN EFFECT OF PROGRAM FOR MULTIVARIATE TEST OF EQUALITY OF MEAN VECTORS

$F = 2.6719^*$ p less than 0.0182 $df = 6$ and 118.0000

Variable	Between Mean Square	Univariate F	p Less Than
1. Peabody	72.3277	5.2918	0.0027
2. Bender	1.2942	0.4049	0.7501

df *for Hypothesis* = *3,* df *for Error* = *60, 2 covariates had been eliminated.*
**Null hypothesis rejected at the 5 percent level.*

The adjusted means for the Peabody Test and the Bender Test, grouped according to treatment, are shown in Figure 10.9. It is evident that the adjusted means of the Peabody Test favor the experimental groups rather than the control group. The adjusted means of the Bender Test do not show

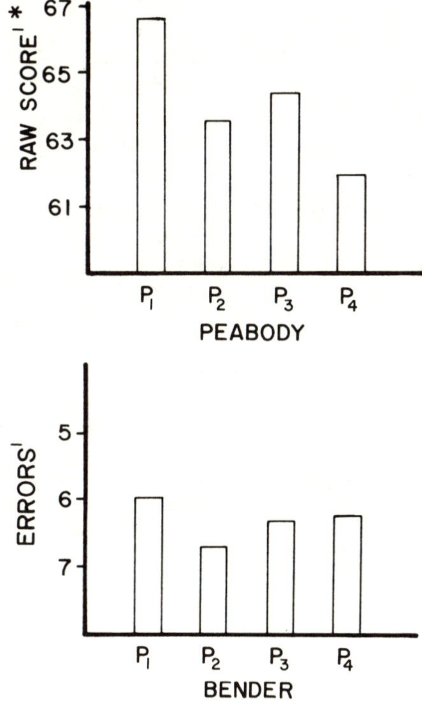

Fig. 10.9 Intellectual development: main effect of program, for the Peabody and Bender Tests. Program 1: individualized program; program 2: group-oriented program; program 3: art program; program 4: control or usual program.

as obvious a pattern and are more difficult to interpret. Tables 10.15, 10.16, and 10.17 include the results of the three planned comparisons. In Table 10.15, the null hypothesis was rejected ($F = 3.7882; p < 0.0284$). Taken with Figure 10.9, Table 10.15 clearly shows that the performance of the classes in the three special programs was significantly superior to that of the groups who were denied the special treatment. Note that in interpreting the adjusted means, the fewer the errors on the Bender Test, the better the performance. What appears to be a limited role of this test is shown both in the univariate test results of Table 10.15 and in Figure 10.9. Thus, the Hawthorne effect was operating and was measured. While all four treatment groups were subject to the same influences of maturation, only three groups of classes had had special treatment. This effect was apparent in measured terms.

The second comparison questioned whether the mean changes in intelligence test scores of those children in the two physical education programs differed from those of the children in the special art program. Reference to Table 10.16 demonstrates that no such differences existed ($F =$

Table 10.15

PLANNED COMPARISON FOR INTELLECTUAL TEST ITEMS: MAIN EFFECT OF PROGRAM—HYPOTHESIS ONE

That no differences exist between the performance on the intellectual test items of those children having Special Programs and those having no Special Program.

FOR MULTIVARIATE TEST OF EQUALITY OF MEAN VECTORS

F = 3.7882* *p* less than 0.0284 *df* = 2 and 59.0000

Variable	*Between Mean Square*	*Univariate* F	p *Less Than*
1. Peabody	89.6769	6.5611	0.0130
2. Bender	3.4424	1.0769	0.3036

df *for Hypothesis* = *1,* df *for Error* = *60, 2 covariates had been eliminated.*
**Null hypothesis rejected at the 5 percent level.*

Table 10.16

PLANNED COMPARISON FOR INTELLECTUAL TEST ITEMS: MAIN EFFECT OF PROGRAM—HYPOTHESIS TWO

That no differences exist between the performance on the intellectual test items of those children having Physical Education Programs and those having the Art Program.

FOR MULTIVARIATE TEST OF EQUALITY OF MEAN VECTORS

F = 0.2534 *p* less than 0.7771 *df* = 2 and 59.0000

Variable	*Between Mean Square*	*Univariate* F	p *Less Than*
1. Peabody	6.2397	0.4565	0.5019
2. Bender	0.2013	0.0630	0.8028

df *for Hypothesis* = *1,* df *for Error* = *60, 2 covariates had been eliminated.*

0.2534; $p < 0.7771$). Failure to reject the hypothesis for the multivariate test was supported by the univariate tests. Figure 10.9, showing the relative positions of the adjusted means, provided evidence that the adjusted means of the classes in the art program closely approximated those of the average of the two physical education programs.

The third planned comparison examined the respective roles of the two physical education programs, observing whether there were differences in the intellectual development of the children in the individualized program as compared to those whose special program had been group-oriented. The result of the planned comparison is shown in Table 10.17 ($F = 5.8279$;

Table 10.17

PLANNED COMPARISON FOR INTELLECTUAL TEST ITEMS: MAIN EFFECT OF PROGRAM—HYPOTHESIS THREE

That no differences exist between the performance on the intellectual test items of those children having the Individualized Physical Education Program and those having the Group-Oriented Physical Education Program.

FOR MULTIVARIATE TEST OF EQUALITY OF MEAN VECTORS

F = 5.8279* *p* less than 0.0050 *df* = 2 and 59.0000

Variable	*Between Mean Square*	*Univariate* F	p *Less Than*
1. Peabody	161.1380	11.7895	0.0011
2. Bender	0.2785	0.0871	0.7689

df *for Hypothesis* = *1,* df *for Error* = *60, 2 covariates had been eliminated.*
**Null hypothesis rejected at the 5 percent level.*

$p < 0.0050$). As can be noted from Figure 10.9, the significant difference favors the individualized program, with the adjusted means being superior for that program on both the Peabody and the Bender Tests. The univariate F values in Table 10.17 indicate again that, as for each of the three planned comparisons for the overall significance of the main effect of program, the Peabody Test was the influential test.

Main Effect of Chronological Age

The design of the study was such that the classes of children were divided according to their chronological age. One group of classes was composed of children ages 6 to 9 years, and the other group children ages 10 to 13 years. This age grouping made it possible to determine the probable differential effects of the treatments on children of different age levels.

The hypothesis that no statistically significant differences would exist between the younger and older children was rejected. See Table 10.18 ($F = 6.4805$; $p < 0.0029$). Both the Peabody and Bender Tests contributed

Table 10.18

INTELLECTUAL DEVELOPMENT: MAIN EFFECT OF AGE FOR MULTIVARIATE TEST OF EQUALITY OF MEAN VECTORS

$F = 6.4805$* p less than 0.0029 $df = 2$ and 59.0000

Variable	*Between Mean Square*	*Univariate* F	p *Less Than*
1. Peabody	99.7455	7.2977	0.0090
2. Bender	18.2880	5.7211	0.0200

df *for Hypothesis* = *1,* df *for Error* = *60, 2 covariates had been eliminated.*
**Null hypothesis rejected at the 5 percent level.*

significantly to the rejection of the null hypothesis. The adjusted means, shown in Figure 10.10, indicate the superiority of the older children on both tests. Thus, on both tests the greater gains were made by the older children; but since there was no significant interaction between age and program, there is no evidence of a differential effect of program on the gains in the measures of intelligence for the two age levels.

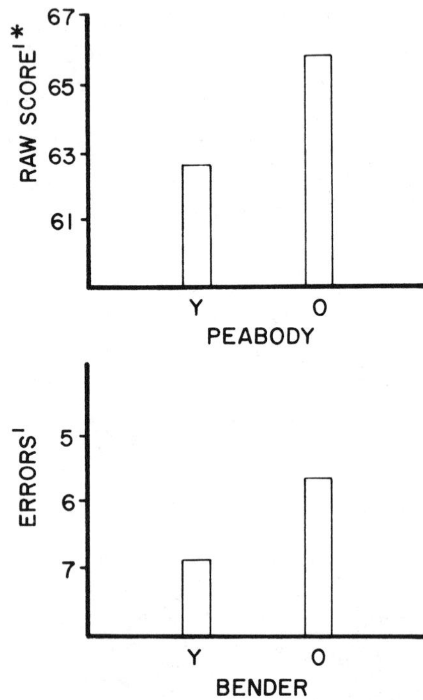

Fig. 10.10 Intellectual development: main effect of age for the Peabody and Bender Tests.

Main Effect of Disability

The results of the multivariate and univariate tests for the effect of educational disability on the measures of intelligence are given in Table 10.19. The hypothesis that the changes in this parameter of development were not different for the two disability groups was not tenable ($F = 6.7117$; $p < 0.0024$). The significant univariate F values for each variable demon-

Table 10.19

INTELLECTUAL DEVELOPMENT: MAIN EFFECT OF DISABILITY FOR MULTIVARIATE TEST OF EQUALITY OF MEAN VECTORS

$F = 6.7117$* p less than 0.0024 $df = 2$ and 59.0000

Variable	*Between Mean Square*	*Univariate* F	p *Less Than*
1. Peabody	90.4647	6.6187	0.0126
2. Bender	21.9396	6.8635	0.0112

df *for Hypothesis = 1,* df *for Error = 60, 2 covariates had been eliminated.*
**Null hypothesis rejected at the 5 percent level.*

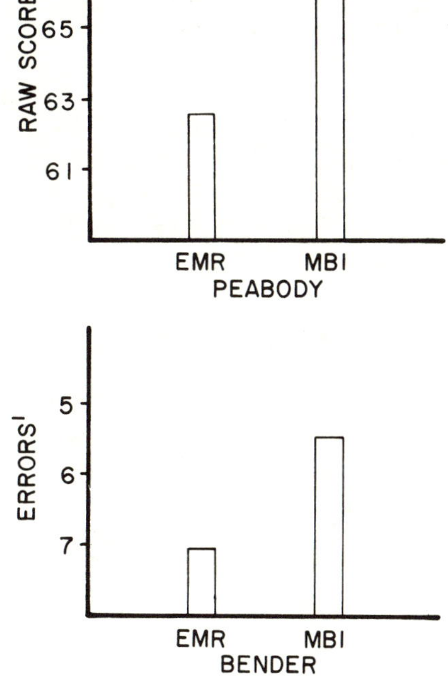

*Cell means adjusted for covariates

Fig. 10.11 Intellectual development: main effect of disability for the Peabody and Bender Tests.

strate that both the Peabody and Bender Tests contributed to the overall significant *F* value. An examination of the adjusted means in Figure 10.11 indicates that for both tests, the mean of the classes of minimally brain-injured children is higher than for the educable mentally retarded classes, taking into account pre-test differences.

The relatively greater gains of the brain-injured children in these tests of intelligence can in no way be attributed to treatment effects, for there was no significant interaction between educational disability and program for this aspect of development.

Observations on the Findings

The results given in this section are believed to be of considerable importance, since the question of the effect of physical activity programs on intellectual development has been the center of controversy and interest for some time. The following observations are justified:

1. No differences were found in the extent to which improved intellectual development was characteristic of the children in the physical education programs (data pooled) in comparison to the changes for those in the art program.

2. The magnitude of the improved intellectual development favored the children in the individualized physical education program as compared to those in the group-oriented program.

3. The role of the experimental treatments in eliciting positive change in the intellectual development of the children was indicated. Over and above the changes noted for the children involved in the usual classroom instructional program, which were changes attributable to maturation, the performance of the children in the three special programs was markedly superior to that of the control group.

4. By examining the degree to which changes in the magnitude of performance increase were attributable to chronological age, the greater improvements favored the older children.

5. From the analysis of the main effect of educational disability, the extent of positive change in intellectual development favored the minimally brain-injured children. This was a pattern also noted in the motor performance of the children.

In summarizing the effects of treatment, age, disability, and sex upon performance changes in the Peabody and Bender Test scores, mean pre- and post-test scores on these two measures have been plotted in Figures 10.12 and 10.13. As pointed out earlier, the older children showed relatively greater gains in test scores on both tests than did the younger children. These differences could not be attributed to the special treatments. However, it should be recalled that the special treatments did bring about greater changes in the measures of intelligence than those occurring in the control group.

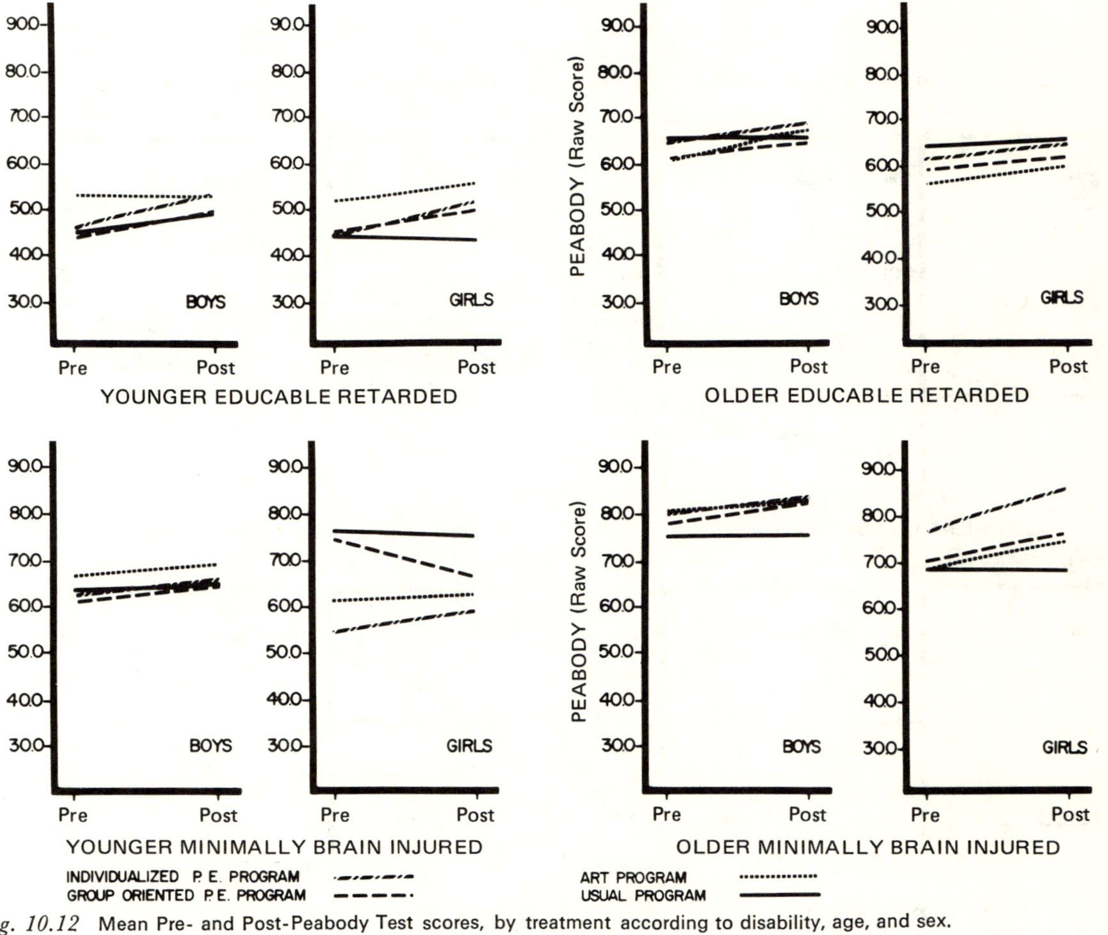

Fig. 10.12 Mean Pre- and Post-Peabody Test scores, by treatment according to disability, age, and sex.

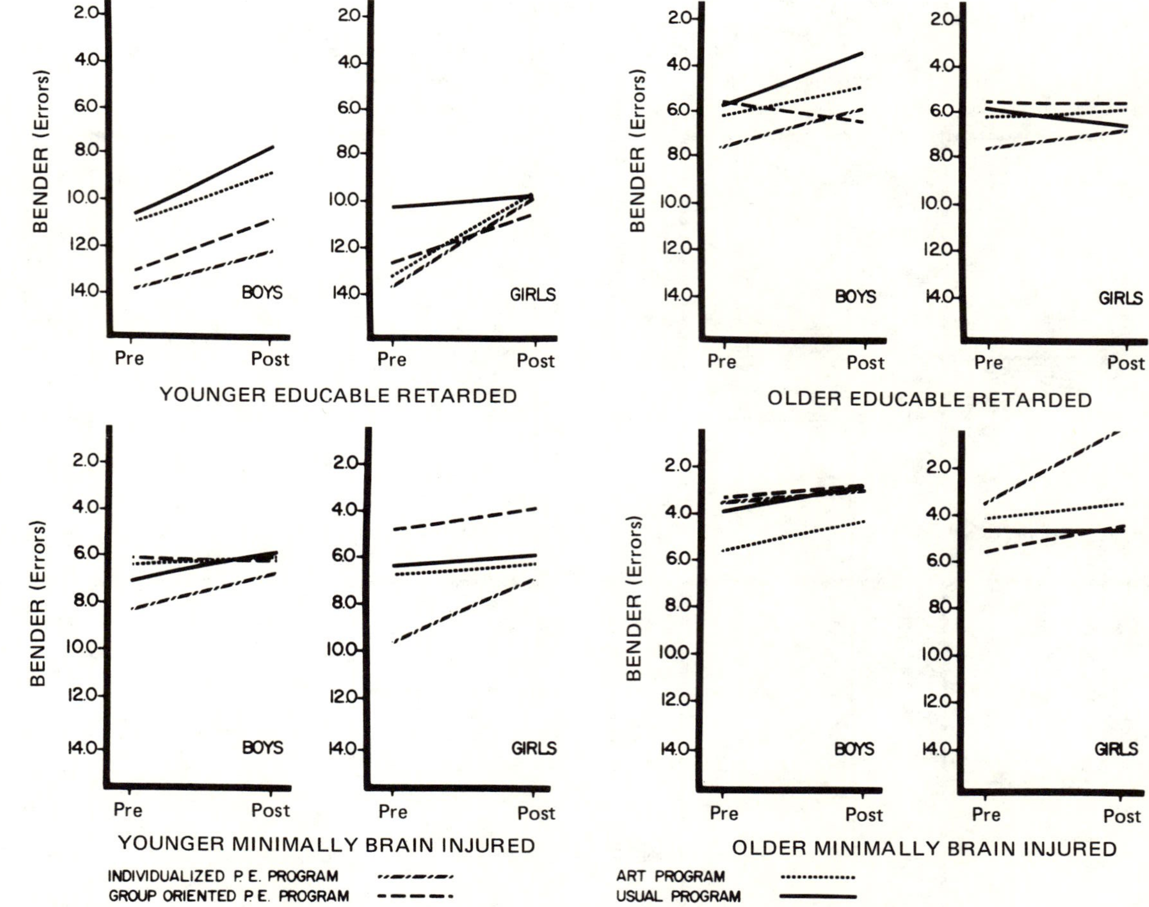

Fig. 10.13 Mean Pre- and Post-Bender Test scores, by treatment according to disability, age, and sex.

An examination of the effect of the educational disability on the performance of the children reveals that relative performance increases favor the brain-injured children. This finding is consistent with that reported for the motor performance results. It was evident that the greater gains in the intellectual and motor tests were made by the children who, in this research, were of superior intellect.

The data presented in Figures 10.12 and 10.13 indicate that the magnitude of the change in behavior favored the classes involved in the special programs rather than those classes which had no special programs. Figure 10.12 shows that on the Peabody Test, the latter decreased their scores in five of the eight cells over a period of 6 months. The pattern for the children in the special programs was distinctly different, for there was a tendency for an increase in performance.

An examination of Figures 10.12 and 10.13 reveals the differential response of the two physical education programs. On the Peabody Picture Vocabulary Test, the tendency was for the children in the individualized program to increase their scores to a greater extent than those in the group-oriented program. It can be seen that the results for five cells favor the individualized program, and on the Bender Test (Figure 10.13) the result is even more clearly shown. Such observations confirm the multivariate test results and the previous examination of the adjusted means.

As a result of the planned comparisons, it was noted that for the main effect of program, the art program was as effective as the two physical education programs (taken collectively) in eliciting change in performance on the two tests. This level of performance was more than that exhibited by the classes for which such change could be explained by maturational factors. It appeared, therefore, that it was the existence of a special program, rather than maturation or particular lesson content alone, which elicited such responses. From Figures 10.12 and 10.13, it is evident that the improvement of the classes which participated in the art program was generally consistent across disability, age, and sex. No sharp increase or regression was observed for either test for classes in this program.

Modifications in Emotional Development

Overview

Two tests were used to assess the changes in emotional development of the educable mentally retarded children and the minimally brain-injured children as a result of the instructional programs. First, a score from the protocol of the Bender Motor Gestalt Test was obtained for the number of "emotional indicators" exhibited in the children's drawings. Second, scores from 13 factors common to two of the Cattell series of personality questionnaires were obtained. The younger children were given the Early School Personality Questionnaire, and the Children's Personality Questionnaire was used with the older children. To retain the discriminatory powers of the tests, raw scores were used and separate covariance analyses were employed for each age group. Hence, the design for the younger children was one of three factors: educational disability, sex, and program.

Some words of caution are necessary in interpreting the results coming from this parameter of development. On the pre-test and on the post-test, several children had difficulty completing the questionnaire, even when assisted by the classroom teacher. On the pre-test especially, possibly because of their very limited intellectual level, a few of the children were unable to complete the test. Other children produced answers which indicated perseveration, a characteristic which is well known in brain-injured children, though in this research the trait was exhibited more by the very youngest retardates. Where obvious perseveration occurred, the protocol was not scored. However, it is not known whether other questionnaires, which did not show a patterned response that was easily noticeable, were in fact a series of haphazard answers. The difficulties in selecting tests for this parameter of development are well known. The choice is obviously limited. It may well be that some of the responses obtained were invalid, and care must therefore be taken in interpreting this section of the results.

For each age level, seven hypotheses were tested by the use of the multivariate analyses referred to earlier. The results, given in Table 10.4, indicate that while five of the seven hypotheses were rejected for the younger children, in only one of the seven hypotheses for the older children did a significant difference occur. Whether this was a function of a greater impact of the treatment on the younger children; whether the younger children, by virtue of their maturity level, were less resistant to personality changes; or whether the differences observed were a function of the measures, is not known.

Effects on the Younger Children

MAIN EFFECT OF PROGRAM. The results of the multivariate analysis, which revealed a significant main effect of program on the emotional development of the younger children, is shown in Table 10.20. Clearly, the programs had different effects on this parameter of development ($F = 8.2730$; $p < 0.0043$), with personality factors B and Q_4 both significantly influencing the result. Since the personality factors B and Q_4 contributed most to this difference, they have been shown in Figure 10.14. This Figure shows that for both of these traits, intelligence and tension, the direction of the differences favors the special experimental programs.

It may be noted from Table 10.21 that the multivariate test for the first

Table 10.20

EMOTIONAL DEVELOPMENT (YOUNGER): MAIN EFFECT OF PROGRAM FOR MULTIVARIATE TEST OF EQUALITY OF MEAN VECTORS

F = 8.2730* p less than 0.0043 df = 42 and 6.6983

	Variable	Between Mean Square	Univariate F	p Less Than
1.	Emotional Indicators	0.2009	0.6498	0.5953
2.	Personality *A*	1.9619	1.7363	0.2025
3.	*B*	5.0945	3.2897	0.0500
4.	*C*	1.5168	0.8852	0.4712
5.	*D*	1.3325	0.4688	0.7085
6.	*E*	2.0444	2.1677	0.1344
7.	*F*	2.9952	1.6647	0.2171
8.	*G*	0.7993	1.7052	0.2087
9.	*H*	1.0052	0.5438	0.6598
10.	*I*	0.9047	0.7407	0.5442
11.	*J*	0.9620	1.0397	0.4035
12.	*N*	1.7542	2.1486	0.1369
13.	*O*	1.8154	1.2246	0.3353
14.	Q_4	4.1634	5.7802	0.0079

df *for Hypothesis = 3,* df *for Error = 15, 14 covariates had been eliminated.*
**Null hypothesis rejected at the 5 percent level.*

Table 10.21

PLANNED COMPARISON FOR EMOTIONAL TEST ITEMS (YOUNGER): MAIN EFFECT OF PROGRAM—HYPOTHESIS ONE

That no differences exist between the performance on the emotional test items of those children having Special Programs and those having no Special Program.

FOR MULTIVARIATE TEST OF EQUALITY OF MEAN VECTORS

F = 49.1519* p less than 0.0202 df = 14 and 2.0000

	Variable	Between Mean Square	Univariate F	p Less Than
1.	Emotional Indicators	0.0922	0.2981	0.5931
2.	Personality *A*	0.6333	0.5605	0.4657
3.	*B*	1.7149	1.1074	0.3094
4.	*C*	1.1813	0.6894	0.4194
5.	*D*	2.3859	0.8393	0.3741
6.	*E*	0.1239	0.1314	0.7221
7.	*F*	2.4768	1.3764	0.2591
8.	*G*	0.0814	0.1737	0.6828
9.	*H*	0.9147	0.4949	0.4926
10.	*I*	0.0000	0.0000	0.9952
11.	*J*	0.7564	0.8174	0.3803
12.	*N*	0.0289	0.0354	0.8533
13.	*O*	3.3612	2.2674	0.1529
14.	Q_4	2.7784	3.8573	0.0684

df *for Hypothesis = 1,* df *for Error = 15, 14 covariates had been eliminated.*
**Null hypothesis rejected at the 5 percent level.*

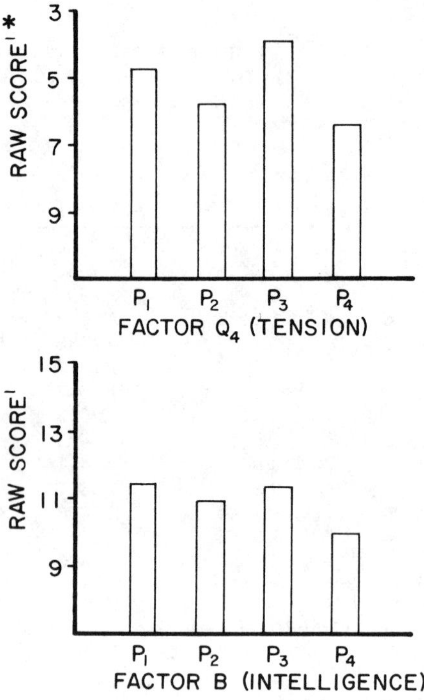

Fig. 10.14 Emotional development (younger): main effect of program for personality factors Q_4 (tension) and B (intelligence). Program 1: individualized program; program 2: group-oriented program; program 3: art program; program 4: control or usual program.

planned comparison, which examined the effect of the special treatments compared with the usual classroom instructional program, resulted in the null hypothesis being rejected ($F = 49.1519$; $p < 0.0202$). This indicates that the differences between those classes having special programs and those having the usual program cannot be attributed to chance.

The second planned comparison was used to note if differences existed between those in the art program and those in the physical education programs for the variables which assessed emotional development. From Table 10.22 it is seen that the null hypothesis was rejected ($F = 73.4754$; $p < 0.0136$). Figure 10.14 shows that the classes involved in the art education program improved their performance to a greater degree than the classes in the physical education programs. This was particularly noticeable for factor Q_4, which measures the extent to which a subject is tense or overwrought. One might infer from this that the art program had a more soothing and relaxing influence than the physical activity programs.

Table 10.22

PLANNED COMPARISON FOR EMOTIONAL TEST ITEMS (YOUNGER): MAIN EFFECT OF PROGRAM—HYPOTHESIS TWO

That no differences exist between the performance on the emotional test items of those children having Physical Education Programs and those having the Art Program.

FOR MULTIVARIATE TEST OF EQUALITY OF MEAN VECTORS

$F = 73.4754$* p less than 0.0136 $df = 14$ and 2.0000

Variable	*Between Mean Square*	*Univariate* F	p *Less Than*
1. Emotional Indicators	0.0769	0.2488	0.6252
2. Personality *A*	2.4021	2.1259	0.1655
3. *B*	0.2355	0.1521	0.7021
4. *C*	0.7426	0.4334	0.5204
5. *D*	0.8540	0.3004	0.5917
6. *E*	0.7219	0.7655	0.3955
7. *F*	4.5084	2.5057	0.1343
8. *G*	0.0266	0.0567	0.8150
9. *H*	2.4855	1.3447	0.2644
10. *I*	0.6474	0.5301	0.4778
11. *J*	0.0673	0.0728	0.7911
12. *N*	0.0048	0.0058	0.9402
13. *O*	1.0967	0.7404	0.4031
14. Q_4	6.2235	8.6402	0.0102

df *for Hypothesis = 1,* df *for Error = 15, 14 covariates had been eliminated.*
**Null hypothesis rejected at the 5 percent level.*

The multivariate analysis used in the third planned comparison (effect of the individualized versus the group-oriented physical education program) resulted in the rejection of the null hypothesis, with $F = 111.6123$ and $p < 0.0090$ (see Table 10.23). This showed that differences existed between the two types of physical activity programs. In order to determine the direction of the differences, the adjusted means were examined. From Figure 10.14 it can be seen that for personality trait B (intelligence), the superior position favored the classes in the individualized program. Similarly, for factor Q_4 (tension), the direction of the differences favored that program.

Main Effect of Disability. An examination of Table 10.24 reveals that the educational disability of the children was a factor which accounted for differences in the performance of the classes for the vector of variables which assessed emotional development ($F = 40.0004$; $p < 0.0247$). In other words, the changes in performance of the brain-injured children, on the emotional test items taken collectively, differed significantly from the performance of the retarded children. The only variable having a significant univariate F value was factor B, intelligence ($p < 0.0015$). From Figure 10.15,

Table 10.23

PLANNED COMPARISON FOR EMOTIONAL TEST ITEMS (YOUNGER): MAIN EFFECT OF PROGRAM—HYPOTHESIS THREE

That no differences exist between the performance on the emotional test items of those children having the Individualized Physical Education Program and those having the Group-Oriented Physical Education Program.

FOR MULTIVARIATE TEST OF EQUALITY OF MEAN VECTORS

F = 111.6123* p less than 0.0090 df = 14 and 2.0000

Variable		*Between Mean Square*	*Univariate* F	p *Less Than*
1.	Emotional Indicators	0.5532	1.7894	0.2010
2.	Personality *A*	1.4936	1.3219	0.2683
3.	*B*	16.7838	10.8378	0.0050
4.	*C*	1.4345	0.8372	0.3747
5.	*D*	0.7815	0.2749	0.6077
6.	*E*	5.1074	5.4154	0.0344
7.	*F*	1.1038	0.6135	0.4457
8.	*G*	1.4239	3.0377	0.1019
9.	*H*	0.0007	0.0004	0.9854
10.	*I*	1.9047	1.5595	0.2309
11.	*J*	1.4454	1.5621	0.2306
12.	*N*	2.9848	3.6560	0.0752
13.	*O*	0.3978	0.2683	0.6121
14.	Q_4	2.7432	3.8084	0.0700

df *for Hypothesis = 1,* df *for Error = 15, 14 covariates had been eliminated.*
**Null hypothesis rejected at the 5 percent level.*

Table 10.24

EMOTIONAL DEVELOPMENT (YOUNGER): MAIN EFFECT OF DISABILITY FOR MULTIVARIATE TEST OF EQUALITY OF MEAN VECTORS

F = 40.0004* p less than 0.0247 df = 14 and 2.0000

Variable		*Between Mean Square*	*Univariate* F	p *Less Than*
1.	Emotional Indicators	0.0011	0.0034	0.9540
2.	Personality *A*	0.0042	0.0037	0.9524
3.	*B*	23.5378	15.1991	0.0015
4.	*C*	1.9177	1.1192	0.3069
5.	*D*	1.0898	0.3834	0.5451
6.	*E*	0.5401	0.5727	0.4610
7.	*F*	0.0560	0.0311	0.8624
8.	*G*	0.0845	0.1803	0.6772
9.	*H*	0.8087	0.4375	0.5184
10.	*I*	0.5769	0.4724	0.5024
11.	*J*	0.2103	0.2272	0.6405
12.	*N*	0.3723	0.4560	0.5098
13.	*O*	0.0021	0.0014	0.9706
14.	Q_4	0.0260	0.0361	0.8518

df *for Hypothesis = 1,* df *for Error = 15, 14 covariates had been eliminated.*
**Null hypothesis rejected at the 5 percent level.*

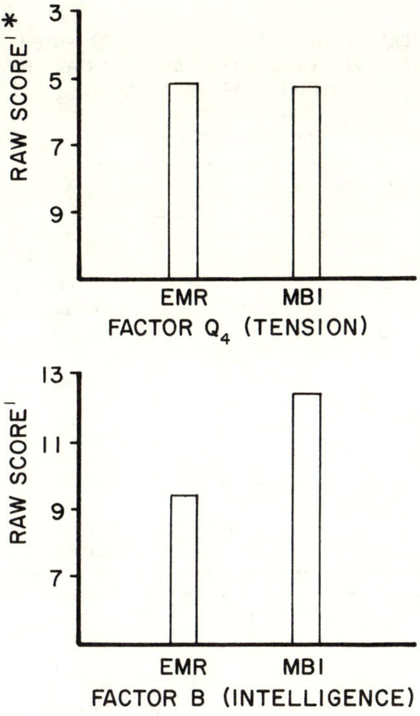

Fig. 10.15 Emotional development (younger): main effect of disability for personality factors Q_4 (tension) and B (intelligence).

it may be noted that the adjusted mean of the brain-injured children is higher than that of the retarded children. Over the period of the experiment, the brain-injured children made greater gains than the retardates on this trait.

MAIN EFFECT OF SEX. The results of the multivariate analysis examining the effect of sex on the changes in the emotional development of the classes of children are given in Table 10.25, in which the null hypothesis was rejected ($F = 25.7527$; $p < 0.0380$). Reference to this table shows that only two factors had a significant univariate F value, namely, factors G and Q_4. The adjusted means for factor B (univariate F not significant) and factor Q_4 are graphically shown in Figure 10.16. The adjusted means for factor Q_4 favor the boys rather than the girls. The direction of the change for factor G was also examined, with changes also favoring the boys. Thus, it would appear that over the period of the study, tension reduction on the one hand, and determination and emotional stability on the other, as assessed by this test, were greater for the boys than for the girls. It would seem, therefore, that the

Table 10.25

EMOTIONAL DEVELOPMENT (YOUNGER):
MAIN EFFECT OF SEX FOR MULTIVARIATE TEST OF
EQUALITY OF MEAN VECTORS

$F = 25.7527$* *p* less than 0.0380 *df* = 14 and 2.0000

Variable	*Between Mean Square*	*Univariate* F	p *Less Than*
1. Emotional Indicators	0.2032	0.6575	0.4302
2. Personality *A*	0.0555	0.0491	0.8276
3. *B*	3.1202	2.0148	0.1763
4. *C*	0.0452	0.0264	0.8731
5. *D*	1.4588	0.5132	0.4828
6. *E*	0.2333	0.2473	0.6262
7. *F*	0.4731	0.2629	0.6156
8. *G*	2.1245	4.5325	0.0503
9. *H*	0.0291	0.0157	0.9019
10. *I*	0.6209	0.5084	0.4868
11. *J*	0.0002	0.0003	0.9873
12. *N*	0.0643	0.0787	0.7829
13. *O*	1.2240	0.8257	0.3779
14. Q_4	7.2162	10.0184	0.0065

df *for Hypothesis = 1,* df *for Error = 15, 14 covariates had been eliminated.*
**Null hypothesis rejected at the 5 percent level.*

change in emotional development as assessed here was more pronounced for the boys than for the girls.

INTERACTION EFFECT OF DISABILITY × PROGRAM. As is shown in Table 10.26, the multivariate test yielded a statistically significant interaction effect between educational disability and program ($F = 3.6302; p < 0.0439$). From this analysis, the contributions of factor *B* (intelligence) and the emotional indicators from the Bender Test are both highly significant. To determine the effects of the various treatments on this interaction, the planned comparisons were made. No differences were found at the 5 percent level of significance when the performance of the classes involved in the special programs was compared to that of the classes having no special program ($F = 17.8826$; $p < 0.0542$). (see Table 10.27.) Reference to Table 10.28 shows that the differences between the responses of the children in the two physical education programs and those in the special art program varied with the educational disability of the children ($F = 123.1066; p < 0.0081$). No differences, however, were noted between the classes having the individualized physical education program and the group-oriented physical education program ($F = 5.1916; p < 0.1731$). (See Table 10.29.)

Figure 10.17 presents the relative positions of the adjusted cell means of both disability groups for each of the four programs and for factors Q_4 (tension) and *B* (intelligence) of the personality profile, thus providing a

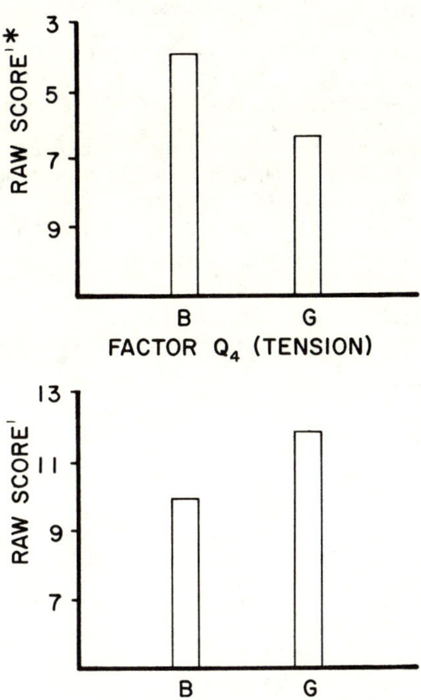

Fig. 10.16 Emotional development (younger): main effect of sex for personality factors Q_4 (tension) and B (intelligence).

Table 10.26

EMOTIONAL DEVELOPMENT (YOUNGER):
INTERACTION EFFECT OF DISABILITY × PROGRAM

FOR MULTIVARIATE TEST OF EQUALITY OF MEAN VECTORS
F = 3.6302* p less than 0.0439 df = 42 and 6.6983

	Variable	*Between Mean Square*	*Univariate* F	p *Less Than*
1.	Emotional Indicators	1.3671	4.4222	0.0204
2.	Personality *A*	0.8171	0.7231	0.5538
3.	*B*	8.5383	5.5135	0.0094
4.	*C*	1.8884	1.1021	0.3790
5.	*D*	3.4004	1.1963	0.3449
6.	*E*	1.6215	1.7193	0.2059
7.	*F*	1.0865	0.6038	0.6226
8.	*G*	0.2963	0.6321	0.6057
9.	*H*	1.8344	0.9924	0.4231
10.	*I*	0.9483	0.7765	0.5252
11.	*J*	0.1603	0.1732	0.9129
12.	*N*	0.4167	0.5104	0.6812
13.	*O*	0.2847	0.1921	0.9002
14.	Q_4	0.8105	1.1252	0.3703

df *for Hypothesis = 3,* df *for Error = 15, 14 covariates had been eliminated.*
**Null hypothesis rejected at the 5 percent level.*

Table 10.27

PLANNED COMPARISON FOR EMOTIONAL TEST ITEMS (YOUNGER): INTERACTION EFFECT OF DISABILITY × PROGRAM—HYPOTHESIS ONE

That no differences exist between the performance on the emotional test items of those children having Special Programs and those having no Special Program.

FOR MULTIVARIATE TEST OF EQUALITY OF MEAN VECTORS

$F = 17.8826$ p less than 0.0542 $df = 14$ and 2.0000

Variable	*Between Mean Square*	*Univariate* F	p *Less Than*
1. Emotional Indicators	0.6655	2.1529	0.1630
2. Personality *A*	1.5832	1.4012	0.2550
3. *B*	10.5741	6.8281	0.0196
4. *C*	1.2895	0.7526	0.3994
5. *D*	6.6590	2.3426	0.1467
6. *E*	3.4775	3.6872	0.0741
7. *F*	0.4250	0.2362	0.6340
8. *G*	0.1591	0.3395	0.5688
9. *H*	0.4927	0.2665	0.6132
10. *I*	1.4919	1.2215	0.2865
11. *J*	0.0884	0.0955	0.7616
12. *N*	0.2143	0.2626	0.6159
13. *O*	0.0006	0.0004	0.9846
14. Q_4	0.1995	0.2770	0.6064

df *for Hypothesis = 1,* df *for Error = 15, 14 covariates had been eliminated.*

Table 10.28

PLANNED COMPARISON FOR EMOTIONAL TEST ITEMS (YOUNGER): INTERACTION EFFECT OF DISABILITY × PROGRAM—HYPOTHESIS TWO

That no differences exist between the performance on the emotional test items of those children having Physical Education Programs and those having the Art Program.

FOR MULTIVARIATE TEST OF EQUALITY OF MEAN VECTORS

$F = 123.1066^*$ p less than 0.0081 $df = 14$ and 2.0000

Variable	*Between Mean Square*	*Univariate* F	p *Less Than*
1. Emotional Indicators	3.5175	11.3786	0.0042
2. Personality *A*	0.5621	0.4975	0.4915
3. *B*	2.4088	1.5555	0.2315
4. *C*	3.7582	2.1934	0.1594
5. *D*	1.8473	0.6499	0.4328
6. *E*	0.2258	0.2394	0.6318
7. *F*	2.6142	1.4530	0.2468
8. *G*	0.6256	1.3346	0.2661
9. *H*	4.6841	2.5341	0.1323
10. *I*	0.2506	0.2052	0.6571
11. *J*	0.3803	0.4110	0.5312
12. *N*	0.0352	0.0431	0.8383
13. *O*	0.1196	0.0807	0.7803
14. Q_4	0.8451	1.1732	0.2959

df *for Hypothesis = 1,* df *for Error = 15, 14 covariates had been eliminated.*
**Null hypothesis rejected at the 5 percent level.*

Table 10.29

PLANNED COMPARISON FOR EMOTIONAL TEST ITEMS (YOUNGER): INTERACTION EFFECT OF DISABILITY × PROGRAM—HYPOTHESIS THREE

That no differences exist between the performance on the emotional test items of those children having the Individualized Physical Education Program and those having the Group-Oriented Physical Education Prcgram.

FOR MULTIVARIATE TEST OF EQUALITY OF MEAN VECTORS

$F = 5.1916$ p less than 0.1731 $df = 14$ and 2.0000

	Variable	*Between Mean Square*	*Univariate* F	p *Less Than*
1.	Emotional Indicators	0.0006	0.0021	0.9643
2.	Personality *A*	0.0032	0.0029	0.9581
3.	*B*	4.3576	2.8138	0.1142
4.	*C*	0.0509	0.0297	0.8655
5.	*D*	1.9764	0.6953	0.4175
6.	*E*	0.1623	0.1720	0.6842
7.	*F*	1.3531	0.7520	0.3995
8.	*G*	0.0400	0.0854	0.7742
9.	*H*	0.0074	0.0040	0.9505
10.	*I*	0.3452	0.2826	0.6028
11.	*J*	0.0125	0.0135	0.9089
12.	*N*	0.4925	0.6032	0.4495
13.	*O*	0.6089	0.4108	0.5313
14.	Q_4	1.0491	1.4565	0.2462

df *for Hypothesis = 1,* df *for Error = 15, 14 covariates had been eliminated.*

graphic description of the interaction between disability and program. For both factors, it can be noted that the brain-injured children, on the average, hold a superior position to the educable retarded children; and though not statistically significant ($p < 0.0542$), it would appear that there is a tendency for the average of the special program classes to be higher than that of the control group. The significant F value noted in Table 10.28, showing a difference between the disability groups with respect to a comparison of the physical education and art programs, is not easy to interpret from an examination of Figure 10.17 or from the univariate F values of Table 10.26.

INTERACTION EFFECT OF DISABILITY × SEX × PROGRAM. The second order interaction resulting from the multivariate analysis of the data on the emotional development of the children resulted in rejection of the null hypothesis ($F = 4.0255$; $p < 0.0334$). The greatest single contribution to the significant F value was made by factor Q_4 (see Table 10.30).

To interpret the significant second order interaction effect, two procedures were employed. First, the three planned comparisons were made; and second, the adjusted means were plotted in Figure 10.18. Tables 10.31, 10.32, and 10.33 provide information on the results of the multivariate and univariate analyses obtained in the three comparisons. An examination of Table

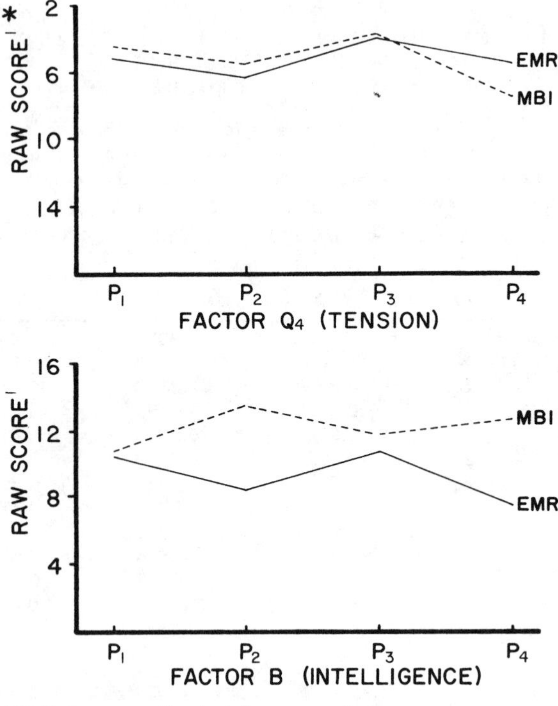

Fig. 10.17 Emotional development (younger): interaction effect of disability × program for personality factors Q_4 (tension) and B (intelligence). Program 1: individualized program; program 2: group-oriented program; program 3: art program; program 4: control or usual program.

10.31 (interaction effect of special programs versus no special program) reveals that the null hypothesis was upheld ($F = 17.2789; p < 0.0561$). It was concluded, therefore, that while the effects on the measures of emotion of the three special programs, taken collectively, were superior to the effects of the usual classroom instructional program, these effects did not differ significantly by disability or sex. A perusal of Table 10.32 likewise shows that while a comparison of the effects of the physical education programs, taken as a whole, with the effects of the art education program favored the groups in the latter program, the differences did not vary significantly by either disability or sex ($F = 0.4580; p < 0.8505$).

Table 10.33 shows the results of the testing of hypothesis three, which questioned whether the previously noted differences on the emotional test items between the classes in the individualized physical education program and those in the group-oriented physical education program varied with disability and sex. The multivariate F of 57.0942, with a probability of 0.0174,

Table 10.30

EMOTIONAL DEVELOPMENT (YOUNGER):
INTERACTION EFFECT OF DISABILITY × SEX × PROGRAM

FOR MULTIVARIATE TEST OF EQUALITY OF MEAN VECTORS

F = 4.0255* p less than 0.0334 df = 42 and 6.6983

Variable	Between Mean Square	Univariate F	p Less Than
1. Emotional Indicators	0.0768	0.2484	0.8612
2. Personality *A*	1.9740	1.7470	0.2005
3. *B*	1.5214	0.9824	0.4274
4. *C*	0.7198	0.4201	0.7413
5. *D*	0.5069	0.1783	0.9095
6. *E*	0.8257	0.8755	0.4757
7. *F*	0.6974	0.3876	0.7636
8. *G*	0.7554	1.6117	0.2286
9. *H*	1.6656	0.9011	0.4637
10. *I*	0.2043	0.1672	0.9169
11. *J*	1.9926	2.1534	0.1362
12. *N*	1.4023	1.7177	0.2062
13. *O*	0.7338	0.4950	0.6912
14. Q_4	3.0581	4.2456	0.0233

df *for Hypothesis* = *3,* df *for Error* = *15, 14 covariates had been eliminated.*
**Null hypothesis rejected at the 5 percent level.*

Table 10.31

PLANNED COMPARISON FOR EMOTIONAL TEST ITEMS
(YOUNGER): INTERACTION EFFECT OF
DISABILITY × SEX × PROGRAM—HYPOTHESIS ONE

That no differences exist between the performance on the emotional test items of those children having Special Programs and those having no Special Program.

FOR MULTIVARIATE TEST OF EQUALITY OF MEAN VECTORS

F = 17.2789 p less than 0.0561 df = 14 and 2.0000

Variable	Between Mean Square	Univariate F	p Less Than
1. Emotional Indicators	0.1006	0.3255	0.5768
2. Personality *A*	1.4353	1.2702	0.2775
3. *B*	3.0928	1.9971	0.1781
4. *C*	0.2061	0.1203	0.7336
5. *D*	1.3763	0.4842	0.4972
6. *E*	1.8977	2.0121	0.1765
7. *F*	0.3449	0.1917	0.6678
8. *G*	0.4202	0.8964	0.3588
9. *H*	0.3674	0.1988	0.6621
10. *I*	0.5464	0.4474	0.5138
11. *J*	0.9320	1.0071	0.3316
12. *N*	3.0026	3.6778	0.0744
13. *O*	0.1520	0.1025	0.7533
14. Q_4	2.7929	3.8775	0.0677

df *for Hypothesis* = *1,* df *for Error* = *15, 14 covariates had been eliminated.*

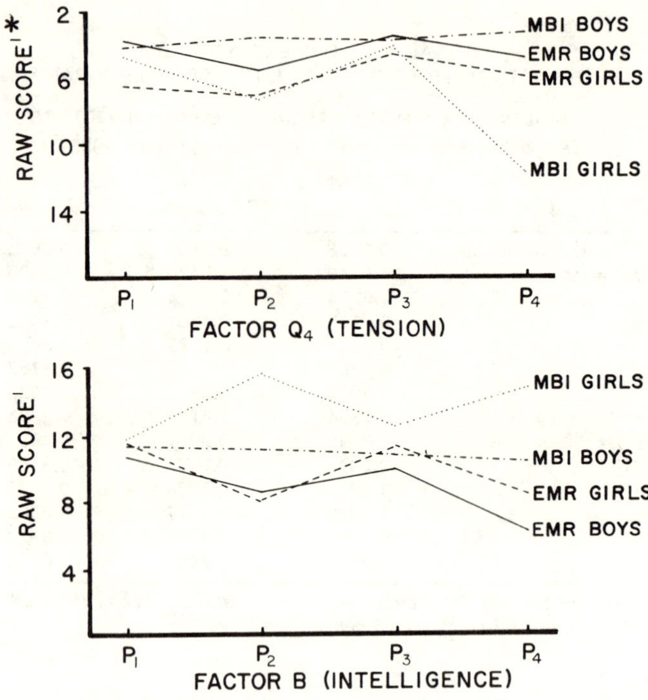

Fig. 10.18 Emotional development (younger): interaction effect of disability × sex × program for personality factors Q_4 (tension) and B (intelligence). Program 1: individualized program; program 2: group-oriented program; program 3: art program; program 4: control or usual program.

clearly indicated that such differences did exist. Figure 10.18 shows the relative position of the adjusted means for two personality factors, B and Q_4. It is evident that the effect of the programs on factor Q_4 varied markedly with disability and sex. The relative position of the adjusted means indicates a superior degree of change favoring the boys rather than the girls on factor Q_4, but also indicates a tendency for the difference to be in favor of the minimally brain-injured children rather than the educable retarded on factor B. As was pointed out earlier, the changes in this aspect of development shown by the classes in the individualized physical education program were superior to those of the classes in the group-oriented program.

Effects on Older Children

Only one of the seven hypotheses tested for the older children was rejected. This was the interaction effect of disability and program. From Table 10.34 it is seen that the null hypothesis was rejected at the 5 percent level ($p < 0.0364$).

Table 10.32

PLANNED COMPARISON FOR EMOTIONAL TEST ITEMS (YOUNGER): INTERACTION EFFECT OF DISABILITY × SEX × PROGRAM—HYPOTHESIS TWO

That no differences exist between the performance on the emotional test items of those children having Physical Education Programs and those having the Art Program.

FOR MULTIVARIATE TEST OF EQUALITY OF MEAN VECTORS

$F = 0.4580$ p less than 0.8505 $df = 14$ and 2.0000

	Variable	*Between Mean Square*	*Univariate* F	p *Less Than*
1.	Emotional Indicators	0.0927	0.3000	0.5920
2.	Personality *A*	2.6784	2.3704	0.1445
3.	*B*	0.3583	0.2313	0.6375
4.	*C*	1.9419	1.1333	0.3040
5.	*D*	0.0675	0.0237	0.8796
6.	*E*	0.1754	0.1860	0.6725
7.	*F*	0.6984	0.3882	0.5427
8.	*G*	0.2005	0.4278	0.5230
9.	*H*	1.2654	0.6846	0.4210
10.	*I*	0.0123	0.0100	0.9216
11.	*J*	0.0006	0.0006	0.9807
12.	*N*	1.4826	1.8161	0.1978
13.	*O*	0.2490	0.1680	0.6878
14.	Q_4	0.0081	0.0113	0.9169

df *for Hypothesis = 1,* df *for Error = 15, 14 covariates had been eliminated.*

Table 10.33

PLANNED COMPARISON FOR EMOTIONAL TEST ITEMS (YOUNGER): INTERACTION EFFECT OF DISABILITY × SEX × PROGRAM—HYPOTHESIS THREE

That no differences exist between the performance on the emotional test items of those children having the Individualized Physical Education Program and those having the Group-Oriented Physical Education Program.

FOR MULTIVARIATE TEST OF EQUALITY OF MEAN VECTORS

$F = 57.0942$* p less than 0.0174 $df = 14$ and 2.0000

	Variable	*Between Mean Square*	*Univariate* F	p *Less Than*
1.	Emotional Indicators	0.0053	0.0171	0.8978
2.	Personality *A*	2.3513	2.0809	0.1698
3.	*B*	1.8418	1.1893	0.2927
4.	*C*	0.0961	0.0561	0.8160
5.	*D*	0.0268	0.0094	0.9240
6.	*E*	0.6086	0.6453	0.4344
7.	*F*	0.6869	0.3818	0.5460
8.	*G*	1.8537	3.9547	0.0654
9.	*H*	2.6212	1.4181	0.2523
10.	*I*	0.1306	0.1069	0.7482
11.	*J*	5.6127	6.0655	0.0264
12.	*N*	0.1578	0.1933	0.6665
13.	*O*	1.9598	1.3220	0.2683
14.	Q_4	4.9677	6.8968	0.0191

df *for Hypothesis = 1,* df *for Error = 15, 14 covariates had been eliminated.*
**Null hypothesis rejected at the 5 percent level.*

Table 10.34

EMOTIONAL DEVELOPMENT (OLDER): INTERACTION EFFECT OF DISABILITY × PROGRAM

FOR MULTIVARIATE TEST OF EQUALITY OF MEAN VECTORS

$F = 2.1767$* *p* less than 0.0364 *df* = 42 and 18.5642

	Variable	*Between Mean Square*	*Univariate* F	p *Less Than*
1.	Emotional Indicators	0.0704	0.2416	0.8663
2.	Personality *A*	0.3197	0.5001	0.6867
3.	*B*	3.0236	3.6090	0.0324
4.	*C*	0.6111	1.0148	0.4081
5.	*D*	0.2476	0.4067	0.7500
6.	*E*	2.3229	2.3992	0.0998
7.	*F*	2.1805	2.4133	0.0985
8.	*G*	0.5622	1.1380	0.3591
9.	*H*	1.7917	3.2324	0.0455
10.	*I*	4.2945	3.4173	0.0384
11.	*J*	1.8066	2.6595	0.0776
12.	*N*	0.0447	0.0486	0.9854
13.	*O*	0.5398	0.7876	0.5157
14.	Q_4	0.4217	0.3681	0.7769

df *for Hypothesis* = *3,* df *for Error* = *19, 14 covariates had been eliminated.*
**Null hypothesis rejected at the 5 percent level.*

Table 10.35

PLANNED COMPARISON FOR EMOTIONAL TEST ITEMS (OLDER): INTERACTION EFFECT OF DISABILITY × PROGRAM—HYPOTHESIS ONE

That no differences exist between the performance on the emotional test items of those children having Special Programs and those having no Special Program.

FOR MULTIVARIATE TEST OF EQUALITY OF MEAN VECTORS

$F = 3.3309$ *p* less than 0.0735 *df* = 14 and 6.0000

	Variable	*Between Mean Square*	*Univariate* F	p *Less Than*
1.	Emotional Indicators	0.0152	0.0523	0.8217
2.	Personality *A*	0.3263	0.5104	0.4837
3.	*B*	4.9737	5.9365	0.0249
4.	*C*	0.0950	0.1577	0.6958
5.	*D*	0.0931	0.1529	0.7001
6.	*E*	4.3764	4.5203	0.0469
7.	*F*	4.0527	4.4854	0.0476
8.	*G*	0.1214	0.2456	0.6259
9.	*H*	0.7746	1.3974	0.2518
10.	*I*	8.6958	6.9196	0.0165
11.	*J*	0.0086	0.0126	0.9118
12.	*N*	0.1381	0.1502	0.7027
13.	*O*	0.1703	0.2484	0.6239
14.	Q_4	0.5209	0.4547	0.5083

df *for Hypothesis* = *1,* df *for Error* = *19, 14 covariates had been eliminated.*

Table 10.36

PLANNED COMPARISON FOR EMOTIONAL TEST ITEMS (OLDER): INTERACTION EFFECT OF DISABILITY × PROGRAM—HYPOTHESIS TWO

That no differences exist between the performance on the emotional test items of those children having Physical Education Programs and those having the Art Program.

FOR MULTIVARIATE TEST OF EQUALITY OF MEAN VECTORS

$F = 3.2341$ p less than 0.0783 $df = 14$ and 6.0000

Variable	*Between Mean Square*	*Univariate* F	p *Less Than*
1. Emotional Indicators	0.0690	0.2367	0.6322
2. Personality *A*	0.3615	0.5654	0.4613
3. *B*	2.8490	3.4005	0.0809
4. *C*	1.8136	3.0115	0.0989
5. *D*	0.2070	0.3401	0.5667
6. *E*	4.2961	4.4373	0.0487
7. *F*	1.8152	2.0091	0.1726
8. *G*	0.1404	0.2842	0.6002
9. *H*	0.6107	1.1018	0.3071
10. *I*	0.7408	0.5895	0.4521
11. *J*	2.8616	4.2128	0.0542
12. *N*	0.0006	0.0007	0.9794
13. *O*	0.6882	1.0041	0.3290
14. Q_4	0.1367	0.1193	0.7336

df *for Hypothesis = 1,* df *for Error = 19, 14 covariates had been eliminated.*

Table 10.37

PLANNED COMPARISON FOR EMOTIONAL TEST ITEMS (OLDER): INTERACTION EFFECT OF DISABILITY × PROGRAM—HYPOTHESIS THREE

That no differences exist between the performance on the emotional test items of those children having the Individualized Physical Education Program and those having the Group-Oriented Physical Education Program.

FOR MULTIVARIATE TEST OF EQUALITY OF MEAN VECTORS

$F = 2.7080$ p less than 0.1136 $df = 14$ and 6.0000

Variable	*Between Mean Square*	*Univariate* F	p *Less Than*
1. Emotional Indicators	0.0824	0.2829	0.6010
2. Personality *A*	0.0411	0.0642	0.8027
3. *B*	2.4777	2.9573	0.1018
4. *C*	0.0402	0.0667	0.7990
5. *D*	0.4849	0.7965	0.3833
6. *E*	0.1866	0.1927	0.6657
7. *F*	2.2999	2.5455	0.1272
8. *G*	1.2324	2.4944	0.1308
9. *H*	4.5398	8.1900	0.0100
10. *I*	3.3298	2.6496	0.1201
11. *J*	2.4780	3.6480	0.0714
12. *N*	0.0030	0.0033	0.9551
13. *O*	0.4065	0.5932	0.4507
14. Q_4	0.8092	0.7064	0.4111

df *for Hypothesis = 1,* df *for Error = 19, 14 covariates had been eliminated.*

An examination of Tables 10.35, 10.36, and 10.37 reveals that none of the three planned comparisons showed a significant difference. Each null hypothesis was upheld. It is evident that the interaction between disability and program for the older children, ages 10 to 13 years, was not an effect which gave useful information in answering the questions posed in this study.

Discussion

To assess the emotional development of the educable mentally retarded children and the minimally brain-injured children, two tests were used: the emotional indicators of the Bender Test, and Cattell personality questionnaires. Separate but identical analyses were completed for the younger and the older children, with seven hypotheses being tested for each age level.

Figures 10.19 and 10.20, which show the pre- and post-test mean scores for two personality traits, support the results previously reported. For both traits—tension and intelligence—the younger children changed the magnitude and direction of their scores much more than did the older children. The best example of this is in factor *B*, where for each of the four cells the pre- and post-test scores for each program, for boys and girls, and for both disabilities are clustered. The scores of the younger children on the same factor are not nearly so close together.

It can be seen from Figure 10.19 that some of the changes on factor Q_4 (tension) were quite sharp, but that the direction of change was not consistent. A remarkable and unexplainable change in position occurred for the younger minimally brain-injured girls who were not involved in any of the special programs. According to the results, these girls changed from one end of the bipolar scale to the other end. This is probably a reflection of the very small number of girls in the group and the variability in their response patterns.

The results can at best be regarded as tentative. While some consistency was noted in the changes that occurred for this and other parameters of development, the difficulty with which the personality questionnaire was handled by the younger children should be borne in mind. Perhaps it is worthwhile to propose possible reasons why differences occurred in the younger children and not in the older children on this parameter of development. One can suppose, for example, that with increasing chronological age, several aspects of the personality of children are not easily altered. Although the oldest children in the research were only 13, it could well be that some stability in personality was already established. A second point would be to reiterate a statement made earlier in this report, that inasmuch as change was to occur, the degree to which it was measured was largely a matter of the precision or sophistication of the tests.

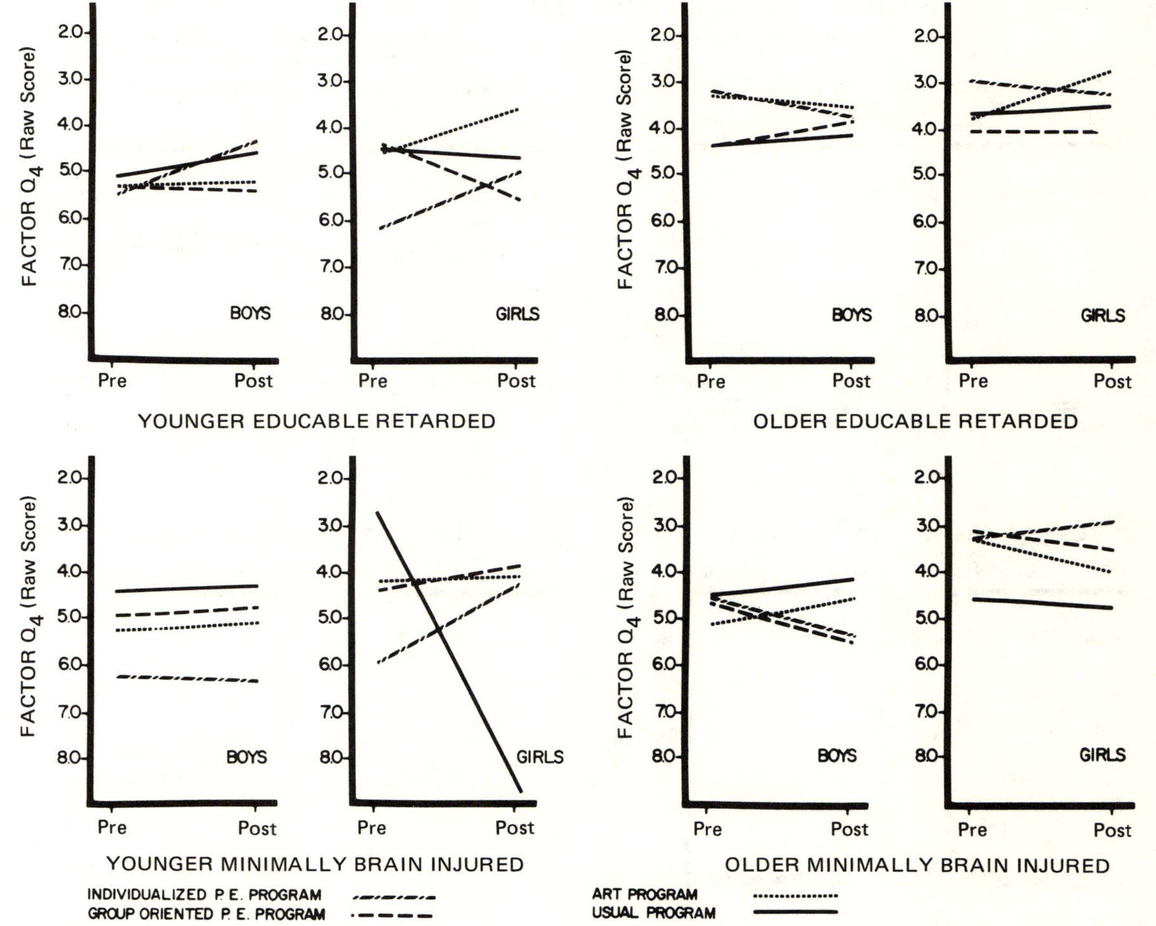

Fig. 10.19 Mean pre- and post-test scores for personality factor Q_4 (tension), by treatment according to disability, age, and sex.

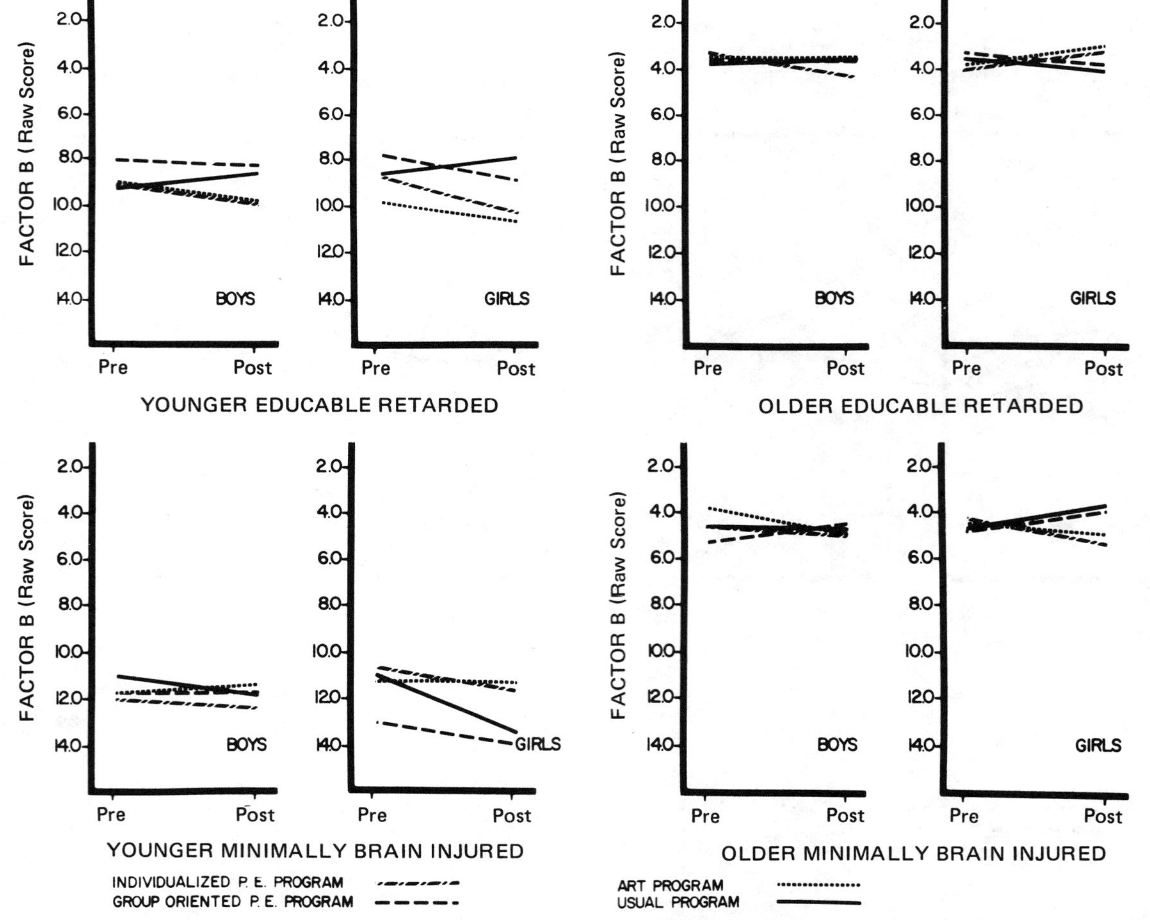

Fig. 10.20 Mean pre- and post-test scores for personality factor *B* (intelligence), by treatment according to disability, age, and sex.

Keeping these comments in mind, we find that the following general observations appear to be supported by the results of the multivariate and univariate covariance analyses, the examination of the adjusted means, and the examination of the pre- and post-test means:

1. Positive changes in emotional development were more evident in the younger than in the older children.

2. Changes in development did not appear to be obviously or consistently in favor of either the boys or the girls.

3. The emotional development of the minimally brain-injured children changed in a more positive manner than that of the educable mentally retarded children.

4. Measured changes in emotional development occurred consistently in only 2 of the 14 test items. In general, positive changes in the intelligence of the children were shown, and many of the children appeared to become more composed and relaxed as a result of the experiment. Whether this latter trait is desirable or not is open to individual interpretation. The opinions of the teachers indicated that the trend was toward more socially acceptable patterns of behavior as the special programs progressed. This would suggest that the degree of composure exhibited by the children resulted in improved classroom behavior.

5. It was demonstrated that the special experimental programs were more successful at eliciting positive developmental changes than was the nonspecial program. In general, the art program was the most successful program in this regard. Of the two physical education programs, the individualized program appeared to elicit more positive changes than the program that was oriented toward the group.

Chapter 11 / Discussion and Conclusions of the Experiment

Overview

This investigation sought to assess the role of educational physical activity in the modification of the motor, strength, intellectual, social, and emotional development of educable mentally retarded children and minimally brain-injured children of elementary school age. Previous research had indicated that changes not only in motor performance but in measured intelligence had occurred when physical activity lessons were added to the daily school schedule of mentally retarded children. Problems in the research designs of the earlier studies and in the treatment of the data had made it difficult to interpret the results.

In view of the possible confounding effect of special kinds of programs on the behavior of children, the present research set out to answer three major questions. First, what were the differential effects of selected motor, strength, intellectual, social, and emotional parameters on the development of educable mentally retarded and minimally brain-injured children who followed special experimental programs (two types of physical education programs and an art education program) as compared to those who pursued their usual classroom instructional program? Second, were there differences in any of these five parameters of development on those who followed the two types of physical education programs as compared to those included in the art program? And third, were any differences noted in the development of the children in an individualized physical education program as compared to those in a group-oriented physical education program? Due consideration was given to the educational disability, chronological age, and sex of the children in answering these questions.

Forty-nine classes of children in the special education program in the Galena Park, Pasadena, and Deer Park Independent School Districts of Harris County, Texas, participated in 20 weeks of instructional programs. Of the 481 children who completed the programs, 275 were educable mentally retarded children and 206 were minimally brain-injured children.

The design of the study required that four treatments or programs of instruction be used. Of the four, two involved special physical activity programs, the one being individually oriented, the other group-oriented. A third treatment was an art education program, included to assess the Hawthorne effect and to provide information regarding the effects which might be brought about by differing special programs. The fourth treatment, which served as an experimental control, was the usual classroom instructional program. Classes were randomly assigned by educational disability and age to one of the four treatments. As implied earlier, four factors were included within the design, namely program (four treatments), disability (EMR and MBI), sex (male and female), and age (younger and older children).

To measure the five parameters of the development of the children, a large battery of tests was administered prior to, and at the conclusion of, the treatments. Motor performance was assessed by a modified version of the AAHPER Test Battery suitable for use with EMR and MBI children. The dynamometric strength of the children was assessed from scores of the right hand and left hand grips and the double-handed pull and push. Intellectual development was assessed by the Peabody Picture Vocabulary Test and the Bender Motor Gestalt Test. The Cowell Social Behavior Trend Index and sociometric evaluations of peer acceptance and rejection gave assessments of social development. The emotional indicators from the Bender Test and a Cattell personality questionnaire provided information on the emotional parameter of development.

The three experimental programs were taught for approximately 35 minutes each school day for 20 weeks by the classroom teachers who had been prepared for the teaching and testing programs through in-service meetings. The experimental programs were supervised by one of the investigators, who consulted with each teacher in person at least twice in every three weeks.

The construction of the experimental programs was of particular importance, since the length of the project was such that the teaching material and presentation had to be both worthwhile and stimulating. Care was taken that the experiences afforded to the children in the respective special programs were educational, with each child not only being in active pursuit of the task at hand but aware of what the implications of the task were. The special art education program was planned and supervised with thought and care equal to that given the physical education programs.

The data were treated by multivariate analysis of covariance. Where significant *F* values occurred for the hypotheses for the main effects and interaction effects, the direction of the differences was examined in the following way. When the difference was with a two-level factor—for example, educational disability—the direction of the differences was determined by examining the adjusted means of the variables in the vector which appeared to be affecting the multivariate *F* value the most. Where the differences were with the four-level factor, namely, program, three planned orthogonal comparisons provided information which could be supplemented by an examination of the adjusted means.

General Discussion of the Results

The premise—that changes in some aspects of the development of educable mentally retarded children and minimally brain-injured children in elementary school special education classes can be elicited—was supported by this research. Where changes occurred, they were toward behaviors which are well regarded in society.

Changes attributable to the planned physical education and art education programs occurred in three of the five parameters of development. While differential changes in the performance of the children on the strength test items were not altogether expected, changes were anticipated in the measured aspects of social development. Significant changes in the latter were not apparent. However, classroom teachers did report that positive changes in social development occurred, and it appeared that many of the children became more "at ease," "outgoing," and "accepted." Since the Cowell Social Behavior Trend Index measured outgoing social behavior, positive changes in scores on this test were expected for those included in the three experimental programs. The children in the special programs were given a great deal of attention. Specially planned lessons, new equipment, and successful learning experiences could reasonably be expected to affect the way the children felt about themselves and acted toward others in the class.

Differential changes in behavior related to the special treatments were noted in the motor, intellectual, and emotional parameters of development. Of the 23 variables which were selected to measure these three aspects of development, 8 variables consistently worked in identifying differential changes in development. In motor performance the items were the arm hang, sit-ups, standing broad jump, and softball throw. Both the Peabody and Bender Tests, assessing intellectual development, were included; and two factors from the personality questionnaires, measuring intelligence and tension, made up the 8 items.

For each of the three parameters of development, a distinct and consistent difference was noted between the behavioral changes of the minimally brain-injured children compared with the educable retarded. At the end of the project, even allowing for differences between pre-test scores, the minimally brain-injured children demonstrated superior performance changes in most of the measured traits. In several ways, this result was both surprising and unexpected. In the first place, the inclusion of the children in the special educational treatment programs involved changes in routine. The programs, both in physical education and in art, involved the children in a spatial orientation with which they were unfamiliar and from which it was expected that difficulties might arise. Many authorities in special education hold the view that these children need a tightly structured school routine, where contact with others in a classroom work situation is limited. The partitioned classroom is seen as a mechanism for excluding undesirable and distracting stimuli. This research did not intend to question or test this theory, but the inclusion of these children in one of the three experimental programs made it necessary for the children to work away from the cubicles and, in the case of the physical education classes, away from the classrooms. In the second place, it had been expected that differential changes would favor the educable retardates. The level of intellectual ability of these children was limited, and it was thought that those with the greatest initial deficits in motor performance, measured intelligence, or emotional traits might reasonably be expected to show the greatest gains. This did not occur. Despite the improved scores of the retarded children, superior change was demonstrated by the minimally brain-injured children. A third reason concerned the experiences of those in special education in the three school districts in their work with the brain-injured. Although the brain-injured were superior to the retarded children in intellectual ability, it had been noted that despite excellent programs, their classroom achievement tended to regress with time, toward the level of the educable retardates. It could therefore have been expected that in a special program which lasted for some 6 months, the brain-injured might be subject to a decline rather than an improvement in performance.

The range of the chronological ages of the children was from 6 to 13 years, with the vast majority of the children being from 7 to 12 years of age. Because it is well known that chronological age is a factor of considerable consequence in affecting many abilities in childhood, the children were placed in one of two age groups. The younger children were from 6 to 9 years old, and the older children were from 10 to 13 years old. Although the level of performance on most tests is superior for older children, there seemed few reasons to suggest that the research might elicit changes in development that differed for children of different ages. Differential change, indeed, did occur.

For the motor and intellectual parameters of development, changes favored the older children. On the other hand, changes favoring the younger children were found for the emotional parameters of development.

Reasons have been given to explain why changes were noted for the emotional test items. The possible variability or inconsistency in response shown by the younger children could have resulted in differential changes in behavioral response. On the other hand, the older children might have been more resistant to changes other than those attributable to maturation, simply because they exhibited more stable personality characteristics. It could be expected that if changes were to favor one group, then they would consistently favor the younger group. For the motor and intellectual parameters of development, the reverse occurred. The fact that the older children did make noteworthy gains, which were attributable to the special programs, provides rather concrete evidence that regression in performance or behavior does not need to happen to the older children in the special education classes.

It is perhaps important to note that the response of the boys and girls to the treatments was not materially different. In only one parameter of development was sex a significant factor as either a main effect or an interaction effect. The effect of sex on the measures of the emotional development of the children was in a sense conflicting. While the girls showed the greater gains in the intelligence factor, the reverse was true for factor Q_4 (tension). Factor G, which is assumed to measure determination and emotional stability, showed greater changes for the boys than the girls. The reasons for the variability in change noted are not known. There is little to make one believe that the programs brought about differential changes in emotional development for the two sexes.

With respect to the three questions the research sought to answer, the answer to the first question was positive, namely, that differences did occur in the classes given the special programs in physical education and art. These changes in performance were over and above those that could be attributed to maturation. The second question which the research sought to answer concerned the comparative effect of physical education versus art education in eliciting measurable changes. Of the three parameters of development where statistically significant differences were apparent, only one was in favor of the physical education programs. Such changes occurred in the motor performance of the children. It is important to note that the physical education programs did not include any of the test items, as had been the case in several other investigations. The programs were designed to provide a wide range of the movement experiences which are important in the motor development of children. It was planned that the children should make progress toward what some people have termed motoric wisdom. It was not altogether unexpected that the physical education experiences might have some carry-over value. One can but assume that more difficult or complex tasks can be acquired only when a good basis of experiences in movement exists.

For the emotional test items, the position of the classes involved in the art education program was superior to that of the classes following the physical education programs. This occurred only for the younger children. The two test items which appeared to be contributing the greatest were the personality characteristics of intelligence and tension. It was clear that the art program elicited greater gains in these aspects of development than the other special programs (taken collectively), and the art program seems to have provided the children with an atmosphere which was conducive to developing improved patterns of emotional behavior.

In view of the earlier research which had shown positive effects of physical activity programs on the intelligence of retarded children, it is interesting to note that in the present investigation the changes in performance on the Peabody and Bender Tests were not different for the children in the physical education programs as compared to those in the art program. Previous research has attempted unsuccessfully to include an experimental group in the design to counter the effects that the research might elicit which were explained by factors other than those being studied. Since all three programs in the present study were specially planned, and because equal attention was given to all programs, any differences between these programs could be attributed to the particular nature of the program—in this case, to the physical education programs or to the art program. For the motor performance items, the difference favoring the physical education programs can be explained by the nature of these programs, as opposed to the art program. The emotional parameter of development (younger children only) produced results in favor of the art program.

Perhaps one can conclude that both physical education and art programs were of importance in modifying and improving certain aspects of the development of these children. It is suggested that other programs for which easily identifiable child objectives are present, and in which progress is linked with feelings of achievement, might be equally successful in this regard.

The third question of the research centered upon the social organization of the children within the special education class. For each of the three parameters of development, the position of the classes which participated in the individualized program was superior to that of the classes involved in the group-oriented physical education program. It appears that individual attention is vital in providing for optimal performance. However, the same point may be described in a different way. In a program where the focus is upon the individual rather than upon the group, the objectives and the explanation of an activity can be modified or reworded for an individual so that the vast individual differences within and between children, both in ability and performance, can be taken into account. When a child is part of a group, then some personal identity, some attention, is lost; the group is like an umbrella in that several individuals are brought together under a common label. On the other hand, children must learn to function in a social group. Unfortunately, methods of measuring the interaction of young children in special education in social groups have not reached the point of refinement where adequate assessments of this parameter of development can be made. The results described are therefore limited by the measures employed. Conceivably, positive social changes occurred in the children in the group-oriented programs which, though not assessed, may well have been of greater educational significance than those noted in the individualized program.

Conclusions

Subject to the limitations previously described, the following conclusions would appear to be warranted:

1. Special treatment in the way of well-designed programs of physical education or art education elicited greater changes in motor, intellectual, and emotional development of retarded and brain-injured children than occurred from the usual classroom instructional program.

2. Of the specially planned experimental programs, the physical education programs demonstrated a superior role in modifying motor performance; the art program indicated a superior role in modifying emotional development of the younger children; and the programs played a similar role in modifying the intellectual development of the children.

3. The physical education program which was oriented toward the individual rather than the group was more successful in eliciting change in the motor, intellectual, and emotional parameters of the development of the children.

4. Positive changes in development were shown more by the older than by the younger children, were manifested more frequently by the brain-injured than by the retarded children, and appeared marginally more likely to occur in the boys than in the girls.

Bibliography, Part II

1. A.A.H.P.E.R. *Youth Fitness Test Manual.* Washington, D.C.: American Association for Health, Physical Education, and Recreation, 1961.
2. A.A.H.P.E.R. *Special Fitness Test Manual for the Mentally Retarded.* Washington, D.C.: American Association for Health, Physical Education, and Recreation, 1968.
3. Bilborough, A., and P. Jones. *Physical Education in the Primary School.* London: University of London Press, 1963.
4. Bonney, M. E. "Values of Sociometric Studies in the Classroom." *Sociometry* 6 (1943), 251–54.
5. Bronfenbrenner, U. "A Constant Frame of Reference for Sociometric Research, Part II." *Sociometry* 7 (1944), 40–75.
6. Budoff, M., and Eleanor M. Purseglove. "Peabody Picture Vocabulary Test Performance of Institutionalized Mentally Retarded Adolescents." *American Journal of Mental Deficiency* 67 (1963), 756–60.
7. Cameron, W. McD., and Peggy Pleasance. *Education in Movement—School Gymnastics.* Oxford, England: Basil Blackwell, 1963.
8. Coan, Richard W., and Raymond Cattell. *Guidebook for the Early School Personality Questionnaire.* Champaign, Ill.: Institute for Personality and Ability Testing, 1966.
9. Cook, D. "The Hawthorne Effect in Educational Research." *Phi Delta Kappa* 44 (1962), 116–22.
10. Corder, W. O. "Effects of Physical Education on the Intellectual, Physical, and Social Development of Educable Mentally Retarded Boys." *Exceptional Children* 32 (1966), 357–64.
11. Cowell, Charles C. "Validating an Index of Social Adjustment for High School Use." *Research Quarterly* 29 (1958), 7–18.
12. Cruickshank, William M., F. A. Bentzen, F. H. Ratzeburg, and M. T. Tannhauser. *A Teaching Method for Brain-Injured and Hyperactive Children: A Demonstration Pilot Study.* Syracuse, N.Y.: Syracuse University Press, 1961.

13. Dunn, L. M. (Ed.). *Exceptional Children in the Schools.* New York: Holt, Rinehart & Winston, 1963.

14. Dunn, L. M. *Peabody Picture Vocabulary Test: Expanded Manual.* Minneapolis, Minn.: American Guidance Service, 1965.

15. Espenschade, Anna. "Motor Performance in Adolescence Including the Study of Relationships with Measures of Physical Growth and Maturity." *Monographs of the Society for Research in Child Development* 5 (1940), 1–126.

16. Francis, R. J., and G. L. Rarick. "Motor Characteristics of the Mentally Retarded." *American Journal of Mental Deficiency* 63 (1959), 792–811.

17. Gronlund, Norman E. *Sociometry in the Classroom.* New York: Harper and Bros., 1959.

18. Hayden, Frank J. *Physical Fitness for the Mentally Retarded.* Toronto: Toronto Association for Retarded Children, 1964.

19. Hays, W. *Statistics for Psychologists.* New York: Holt, Rinehart & Winston, 1963.

20. Heber, Rick (Ed.). "A Manual on Terminology and Classification in Mental Retardation." *American Journal of Mental Deficiency,* 64 (2), Suppl: 1–111, Sept. 1959.

21. Hunsicker, P. A., and G. G. Reiff. "A Survey and Comparison of Youth Fitness 1958–65." Cooperative Research Project No. 2418. Ann Arbor, Mich.: University of Michigan Press, 1965.

22. Koppitz, E. M. *The Bender Motor Gestalt Test for Young Children.* New York: Grune & Stratton, 1966.

23. Lowe, Benjamin J. *The Effects of Physical Conditioning on the Cognitive Functioning of Educationally Sub-Normal Boys.* Department of Psychology, Birmingham University, Birmingham, England, 1966.

24. McCloy, C. H. *The Measurement of Athletic Power.* New York: A. S. Barnes and Co., 1932.

25. Nunley, Rachel L. "A Physical Fitness Program for the Mentally Retarded in the Public Schools." *Physical Therapy* 45 (1965), 949–54.

26. Oliver, J. N. "The Effect of Physical Conditioning Exercises and Activities on the Mental Characteristics of Educationally Sub-Normal Boys." *British Journal of Educational Psychology* 28 (1958), 155–65.

27. Oliver, J. N. "The Effects of Physical Conditioning on the Sociometric Status of Educationally Sub-Normal Boys." *Physical Education* 156 (1960), 38–46.

28. Porter, Rutherford B., and Raymond B. Cattell. *Handbook for the IPAT Children's Personality Questionnaire: "The CPQ."* Champaign, Ill.: Institute for Personality and Ability Testing, 1959.

29. Porter, Rutherford B., and Raymond B. Cattell. *Interim Manual for the Children's Personality Questionnaire.* Champaign, Ill.: Institute for Personality and Ability Testing, 1963.

30. Porter, Rutherford B., James L. Collins, and Raymond M. McIver. "A Comparative Investigation of the Personality of Educable Mentally Retarded Children and Those of a Norm Group of Children." *Exceptional Children* 31 (1965), 457–63.

31. Rarick, G. L., and D. A. Dobbins. *Basic Components in the Motor Performance of Educable Mentally Retarded Children: Implications for Curriculum Development.* Department of Physical Education, University of California, Berkeley, 1972.

32. Rarick, G. L., James H. Widdop, and Geoffrey D. Broadhead. *The Motor Performance and Physical Fitness of Educable Mentally Retarded Children.* Department of Physical Education, University of Wisconsin, Madison, Wis., 1967a.

33. Rarick, G. L., James H. Widdop, and Geoffrey D. Broadhead. *Environmental Factors Associated with the Motor Performance and Physical Fitness of Educable Mentally Retarded Children,* Department of Physical Education, University of Wisconsin, Madison, Wis., 1967b.

34. Rarick, G. L., James H. Widdop, and Geoffrey D. Broadhead. "The Physical Fitness and Motor Performance of Educable Mentally Retarded Children." *Exceptional Children* 36 (1970), 509–19.

35. Roethlisberger, F. J., and W. J. Dickson. *The Management and the Worker.* Cambridge, Mass.: Harvard University Press, 1939.

36. Sloan, W. "Motor Proficiency and Intelligence." *American Journal of Mental Deficiency* 55 (1951), 394–406.

37. Solomon, A. H., and R. Pangle. "The Effects of a Structured Physical Education Program on Physical, Intellectual, and Self-Concept Development of Educable Retarded Boys." *Behavioral Science Monograph No. 4.* Nashville, Tenn.: George Peabody College, 1966.

38. Solomon, A. H., and R. Pangle. "Demonstrating Physical Fitness Improvement in the EMR." *Exceptional Children* 34 (1967), 177–81.

39. Stein, Julian U. "Motor Function and Physical Fitness of the Mentally Retarded." *Rehabilitation Literature* 24 (1963), 230–42.

40. Texas Education Agency. *State Plan for Special Education.* Austin, Texas: Texas Education Agency, 1965.

41. Widdop, James H. "The Motor Performance of Educable Mentally Retarded Children with Particular Reference to the Identification of Factors Associated with Individual Differences in Performance." Unpublished Doctoral Dissertation, Department of Physical Education, University of Wisconsin, Madison, Wis., 1967.

Appendix A / Table of Reliabilities of Motor Performance Measures

Test	Normal Boys r_{12}	Normal Boys S.B.*	Old EMR Boys r_{12}	Old EMR Boys S.B.*	Young EMR Boys r_{12}	Young EMR Boys S.B.*	Normal Girls r_{12}	Normal Girls S.B.*	Old EMR Girls r_{12}	Old EMR Girls S.B.*	Young EMR Girls r_{12}	Young EMR Girls S.B.*
Grip Strength (Right)	.911	.953	.927	.962	.902	.948	.882	.938	.975	.987	.917	.957
Grip Strength (Left)	.959	.979	.941	.970	.917	.957	.896	.945	.959	.979	.934	.963
Cybex Elbow Extension Str.	.865	.928	.959	.979	.845	.916	.900	.947	.909	.953	.976	.988
Cybex Elbow Flexion Str.	.897	.946	.972	.985	.851	.920	.717	.835	.909	.953	.972	.985
Cybex Knee Extension Str.	.929	.963	.939	.969	.931	.964	.925	.960	.955	.977	.902	.948
Cybex Knee Flexion Str.	.926	.962	.944	.971	.905	.950	.891	.942	.925	.961	.910	.953
Vertical Jump	.979	.989	.959	.979	.918	.957	.972	.985	.945	.972	.931	.964
Standing Broad Jump	.805	.892	.917	.957	.947	.973	.906	.951	.953	.976	.957	.978
35 Yard Dash (5-35)	.952	.976	.910	.953	.898	.946	.913	.955	.893	.943	.895	.945
Medicine Ball Throw	.979	.989	.920	.958	.936	.967	.967	.983	.948	.973	.796	.886
Bike With Resistance	.970	.985	.938	.968	.938	.968	.927	.962	.946	.972	.943	.971
Bike Without Resistance	.941	.970	.950	.974	.919	.958	.926	.962	.935	.966	.945	.972
Softball Throw	.863	.927	.964	.982	.966	.983	.709	.830	.950	.974	.864	.927
Trunk Raise for Time	.743	.853	.822	.903	.779	.876	.705	.827	.804	.891	.843	.915
Shuttle Run	.955	.977	.915	.956	.940	.969	.947	.973	.905	.950	.926	.962
Edgren Test	.916	.956	.904	.950	.936	.967	.843	.915	.937	.967	.914	.955
Scramble	.916	.956	.935	.966	.924	.960	.882	.937	.943	.971	.913	.955
Mat Crawl	.925	.961	.918	.957	.924	.961	.940	.969	.939	.969	.949	.974
Tire Run	.972	.986	.951	.975	.917	.957	.960	.980	.952	.975	.961	.980
Pursuit Rotor at 20 RPM	.881	.937	.910	.953	.888	.941	.879	.936	.901	.948	.891	.942
Pursuit Rotor at 40 RPM	.862	.928	.922	.959	.873	.932	.847	.917	.878	.935	.910	.953
Target Throw Horizontal	.740	.850	.640	.780	.706	.828	.563	.720	.689	.816	.866	.928
Target Throw Vertical	.768	.869	.524	.688	.578	.738	.506	.671	.695	.820	.744	.853
Visual Coincidence	.534	.696	.776	.874	.722	.839	.716	.834	.898	.946	.657	.792
Minnesota Manipulative	.746	.854	.826	.905	.804	.891	.782	.877	.778	.875	.896	.945
Purdue Pegboard Test	.880	.936	.908	.952	.915	.956	.895	.945	.930	.963	.953	.976
2-Plate Tapping Test	.858	.924	.914	.955	.889	.941	.884	.938	.914	.955	.867	.928
Ring Stacking Test	.757	.862	.783	.878	.769	.869	.709	.830	.775	.873	.779	.876
Golfball Placement	.793	.885	.849	.918	.845	.916	.845	.916	.739	.850	.875	.933
Steadiness Groove	.681	.810	.814	.898	.666	.800	.765	.867	.806	.893	.757	.862
Bass Test	.973	.986	.873	.932	.798	.888	.914	.955	.793	.885	.828	.906
Stabilometer	.746	.855	.866	.928	.785	.880	.694	.819	.869	.930	.788	.881
Stork Test	.790	.883	.781	.877	.791	.883	.798	.888	.727	.841	.818	.900
Angle Reproduction			.422	.594	.321	.486			.483	.651	.446	.617
Comparative Hand Adj.			.470	.639	.423	.595			.489	.657	.362	.532
Force Estimation			.460	.630	.326	.492			.705	.827	.421	.592
Toe Touch	.968	.984	.980	.989	.962	.981	.928	.963	.975	.987	.969	.984
Spinal Extension	.950	.974	.941	.970	.908	.952	.960	.980	.910	.953	.899	.947
Spinal Rotation	.896	.945	.951	.975	.961	.980	.928	.963	.837	.911	.985	.992
Lateral Spinal Extension	.927	.962	.911	.953	.863	.926	.953	.976	.893	.943	.840	.913
3-Plate Foot Tapping	.875	.933	.923	.960	.910	.953	.923	.960	.928	.962	.876	.934
Corner Plate Tapping	.846	.917	.843	.915	.803	.891	.858	.924	.820	.901	.847	.917
Turntable Speed	.841	.914	.884	.938	.911	.953	.879	.936	.914	.955	.900	.947

*Adjusted by Spearman-Brown Prophesy Formula

Appendix B / Table of Intercorrelations Upon Which the Factor Analyses are Based

	TEST	1	2	3	4	5	6	7	8	9	10	11	12	13	14	15	16	17	18	19	20	21	22	23	24	25	26	27	28	29	30	31	32	33	34	35	36	37	38	39	40	41	42	43	44	45	46	47
1	355/35																																															
2	TIRER	68																																														
3	RLWKF	-40	-44																																													
4	RLWKB	-50	-55	57																																												
5	RLWKS	-29	-35	51	64																																											
6	TGTHZ	-64	-72	54	57	41																																										
7	TGTVT	-71	-72	63	55	44	76																																									
8	VERTJ	-79	-62	45	58	46	60	63																																								
9	MATCR	74	66	-50	-63	-34	-73	-69	-69																																							
10	STBRJ	-80	-74	52	62	45	69	71	84	-78																																						
11	SCRMB	76	59	-61	-55	-46	-63	-68	-66	74	-69																																					
12	150YD	87	60	-50	-52	-42	-63	-72	-75	68	-75	72																																				
13	CKFLX	-70	-57	23	45	26	48	51	71	-57	78	-45	-63																																			
14	CKEXT	-64	-51	18	39	27	42	48	66	-50	71	-38	-59	86																																		
15	CEFLX	-70	-47	29	42	19	53	56	68	-59	71	-48	-66	74	63																																	
16	CEEXT	-71	-57	30	59	36	57	58	68	-65	78	-46	-67	81	77	76																																
17	TRICP	14	15	-18	-06	-11	-17	-17	-15	02	-09	27	21	07	11	-07	08																															
18	SUBSC	04	01	-16	-04	-14	-01	-01	-08	-10	-01	23	06	21	25	03	18	77																														
19	ABDOM	02	-01	-10	-03	-12	06	02	-08	-11	01	15	05	24	25	07	17	79	93																													
20	BIACR	-59	-52	16	36	17	37	48	53	-43	64	-37	-59	81	76	60	66	19	32	34																												
21	BIILC	-49	-41	02	22	03	30	32	40	-35	49	-21	-49	66	64	52	54	22	32	35	79																											
22	HTCMS	-59	-49	11	26	15	42	43	53	-38	60	-32	-58	83	77	66	70	06	20	25	85	80																										
23	WTKLS	-50	-40	06	21	08	35	38	45	-37	54	-19	-46	81	78	58	67	37	57	59	83	75	87																									
24	GRPRT	-65	-49	21	42	17	45	45	64	-54	73	-47	-58	81	68	77	74	10	21	25	79	66	83	78																								
25	GRPLT	-62	-58	31	50	30	49	54	61	-57	75	-52	-59	80	70	71	76	10	25	29	80	66	79	77	91																							
26	BK W/	-78	-60	29	52	25	60	59	77	-62	81	-51	-74	89	83	80	83	06	23	23	81	70	82	80	85	82																						
27	BKW/O	-73	-56	38	55	34	54	51	72	-60	76	-53	-72	79	75	70	73	04	15	17	75	63	73	69	76	73	89																					
28	SITUP	-60	-58	30	49	31	37	55	59	-57	66	-45	-59	62	54	59	57	05	13	12	56	36	45	51	55	59	62	62																				
29	TRKRS	-40	-45	39	46	50	40	42	52	-42	62	-47	-45	38	41	35	42	-11	-13	-08	40	34	32	27	42	50	40	43	49																			
30	LEGRS	-04	-24	25	25	26	25	23	18	-19	26	-09	-08	03	06	08	15	-24	-18	-17	-10	-10	-09	-07	-03	08	-03	01	29	42																		
31	PRT40	-64	-66	34	55	31	59	55	64	-64	64	-49	-59	53	44	49	53	-11	-05	-06	44	34	45	32	49	53	60	62	55	23	20																	
32	MINNM	63	62	-40	-64	-38	-50	-49	-64	53	-54	53	53	-40	-33	-35	-44	06	03	06	-36	-19	-28	-22	-40	-42	-53	-58	-52	-24	-07	-66																
33	RINGS	62	70	-43	-60	-45	-54	-57	-65	65	-65	60	61	-54	-48	-40	-50	12	05	04	-52	-32	-41	-33	-48	-51	-56	-60	-52	-39	-05	-58	72															
34	GOLFB	-73	-77	38	54	44	61	62	70	-64	71	-53	-70	66	63	53	63	-09	04	05	63	49	55	47	54	58	69	73	63	44	12	69	-68	-76														
35	BASST	-19	-20	11	25	27	22	16	33	-23	32	-20	-20	11	10	18	17	-11	-08	-12	10	11	06	04	18	25	19	24	23	35	25	37	-11	-10	22													
36	STBTL	-07	11	-21	-26	-47	-09	-10	-10	00	-09	23	02	15	17	05	05	27	37	37	17	30	21	35	06	-01	13	06	04	-15	-16	-11	19	21	-08	-25												
37	STRKT	-40	-52	36	57	47	48	44	46	-45	46	-36	-43	35	27	36	35	-20	-18	-15	27	23	21	09	24	32	37	43	41	32	16	46	-46	-56	62	33	-34											
38	TOE T	-08	-05	17	25	32	20	24	25	-15	24	-19	-13	09	05	05	15	-06	00	00	05	-21	-13	02	02	08	07	16	29	25	34	08	-18	-08	06	37	-22	19										
39	SPEXT	-19	-13	36	36	36	31	21	25	-34	37	-26	-21	17	14	19	31	02	-03	-03	22	07	10	10	26	29	20	34	15	36	16	24	-24	-32	21	16	-22	20	86									
40	SPROT	-01	-09	28	18	15	09	17	11	-13	14	-15	01	06	-02	06	07	-07	-03	-11	03	-01	-01	-04	08	06	11	07	-02	06	-13	13	-09	00	03	01	-05	01	11	22								
41	LTEXT	-38	-31	28	42	20	29	23	26	-39	42	-28	-28	31	23	24	46	13	09	04	30	25	29	24	37	35	36	36	16	20	-03	40	-34	-35	28	18	-08	14	-13	50	22							
42	PW170	-49	-46	25	28	28	41	51	57	-37	61	-36	-51	60	64	52	51	02	08	08	63	50	61	59	54	54	64	58	35	37	11	34	-24	-37	45	09	07	21	11	19	07	29						
43	BKTOT	-75	-57	29	47	29	55	56	76	-57	79	-49	-72	86	81	78	78	03	16	17	81	74	88	80	86	82	93	88	64	46	03	57	-49	-53	66	24	16	36	08	22	06	32	67					
44	2PLTP	-46	-67	41	52	44	41	48	54	-51	61	-47	-42	45	34	32	43	-02	02	05	44	28	36	32	42	51	47	48	51	37	17	56	-63	-69	64	38	-30	45	17	14	06	32	29	47				
45	SFTBL	-63	-63	44	51	36	77	75	62	-66	70	-60	-64	60	51	54	59	-08	-02	04	49	43	49	43	53	55	63	52	38	35	12	48	-38	-55	52	18	-03	41	12	31	04	32	49	61	41			
46	PRDUE	-55	-67	36	57	43	49	57	58	-56	57	-47	-54	38	37	29	38	-12	-03	-03	38	26	30	25	37	40	49	50	55	37	25	61	-74	-77	70	14	-17	51	10	21	03	32	36	45	70	48		
47	CHRON	-66	-59	35	56	43	47	57	65	-55	68	-52	-64	69	68	54	65	04	19	23	68	60	69	63	67	71	72	72	60	42	09	53	-59	-60	70	24	-01	44	07	31	02	41	48	75	56	52	62	
		1	2	3	4	5	6	7	8	9	10	11	12	13	14	15	16	17	18	19	20	21	22	23	24	25	26	27	28	29	30	31	32	33	34	35	36	37	38	39	40	41	42	43	44	45	46	47

	TEST	1	2	3	4	5	6	7	8	9	10	11	12	13	14	15	16	17	18	19	20	21	22	23	24	25	26	27	28	29	30	31	32	33	34	35	36	37	38	39	40	41	42	43	44	45	46	47
1	355/35																																															
2	TIRER	69																																														
3	RLWKF	-47	-48																																													
4	RLWKB	-54	-39	45																																												
5	RLWKS	-19	-26	40	50																																											
6	TGTHZ	-53	-63	34	32	22																																										
7	TGTVT	-49	-44	42	47	26	48																																									
8	VERTJ	-74	-49	26	48	29	38	43																																								
9	MATCR	52	56	-32	-45	-22	-34	-26	-43																																							
10	STBRJ	-75	-68	31	47	31	62	47	69	-62																																						
11	SCRMB	61	49	-41	-56	-33	-36	-31	-56	64	-63																																					
12	150YD	89	62	-43	-52	-19	-55	-50	-70	60	-78	64																																				
13	CKFLX	-47	-39	22	31	04	44	44	30	-19	47	-14	-48																																			
14	CKEXT	-60	-55	34	39	14	49	40	46	-33	63	-36	-57	81																																		
15	CEFLX	-53	-43	22	37	05	51	48	44	-32	55	-20	-60	65	61																																	
16	CEEXT	-51	-39	20	32	07	45	40	47	-20	48	-19	-47	68	57	69																																
17	TRICP	13	16	-15	-22	-15	-15	03	-26	20	-24	53	19	26	02	09	16																															
18	SUBSC	17	24	-30	-18	-18	-16	-01	-21	25	-26	52	21	24	-04	09	22	85																														
19	ABDOM	18	24	-27	-16	-21	-10	03	-21	21	-27	50	19	27	00	08	16	78	90																													
20	BIACR	-36	-33	19	18	-04	44	43	28	-17	37	03	-37	68	61	66	73	44	39	43																												
21	BIILC	-14	-14	-07	05	-15	21	25	03	05	11	29	-13	60	54	50	53	58	55	56	76																											
22	HTCMS	-20	-31	13	08	-03	45	36	12	-06	33	07	-22	50	49	50	43	22	11	18	65	56																										
23	WTKLS	-13	-13	-06	04	-13	26	29	02	05	08	34	-11	67	47	56	64	68	67	69	84	89	61																									
24	GRPRT	-47	-38	19	34	16	42	35	42	-33	50	-15	-52	59	61	69	58	19	10	10	64	47	50	52																								
25	GRPLT	-47	-39	17	29	12	31	32	39	-36	49	-21	-52	62	62	65	57	17	12	13	64	41	48	49	89																							
26	BK W/	-64	-46	23	44	17	53	50	55	-35	63	-35	-61	68	75	65	66	10	10	11	66	56	50	55	66	59																						
27	BKW/O	-73	-53	34	46	21	52	38	57	-46	68	-52	-70	55	68	56	51	-11	-14	-16	43	30	35	26	54	57	78																					
28	SITUP	-39	-35	28	43	17	32	34	30	-28	43	-50	-46	27	36	26	25	-27	-18	-19	03	-04	05	-07	15	15	34	43																				
29	TRKRS	-43	-43	43	40	25	38	40	26	-24	44	-38	-42	37	56	24	26	-04	-13	-15	23	16	23	11	33	41	35	47	52																			
30	LEGRS	-23	-18	18	23	13	01	-04	18	-23	17	-36	-24	-14	08	-06	-01	-32	-24	-30	-19	-26	-31	-31	-03	-02	04	19	48	29																		
31	PRT40	-49	-51	28	54	34	48	43	36	-38	49	-40	-50	46	57	52	37	-02	-02	03	27	25	27	24	51	48	60	57	43	42	08																	
32	MINNM	41	51	-09	-38	-18	-37	-33	-43	40	-49	34	36	-26	-32	-19	-31	-04	-13	-12	-32	-19	-20	-25	-32	-33	-48	-41	-24	-14	-09	-36																
33	RINGS	57	62	-40	-47	-24	-55	-45	-45	46	-59	48	53	-40	-59	-48	-39	07	13	11	-38	-20	-41	-20	-51	-54	-61	-62	-41	-41	-16	-68	64															
34	GOLFB	-60	-64	27	48	14	55	47	44	-41	64	-42	-58	57	69	46	44	11	09	11	52	42	43	40	51	52	66	64	48	47	12	63	-63	-74														
35	BASST	-44	-40	23	34	30	27	22	50	-31	53	-35	-46	37	56	30	23	-05	-07	-11	23	19	05	10	28	28	36	40	24	38	11	35	-21	-35	45													
36	STBTL	24	17	-26	-28	-34	-10	00	-22	29	-26	33	31	05	-10	03	04	27	26	24	13	23	17	31	-08	-06	-09	-21	-24	-17	-35	-36	08	24	-14	-10												
37	STRKT	-41	-41	37	44	37	30	46	30	-30	33	-28	-36	30	44	20	13	-04	-09	-10	17	09	04	08	24	27	36	39	23	41	26	45	-35	-51	42	36	-23											
38	TOE T	-26	-36	35	21	35	22	19	25	-26	27	-36	-28	11	29	18	22	-17	-21	-20	12	-05	-03	-07	11	13	17	22	38	16	26	29	-16	-31	29	13	-31	26										
39	SPEXT	-22	-38	43	29	14	22	23	18	-37	31	-26	-24	21	33	25	24	-16	-08	-10	24	04	10	05	24	27	26	33	25	32	13	32	-36	-43	29	20	-25	20	22									
40	SPROT	-51	-35	28	38	11	42	33	46	-30	50	-31	-53	49	50	48	47	-02	-06	-06	41	23	26	23	50	44	50	41	33	30	12	40	-19	-40	42	26	-29	17	37	18								
41	LTEXT	-33	-40	28	31	08	35	24	21	-28	42	-33	-28	14	24	16	15	-31	-23	-23	10	-07	05	-12	12	09	21	31	30	21	00	21	-34	-35	33	08	-13	17	23	42	23							
42	PW170	-21	-12	-04	14	02	23	12	27	-11	29	-12	-24	40	38	52	38	11	06	03	42	39	46	39	48	43	43	40	00	13	-28	20	-16	-20	15	04	07	-12	-12	09	34	00						
43	BKTOT	-62	-55	25	50	20	61	52	46	-36	61	-27	-63	69	77	70	65	10	07	06	68	61	60	60	68	63	83	71	32	49	00	58	-41	-58	68	35	-06	42	14	28	50	20	43					
44	2PLTP	-56	-72	33	42	16	50	44	41	-48	64	-47	-56	43	60	44	37	-05	-13	-12	41	32	45	25	42	40	60	59	34	37	09	56	-60	-72	75	45	-09	41	32	34	36	37	20	59				
45	SFTBL	-58	-62	36	31	14	63	50	51	-28	54	-37	-60	33	41	51	37	-21	-23	-12	39	13	29	14	33	36	35	43	34	25	12	32	-30	-50	41	26	01	23	36	31	45	37	16	44	44			
46	PRDUE	-54	-56	30	47	32	55	45	49	-40	60	-46	-53	43	59	38	35	-09	-04	-03	36	19	26	20	46	46	62	59	48	38	20	57	-68	-77	76	45	-22	45	38	35	35	32	08	53	63	41		
47	CHRON	-60	-63	41	37	19	63	49	43	-33	62	-26	-55	62	70	52	52	09	01	04	62	45	60	46	54	49	72	64	31	43	06	52	-54	-70	75	28	-16	39	23	32	43	38	30	73	66	43	67	
		1	2	3	4	5	6	7	8	9	10	11	12	13	14	15	16	17	18	19	20	21	22	23	24	25	26	27	28	29	30	31	32	33	34	35	36	37	38	39	40	41	42	43	44	45	46	47

	TEST	1	2	3	4	5	6	7	8	9	10	11	12	13	14	15	16	17	18	19	20	21	22	23	24	25	26	27	28	29	30	31	32	33	34	35	36	37	38	39	40	41	42	43	44	45	46	47
1	355/35																																															
2	TIRER	67																																														
3	RLWKR	-38	-48																																													
4	RLWKB	-46	-58	75																																												
5	RLWKS	-26	-41	59	60																																											
6	TGTHZ	-50	-53	39	46	30																																										
7	TGTVT	-36	-44	43	44	26	70																																									
8	VERTJ	-57	-48	45	52	38	44	44																																								
9	MATCR	68	63	-40	-43	-43	-36	-19	-46																																							
10	STBRJ	-64	-54	37	40	28	54	43	68	-54																																						
11	SCRMB	66	63	-30	-30	-31	-29	-13	-39	68	-51																																					
12	150YD	87	63	-38	-41	-29	-45	-34	-57	67	-65	70																																				
13	CKFLX	-44	-40	18	26	19	40	29	28	-28	44	-29	-39																																			
14	CKEXT	-32	-28	20	26	13	34	35	39	-14	34	-13	-31	72																																		
15	CEFLX	-43	-39	38	32	16	35	26	44	-35	46	-31	-33	52	51																																	
16	CEEXT	-26	-28	18	18	12	32	20	18	-23	35	-28	-16	55	47	70																																
17	TRICP	29	11	-22	-28	-05	-03	-05	-12	29	-20	07	29	-04	10	07	28																															
18	SUBSC	30	21	-20	-23	-15	-01	05	-15	33	-32	37	38	14	35	14	32	56																														
19	ABDOM	40	28	-27	-27	-16	-07	-01	-26	40	-38	37	49	08	29	11	40	72	89																													
20	BIACR	01	-12	-13	-09	-09	10	12	14	01	02	-05	05	29	43	44	57	58	65	68																												
21	BIILC	15	-02	-17	-17	-15	01	07	-04	15	-16	00	14	20	43	40	48	69	66	74	85																											
22	HTCMS	-28	-35	21	20	06	34	38	28	-21	37	-11	-22	51	59	63	59	09	23	24	56	45																										
23	WTKLS	12	-02	01	-03	-02	16	24	07	20	-01	19	21	39	60	50	61	52	76	78	81	75	69																									
24	GRPRT	-39	-42	33	41	30	50	46	50	-34	40	-12	-25	57	54	64	64	11	27	22	45	30	60	54																								
25	GRPLT	-44	-44	42	43	24	47	46	48	-29	55	-21	-38	58	57	60	64	-01	19	11	38	24	56	46	83																							
26	BK W/	-40	-38	20	28	13	35	35	37	-22	39	-15	-33	62	61	53	49	07	23	20	39	24	65	51	55	55																						
27	BKW/O	-71	-60	46	57	42	51	39	61	-62	67	-55	-65	49	45	44	36	-18	-17	-21	04	-05	35	04	45	51	51																					
28	SITUP	-53	-46	34	41	23	25	28	36	-48	44	-49	-51	39	34	40	20	-21	-22	-27	-02	-02	17	-05	30	32	22	43																				
29	TRKRS	-35	-46	30	41	31	28	17	18	-26	26	-35	-29	41	35	47	29	-02	-05	-06	14	16	27	18	25	19	25	37	31																			
30	LEGRS	-05	04	-10	-06	05	-05	-10	00	-16	10	-33	-15	05	01	14	00	-03	-25	-17	-08	04	-25	-20	-13	-11	-11	15	33	32																		
31	PRT40	-42	-54	44	53	35	56	62	53	-35	51	-24	-46	47	47	33	28	02	13	03	19	13	26	24	51	57	40	49	33	23	-06																	
32	MINNM	51	55	-54	-57	-55	-47	-32	-36	53	-42	48	51	-37	-21	-28	-27	23	11	19	09	17	-20	02	-24	-36	-28	-61	-23	-34	04	-48																
33	RINGS	58	60	-53	-60	-43	-46	-38	-40	52	-47	42	52	-47	-20	-24	-19	33	29	34	14	29	-29	10	-32	-39	-45	-62	-28	-35	11	-42	66															
34	GOLFB	-62	-61	55	65	43	52	47	49	-55	56	-41	-60	56	42	40	31	-32	-09	-21	-04	-15	35	09	43	52	57	70	40	40	-02	60	-67	-79														
35	BASST	-37	-39	45	57	45	36	25	22	-36	28	-27	-30	37	16	39	26	-23	-10	-13	05	-08	25	13	37	40	24	38	33	44	07	30	-42	-47	54													
36	STBTL	19	36	-25	-50	-32	-25	-08	-25	33	-16	16	18	-18	-11	-11	-02	23	19	21	18	18	03	17	-22	-23	-14	-45	-15	-21	-10	-39	49	43	-41	-32												
37	STRKT	-44	-50	50	66	51	43	43	49	-40	40	-26	-42	32	28	43	17	-20	-09	-18	10	-03	25	13	45	49	27	51	41	41	05	43	-44	-49	55	71	-36											
38	TOE T	00	-01	12	15	28	14	-01	17	-03	20	-10	-08	-15	-17	-25	-08	-23	-29	-23	-24	-35	-26	-28	-12	-05	-05	14	-08	-04	16	-01	-23	-15	14	04	-10	-02										
39	SPEXT	-32	-27	29	31	22	08	-02	33	-22	35	-26	-30	11	10	17	06	-19	-08	-18	02	-08	05	-10	14	29	12	33	20	12	-06	16	-40	-26	21	20	-23	22	23									
40	SPROT	-30	-24	18	26	07	41	37	44	-18	43	-09	-31	15	22	26	26	-01	-02	-06	13	09	25	12	35	40	23	41	16	20	08	32	-25	-24	32	10	-19	18	27	15								
41	LTEXT	-08	-25	21	31	35	22	19	16	-12	07	-17	-05	13	03	-03	11	01	-04	-01	-05	-05	-14	-14	07	13	03	15	24	01	06	21	-21	-24	08	04	-23	16	20	19	07							
42	PW170	-35	-38	20	19	11	27	35	31	-18	36	-27	-19	37	31	36	35	09	14	11	38	22	51	42	46	45	33	36	26	24	-17	27	-17	-33	33	42	-02	38	-17	04	21	-07						
43	BKTOT	-41	-31	30	25	12	37	32	43	-26	42	-37	-34	42	49	69	60	26	24	22	48	51	49	47	58	59	46	46	32	31	06	37	-17	-20	31	16	-04	34	-13	12	36	-05	48					
44	2PLTP	-45	-62	35	53	47	40	31	45	-56	42	-35	-43	45	37	38	27	-02	01	-06	12	10	34	17	47	42	42	56	32	41	-04	51	-62	-61	66	38	-45	53	-12	29	21	19	29	29				
45	SFTBL	-63	-61	51	59	30	71	67	63	-50	71	-29	-63	44	45	48	32	-24	-18	-25	09	-06	47	12	54	59	48	62	40	35	-02	62	-52	-56	64	41	-31	51	11	30	47	17	33	37	54			
46	PRDUE	-58	-64	67	66	36	56	43	46	-51	43	-43	-51	41	38	44	29	-13	05	-09	07	01	30	12	42	54	44	63	34	37	-17	54	-62	-66	74	45	-30	50	-04	37	20	17	31	40	57	55		
47	CHRON	-34	-35	26	36	14	39	44	42	-28	49	-05	-25	49	50	42	28	-16	09	-01	17	07	57	32	45	45	49	50	29	26	-06	41	-33	-50	46	33	-23	47	-17	22	38	02	44	34	48	59	37	
		1	2	3	4	5	6	7	8	9	10	11	12	13	14	15	16	17	18	19	20	21	22	23	24	25	26	27	28	29	30	31	32	33	34	35	36	37	38	39	40	41	42	43	44	45	46	47

	TEST	1	2	3	4	5	6	7	8	9	10	11	12	13	14	15	16	17	18	19	20	21	22	23	24	25	26	27	28	29	30	31	32	33	34	35	36	37	38	39	40	41	42	43	44	45	46	47
1	355/53																																															
2	TIRER	60																																														
3	RLWKF	-52	-56																																													
4	RLWKB	-50	-54	68																																												
5	RLWKS	-34	-49	60	71																																											
6	TGTHZ	-34	-23	23	23	31																																										
7	TGTVT	-21	-20	27	26	35	69																																									
8	VERTJ	-57	-52	51	55	51	32	32																																								
9	MATCR	66	67	-54	-49	-39	-24	-26	-51																																							
10	STBRJ	-62	-55	52	46	42	31	27	62	-63																																						
11	SCRBL	65	57	-38	-41	-24	-22	-24	-42	67	-63																																					
12	150YD	89	65	-57	-52	-32	-30	-25	-50	67	-64	71																																				
13	CKFLX	-50	-36	31	27	14	21	17	27	-21	32	-26	-39																																			
14	CKEXT	-55	-38	32	21	18	24	24	31	-27	36	-29	-45	76																																		
15	CEFLX	-33	-23	15	16	10	14	23	28	-21	20	-19	-26	35	31																																	
16	CEEXT	-48	-31	26	20	06	-04	06	24	-24	31	-46	-46	60	58	23																																
17	TRICP	19	12	-33	-22	-19	-14	-07	-19	15	-31	06	30	-13	-09	-05	16																															
18	SUBSC	13	08	-35	-24	-14	-04	-14	-18	32	-31	29	26	17	14	09	19	67																														
19	ABDOM	15	16	-35	-23	-17	-13	-14	-27	32	-39	25	29	10	06	02	19	78	88																													
20	BIACR	-09	-13	-16	-10	-10	-03	01	-05	03	-07	-11	04	34	32	20	45	70	65	66																												
21	BIILC	08	05	-23	-19	-20	-08	-03	-12	15	-19	-09	18	11	16	06	39	70	55	58	78																											
22	HTCMS	-33	-16	08	06	-03	03	02	10	-09	25	-06	-18	59	59	31	52	09	28	17	49	36																										
23	WTKLS	-16	-08	-14	-09	-14	-05	-01	02	11	-02	04	01	55	50	23	53	50	72	63	78	65	75																									
24	GRPRT	-48	-33	24	23	12	05	18	22	-39	32	-34	-35	63	59	24	52	14	16	11	48	29	66	61																								
25	GRPLT	-47	-36	25	21	11	14	23	32	-42	42	-44	-38	60	62	20	55	10	08	-02	42	26	61	53	90																							
26	BK W/	-56	-46	24	34	22	15	16	34	-34	33	-38	-45	61	52	35	65	21	38	31	61	39	52	64	59	48																						
27	BKW/O	-72	-66	52	52	42	29	31	45	-62	54	-47	-64	52	50	29	47	-04	02	-05	22	10	39	28	50	43	72																					
28	SITUP	-43	-28	22	41	28	13	20	39	-39	46	-36	-39	05	07	10	22	-06	-10	-12	-06	-14	10	-05	19	23	25	35																				
29	TRKNS	-35	-26	27	26	32	27	25	30	-28	38	-38	-38	-02	23	01	23	-09	-17	-23	-02	-01	04	-12	07	27	04	24	23																			
30	LEGRS	-20	-13	18	15	15	-06	01	07	-20	04	-27	-22	-27	-20	-02	-04	09	-15	-05	-01	-01	-33	-27	-07	-08	02	03	20	31																		
31	PRT40	-45	-47	48	54	50	48	52	50	-45	58	-44	-47	22	40	09	19	-03	-07	-15	09	01	20	08	35	40	31	54	28	42	-02																	
32	MINNM	30	46	-49	-53	-47	-39	-38	-58	44	-54	18	31	-25	-39	-30	-16	02	-04	09	-13	-01	-22	-12	-29	-34	-32	-48	-31	-27	01	-65																
33	RINGS	52	51	-53	-52	-59	-29	-29	-54	69	-57	41	48	-29	-39	-32	-18	18	16	27	01	19	-23	01	-46	-31	-29	-53	-43	-29	02	-59	67															
34	GOLFB	-67	-59	47	50	48	44	39	59	-58	63	-43	-59	51	59	33	36	-04	03	-11	18	-03	41	27	57	57	51	68	38	32	-07	72	-71	-74														
35	BASST	-23	-32	40	49	58	18	23	32	-20	37	-15	-11	28	27	09	19	-13	01	-05	06	-07	14	10	36	36	28	37	26	29	00	43	-43	-47	50													
36	STBTL	23	15	-15	-31	-29	-24	-13	-30	15	-19	23	30	20	04	01	20	27	39	43	33	29	30	44	20	12	15	-14	-13	-41	-20	-23	13	08	-10	-08												
37	STRKT	-36	-39	49	63	54	42	44	62	-27	46	-21	-36	22	27	19	12	-27	-22	-29	-14	-22	04	-04	15	17	23	39	28	39	07	56	-57	-48	54	43	-24											
38	TOE T	-04	-13	14	25	20	05	05	21	-05	04	00	-12	-10	-26	-03	-20	-14	-17	-10	-18	-30	-48	-31	16	-19	-06	-05	-02	-05	26	00	-06	-09	-05	03	-15	25										
39	SPEXT	-28	-32	23	29	28	34	27	24	-24	30	-12	-29	17	14	-04	-05	-13	-12	-12	-12	-35	-07	-09	09	07	06	31	17	21	-09	41	-23	-24	42	21	-30	36	34									
40	SPROT	-41	-30	34	43	27	20	19	28	-28	35	-23	-31	24	18	10	15	06	00	-01	06	-10	12	07	38	36	22	43	32	26	26	24	-37	-35	44	39	-10	37	22	30								
41	LTEXT	-33	-27	33	24	32	30	26	17	-32	19	-29	-23	11	18	21	10	08	-05	-05	13	13	12	07	22	22	14	32	-04	27	11	33	-15	-19	27	24	-25	22	-02	29	14							
42	PW170	-06	09	-03	09	02	16	09	-01	17	11	-02	02	32	26	22	23	05	06	06	32	27	46	33	26	14	24	10	03	-02	-11	20	-20	-10	21	11	16	25	-19	06	-11	14						
43	BKTOT	-55	-45	36	37	30	20	26	29	-34	42	-36	-43	58	61	19	65	24	31	27	60	38	62	64	68	62	79	68	29	16	02	50	-44	-40	59	38	19	30	-05	15	43	29	26					
44	2PLTP	-44	-62	24	38	36	35	25	50	-48	53	-45	-46	29	36	30	23	10	06	-07	31	13	22	18	28	36	43	57	30	32	-06	61	-59	-58	69	20	-12	49	04	38	25	25	24	44				
45	SFTBL	-47	-40	42	41	34	44	50	41	-33	45	-28	-41	48	54	34	24	-11	06	-02	17	-02	31	25	38	34	44	56	17	22	-10	62	-55	-52	64	37	08	62	12	31	36	23	33	55	52			
46	PRDUE	-36	-55	46	53	54	37	41	57	-35	53	-31	-41	27	41	34	25	-01	08	-07	18	04	19	17	26	34	39	56	26	42	01	69	-75	-59	68	47	-27	66	10	32	39	25	16	46	70	67		
47	CHRON	-42	-21	21	27	17	23	19	35	-27	51	-24	-27	46	60	26	33	-07	04	-08	31	18	64	41	54	56	41	47	21	28	-21	45	-53	-47	64	30	02	37	-25	16	34	16	38	55	51	56	49	
		1	2	3	4	5	6	7	8	9	10	11	12	13	14	15	16	17	18	19	20	21	22	23	24	25	26	27	28	29	30	31	32	33	34	35	36	37	38	39	40	41	42	43	44	45	46	47

	TEST	1	2	3	4	5	6	7	8	9	10	11	12	13	14	15	16	17	18	19	20	21	22	23	24	25	26	27	28	29	30	31	32	33	34	35	36	37	38	39	40	41	42	43	44	45	46	47
1	355/35																																															
2	TIRER	45																																														
3	RLWKF	-38	-52																																													
4	RLWKB	-44	-53	69																																												
5	RLWKS	-36	-46	66	66																																											
6	TGTHZ	-40	-37	32	34	20																																										
7	TGTVT	-46	-49	27	39	22	65																																									
8	VERTJ	-62	-43	35	42	31	47	50																																								
9	MATCR	63	66	-51	-61	-48	-32	-34	-61																																							
10	STBRJ	-65	-56	42	51	34	43	45	79	-72																																						
11	SCRMB	48	56	-38	-43	-36	-39	-40	-49	68	-62																																					
12	150YD	72	61	-46	-48	-40	-52	-54	-71	69	-74	55																																				
13	CKFLX	-21	-42	16	15	20	46	42	52	-27	38	-18	-51																																			
14	CKEXT	-26	-39	07	06	07	47	44	51	-24	39	-20	-50	84																																		
15	CEFLX	-10	-12	17	07	06	10	09	23	-03	11	15	-22	48	35																																	
16	CEEXT	-05	-13	16	07	04	13	10	22	02	07	21	-19	46	34	94																																
17	TRICP	38	04	-36	-27	-35	01	02	-15	24	-24	12	12	23	31	17	17																															
18	SUBSC	31	-03	-31	-21	-24	-01	10	-12	27	-24	24	08	37	40	32	36	78																														
19	ABDOM	31	-04	-27	-19	-18	05	12	-15	21	-24	17	05	35	34	24	31	77	91																													
20	BIACR	-18	02	-25	-22	-14	23	18	40	00	20	07	-28	55	58	30	28	39	35	30																												
21	BIILC	-06	-17	-24	-14	-18	20	24	29	01	16	-13	-31	49	56	23	23	71	69	67	62																											
22	HTCMS	-20	-12	-06	-15	-13	29	27	38	00	22	15	-32	56	61	28	31	28	39	35	69	65																										
23	WTKLS	00	-14	-17	-21	-17	19	20	20	12	03	17	-21	64	67	43	49	61	78	75	68	81	78																									
24	GRPRT	-38	-36	10	08	08	38	40	59	-30	51	-12	-54	70	76	41	43	16	31	30	63	56	70	70																								
25	GRPLT	-31	-34	10	03	10	32	28	56	-27	49	-16	-50	70	80	38	42	14	31	27	64	54	68	71	91																							
26	BK W/	-45	-48	08	13	06	43	45	61	-39	51	-29	-53	64	71	30	31	26	36	34	55	62	65	64	70	67																						
27	BKW/O	-53	-77	45	59	49	48	51	62	-66	65	-45	-68	55	53	21	21	-06	07	06	17	19	25	22	48	45	57																					
28	SITUP	-55	-47	46	52	37	50	40	65	-58	69	-58	-62	35	30	11	09	-29	-30	-33	07	-01	01	-08	28	32	32	52																				
29	TRKRS	-52	-53	37	32	22	50	40	46	-58	49	-50	-55	28	32	12	09	-09	-17	-13	06	09	02	03	28	30	40	50	59																			
30	LEGRS	-25	-27	29	23	17	09	04	25	-28	26	-34	-27	18	06	12	13	-09	01	06	-01	13	-07	12	21	19	06	18	37	44																		
31	PRT40	-38	-51	39	43	40	43	41	44	-43	47	-32	-42	49	43	17	14	15	07	03	12	17	22	16	26	24	50	56	35	37	05																	
32	MINNM	35	59	-59	-55	-50	-40	-37	-31	50	-38	33	43	-37	-29	-15	-17	12	04	-04	06	01	-06	-06	-23	-18	-21	-59	-31	-31	-30	-43																
33	RINGS	41	69	-61	-58	-48	-45	-35	-42	62	-48	33	48	-42	-39	-15	-15	15	04	05	-04	00	-17	-09	-31	-27	-34	-68	-35	-37	-22	-56	76															
34	GOLFB	-46	-72	60	64	55	45	46	45	-64	52	-41	-57	42	32	17	17	-23	-09	-09	-08	-04	09	02	23	20	30	68	49	47	29	56	-72	-80														
35	BASST	-43	-42	37	48	49	30	23	31	-50	39	-37	-36	20	17	00	-01	-34	-23	-25	-09	-20	-15	-18	08	06	24	41	46	34	17	46	-35	-41	49													
36	STBTL	48	38	-49	-53	-54	-28	-32	-39	54	-42	47	39	-13	-07	10	13	37	31	29	20	20	19	28	-04	-06	-18	-37	-46	-33	-12	-35	33	41	-42	-50												
37	STRKT	-43	-62	45	55	50	20	30	21	-56	42	-40	-42	11	09	01	-02	-31	-19	-20	-22	-18	-21	-22	02	00	21	56	41	41	13	41	-49	-54	67	61	-50											
38	TOE T	-19	-26	19	16	10	28	14	37	-24	39	-32	-29	44	41	27	21	-05	05	00	18	12	08	16	31	34	25	40	36	19	26	13	-22	-31	26	14	-10	12										
39	SPEXT	-32	-42	34	38	18	33	23	27	-46	36	-32	-28	20	13	21	15	-14	-13	-09	07	00	-04	-01	19	21	21	35	34	49	23	15	-35	-39	41	20	-18	25	34									
40	SPROT	-02	-23	10	06	01	19	07	19	-12	19	-14	-23	24	21	15	18	26	29	30	24	39	32	27	18	15	28	28	08	-02	14	17	-26	-21	08	-03	13	-16	23	06								
41	LTEXT	-18	-31	13	08	11	28	13	42	-33	33	-41	-25	26	29	29	27	15	09	11	15	26	01	16	35	37	34	23	40	46	41	08	-15	-11	11	11	-10	-02	39	36	27							
42	PW170	-34	-18	03	-05	02	25	24	40	-21	29	-06	-42	56	62	38	38	16	23	24	60	44	56	59	67	70	66	29	17	32	00	29	-14	-20	09	13	-08	03	19	14	07	08						
43	BKTOT	-37	-34	08	12	11	44	34	58	-28	42	-16	-53	77	77	49	50	28	40	39	67	57	62	69	77	75	80	55	31	30	21	42	-25	-34	26	14	-10	08	34	14	28	34	65					
44	2PLTP	-40	-63	47	38	44	44	49	43	-52	44	-34	-55	49	46	17	19	01	15	19	18	24	26	30	47	37	50	62	31	46	33	50	-66	-66	66	45	-32	49	21	24	27	19	33	42				
45	SFTBL	-56	-59	42	35	38	68	65	62	-48	58	-45	-71	63	60	27	23	-04	06	06	40	37	45	34	55	50	63	71	47	42	11	53	-46	-56	56	37	-33	38	41	35	29	24	46	62	65			
46	PRDUE	-28	-39	33	37	10	04	10	19	-39	28	-24	-27	09	08	07	05	-15	-11	-12	-01	02	-02	-04	07	06	09	33	13	20	30	20	-47	-45	36	17	-23	31	23	45	26	01	01	05	27	23		
47	CHRON	-17	-16	10	05	04	32	36	33	-09	29	05	-27	47	55	14	20	09	16	16	39	32	46	44	53	48	49	25	19	19	14	17	-13	-17	15	31	-03	09	19	-06	07	11	34	50	35	36	02	

	TEST	1	2	3	4	5	6	7	8	9	10	11	12	13	14	15	16	17	18	19	20	21	22	23	24	25	26	27	28	29	30	31	32	33	34	35	36	37	38	39	40	41	42	43	44	45	46	47
1	355/35																																															
2	TIRER	56																																														
3	RLWLKF	-41	-64																																													
4	RLWLKB	-26	-49	55																																												
5	RLWLKS	-41	-61	57	50																																											
6	TGTHZ	-44	-62	44	47	56																																										
7	TGTVT	-35	-56	20	25	44	53																																									
8	VERTJ	-59	-59	40	30	37	48	47																																								
9	MATCR	46	70	-45	-44	-34	-45	-33	-39																																							
10	STBRJ	-66	-72	54	48	46	58	46	69	-61																																						
11	SCRMB	35	68	-61	-52	-42	-44	-31	-41	63	-64																																					
12	150YD	69	75	-59	-49	-51	-54	-61	-71	58	-78	59																																				
13	CKFLX	-35	-45	23	26	27	45	49	65	-18	51	-22	-54																																			
14	CKEXT	-40	-54	30	34	40	49	58	60	-28	55	-29	-55	88																																		
15	CEFLX	-34	-34	00	22	17	49	57	53	-27	47	-20	-46	67	66																																	
16	CEEXT	-13	-24	13	31	01	35	45	36	-25	34	-17	-30	39	35	39																																
17	TRICP	29	05	-27	02	-12	06	18	02	10	-18	12	10	26	26	32	07																															
18	SUBSC	42	08	-27	04	-15	02	09	-09	13	-21	12	18	24	22	22	03	77																														
19	ABDOM	15	11	-18	01	-20	-03	06	-02	17	-10	10	03	27	23	32	02	67	79																													
20	BIACR	00	-28	03	25	00	23	23	44	-21	27	-21	-30	52	44	46	24	54	85	32																												
21	BIILC	19	-12	-09	23	-01	18	15	20	00	05	-11	-06	39	38	31	14	71	61	54	73																											
22	HTCMS	-26	-24	00	13	01	27	37	56	-07	35	-01	-35	66	63	55	37	35	18	22	62	46																										
23	WTKLS	-06	-27	-02	26	06	34	41	45	-13	31	-04	-25	69	73	66	38	66	60	55	69	70	75																									
24	GRPRT	-37	-45	26	38	27	51	57	61	-26	60	-27	-57	81	83	76	41	32	29	32	57	42	74	81																								
25	GRPLT	-43	-44	28	37	27	51	52	60	-27	60	-27	-55	80	82	75	34	23	21	28	49	37	68	74	95																							
26	BK W/	-42	-58	31	44	36	59	51	61	-44	62	-36	-61	75	77	60	36	21	18	14	59	43	70	71	83	84																						
27	BKW/O	-61	-62	49	43	47	54	39	53	-49	60	-32	-65	53	58	36	34	-21	-22	-14	16	-07	33	29	55	56	66																					
28	SITUP	-57	-67	55	39	40	42	32	-56	-70	69	-69	-62	32	34	21	23	-25	-32	-27	18	-07	21	05	34	37	45	52																				
29	TRKRS	-24	-34	19	27	38	32	11	28	-34	22	-29	-23	07	14	08	01	08	-05	-14	18	10	10	04	11	18	27	26	50																			
30	LEGRS	-02	-20	25	24	01	16	-14	-13	-29	20	-35	-02	-17	-13	-08	-09	-17	-10	-20	-04	-14	-19	-14	-04	01	07	07	35	36																		
31	PROT40	-27	-49	31	46	41	49	38	47	-25	56	-33	-49	61	64	41	16	16	13	11	39	29	42	45	58	57	55	42	32	15	-04																	
32	MINNM	34	69	-51	-42	-60	-37	-48	-44	43	-57	48	56	-42	-56	-27	-13	01	-04	02	-23	-12	-26	-34	-46	-40	-47	-45	-42	-04	04	-56																
33	RINGS	48	75	-52	-44	-54	-47	-40	-46	47	-59	38	55	-49	-59	-30	-14	-04	-12	-09	-16	-06	-30	-39	-50	-47	-53	-56	-47	-21	-10	-52	69															
34	GOLFB	-48	-74	44	44	46	53	58	44	-45	63	-42	-59	60	69	50	30	14	10	08	30	13	43	51	62	60	66	61	40	15	12	52	-69	-81														
35	BASST	-25	-39	40	30	47	15	13	30	-33	45	-40	-28	17	15	01	-05	-17	-20	-23	05	-05	07	-02	14	19	18	14	41	30	11	32	-42	-36	30													
36	STBTL	11	13	-18	-02	-20	-26	-15	01	13	-16	28	05	06	-02	-01	01	21	27	29	21	06	20	17	00	-05	02	-03	-30	-17	-27	05	-09	-06	04	-14												
37	STRKT	-20	-46	45	50	44	31	15	33	-32	44	-46	-37	15	21	18	-02	03	-06	-04	26	13	10	13	25	31	26	13	35	31	08	47	-36	-42	33	61	-09											
38	TOE T	-17	-39	22	23	14	07	11	20	-28	28	-32	-16	-04	01	06	23	-12	-17	-21	01	-10	-08	06	03	04	15	25	21	12	20	-01	-18	-29	32	18	-06	29										
39	SPEXT	-21	-38	11	03	31	29	01	-02	-32	18	-20	-07	05	06	03	05	-08	-12	-15	-04	-06	-19	-08	-06	-09	04	26	06	07	-01	07	-23	-29	33	21	-10	11	29									
40	SPROT	06	-07	-07	10	19	08	07	10	02	00	01	-04	21	14	15	12	-05	12	03	09	12	-04	12	05	09	08	05	-01	-04	-24	10	-03	-07	-03	-08	04	-05	11	-03								
41	LTEXT	-01	-39	18	11	31	32	10	09	-28	13	-34	-06	14	15	10	-01	00	-02	-22	10	14	-08	02	07	10	15	09	19	18	08	24	-20	-18	17	39	-35	29	20	45	06							
42	PW170	-50	-56	35	43	38	46	45	58	-39	61	-26	-58	57	64	52	28	13	01	04	48	32	04	60	65	69	73	49	37	18	03	51	-40	-53	61	29	-04	40	28	03	11	15						
43	BKTOT	-43	-59	36	46	32	53	42	61	-44	60	-38	-62	63	68	49	27	19	09	10	66	45	72	66	74	72	89	61	48	23	06	61	-50	-52	61	22	09	33	15	00	04	12	73					
44	2PLTP	-40	-63	45	38	49	40	44	45	-33	59	-48	-52	47	57	35	13	08	03	04	24	27	36	35	46	46	49	38	34	17	-01	52	-63	-55	60	40	08	38	08	16	-05	17	51	52				
45	SFTBL	-47	-61	47	55	41	61	58	63	-54	69	-45	-64	56	56	46	50	13	06	02	41	27	47	48	66	66	67	50	52	34	10	47	-46	-54	55	37	-07	40	17	06	00	19	61	60	51			
46	PRDUE	-47	-66	61	55	62	46	34	42	-48	53	-50	-54	39	49	20	06	-04	-06	-06	26	07	15	18	39	41	46	45	49	32	09	62	-65	-70	59	43	-05	60	12	24	05	24	45	49	60	52		
47	CHRON	-19	-31	14	24	20	38	43	57	-09	41	-24	-44	63	63	53	30	18	07	11	51	35	68	52	68	66	62	40	30	36	-04	52	-22	-24	35	09	04	21	-07	-20	00	11	42	56	34	52	23	
		1	2	3	4	5	6	7	8	9	10	11	12	13	14	15	16	17	18	19	20	21	22	23	24	25	26	27	28	29	30	31	32	33	34	35	36	37	38	39	40	41	42	43	44	45	46	47

Appendix C / The Individualized Physical Education Program

These descriptions are of two types of work, but it is important to recognize that in this, as in each special program, the teachers adjusted the materials to the student's capabilities. Hence, it is not possible to convey the conceptual base which the teachers were able to form and develop during the experiment.

A. Jumping and Landing

The importance of jumping and landing was stressed in regard to the skills themselves and their inclusion in sequence work. Jumping activities can be exhilarating, stimulating, and worthwhile. The correct techniques of jumping and landing were given immediate attention with careful teaching, and a great deal of practice was needed by the children.

Jumping was practiced with and without apparatus, on the move or on the spot, onto, over, from, or around apparatus, and off one foot, off the other foot, or off both feet. Whatever the practice, the activity could be changed by the varied use of the arms or legs, by the shape and direction of the body, and by the speed of the activity. Since it was important that the children were physically active for the largest portion of the lesson, jumping and landing were combined with walking or running activities. In this way, the practice in jumping was continuous.

Some of the work was done without apparatus, with the children practicing freely any type of jump, but with a special emphasis on height, or stretch, or lightness. It was possible to jump vertically, horizontally, forward, backward, and sideways. In addition, various kinds of apparatus—blocks, balls, canes, hoops, mats, and ropes—were used to jump with, along, around, or over.

The ability of the children to learn ways of landing safely, with good control, was stressed. The children practiced landing from a height so that they could learn to bend their knees fully on impact and avoid jarring themselves. The method of landing suggested by Bilborough and Jones (1963) was practiced.

Much of this work proved quite successful in an informal teaching situation and the children were able to practice freely, at their own level of ability, but still within the general frame of reference of the teacher. The apparatus proved a great motivating force with the children.

B. Using Small Apparatus

Small apparatus was used frequently during the lessons. For example, in jumping and landing activities, apparatus enabled the children to widen their own movement experience and increase their repertoire of movements. Additionally, it was possible to use the apparatus as the focus, for example, in ways of bouncing the ball using only the left hand. The apparatus was used to improve the level of skill attainment in specific activities such as bouncing and throwing. Teachers always had to remember that in this program the child was only to work by himself, never with a partner, a group, or a team. As in other types of the work, use was made of child demonstration and class observation. Children were learning to "look for"; —not only to "look at."

Ball-handling activities were most useful, since such skill is essential to many games. Activities with a ball were very popular, possibly because of the wide variety of ways a ball may be used. In the program, for example, a ball could be thrown, caught, bounced, or rolled, either on the floor or in the air, with a variety of body parts and in various positions. It was moved in different directions and at a variety of speeds.

Appendix D / The Group Oriented Physical Education Program

The three main types of work in this experimental program were relays, partner activities, and class games. Several examples of each type will be described.

A. Relays

1. Straight Relays

The first child on each team runs around a marker and back, tags the outstretched hand of the next child, and goes to the end of the team. The next child must wait behind the starting line until his hand is tagged. When every child on the team has had a turn, the whole team squats. The first team to complete the entire exercise wins.

2. Zigzag Relays

The last child on each team begins to zigzag in and out of the others on his team. He then runs and touches a distant object and runs again to touch a second object behind his team. Finally, he returns to his own position, tagging the next runner.

3. Follow-On Relays

These relays are introduced after the children are familiar with other relays. In this type of relay, instead of each child completing his turn before the next child moves, the second child follows the first child.

4. Over-and-Under Relays

The first player in each line has a ball which, at a signal, he passes over his head to the second player, who passes it between his legs to the third player. In this manner, the ball is passed over and under the entire team. Upon receiving the ball, the last player runs forward to the front of his team and starts the ball going again. This procedure is continued until the team is back in its original line-up and the ball is in the hands of the original first player.

The teachers knew how to manipulate these relays so that they not only could cope with teams of unequal number but could change a relay of two teams with eight players per team into one of four teams with four players per team. As a result, the children were constantly being challenged to adjust to different situations. Relays were walked, run, skipped, hopped, first on one foot, then on the other foot, sometimes using apparatus, and so on. Thus, the variety of relays was great.

B. Partner Activities

1. Knee Tag

Two opponents face each other. At a signal each attempts, by dodging or sparring, to touch his opponent's knee while at the same time protecting his own knee from being touched.

2. Chinese Boxing

Partners stand facing each other with arms raised half-way. With his own right hand, each partner grasps the other's left wrist. With the hand free to move about, i.e., the left hand, each tries to tag the other (gently) on the cheek or on the top of the head, without having his own cheek or head tapped in turn. The partners then change grip hands and repeat the maneuver.

3. Dodge and Mark

Partners stand together, one the "attacker" and the other the "defender." At a given signal, the attacker tries to get free and the defender tries to follow very closely, keeping within touching distance. At a second signal, both stop moving and the defender hopes still to be able to touch his partner.

4. Wheelbarrows

One partner places his hands on the floor, shoulder distance apart, knees straight, weight on his hands and feet. The other partner steps between the legs of the first partner and picks up one leg in each hand. He then walks his partner forward in wheelbarrow fashion.

C. Class Games

1. Crows and Cranes

Children are divided into two groups, the "Crows" and the "Cranes." The groups stand on a line, shoulder to shoulder or a few feet apart. The teacher calls either "Crows" or "Cranes," using a "Crrr" sound at the beginning of the word to mask the result. If "Crows" is the call, the Crows run to their own goal line chased by the Cranes. If a Crane catches a Crow, then the Crow has to carry the Crane back to the starting position. Alternate words of command are "Blue" and "Black," "Rats" and "Rabbits," "Crusts" and "Crumbs."

2. Free and Caught

Two children are the catchers. They try to tag as many players as they can. Whenever a player is tagged, he must stand still with his arms crossed; but if a free player comes along and touches him, he then is free to run around again. The catchers try to get everyone caught and standing still, while the players try to keep everyone free. Two catchers may be insufficient, for the catchers should usually manage to win!

3. Team Dodge Ball

One team makes a circle and the other team stands inside it. The circle team attempts to hit the players in the center of the circle with the ball. Only hits below the waist (or knee) count. Play continues until all the players in the center have been hit, or for a certain length of time, with the hits being counted.

4. Pass Ball

The game between two teams is begun with a jump ball. The team with the ball tries to complete a certain number of passes (e.g., six) to score a point. If the ball is intercepted by the other team, the counting begins again. Players may not run with the ball and must keep within the designated area.

Appendix E / The Art Program

This appendix includes examples of the four types of activity accomplished by the educable mentally retarded children and the minimally brain-injured children.

A. Painting

Painting with finger, brush, or string
Resist painting, using wax crayons and watercolor
Painting action pinmen on newspaper
Scratch pictures
Blow painting
Double crayon scribbling
Potato and handprint painting

B. Pasting

1. Mosaic pictures were made with small squares of different colored papers which were cut, pasted, and assembled.

2. Pasta, macaroni, peas, yarn, and paper cuts were pasted to form pictures and designs.

3. Heart Pet

Use red and white construction paper and paste. Cut one heart shape from a 4″ square for the body; cut a second heart shape from a 2″ square for the head; and cut four heart shapes from $1^{1}/_{2}$″ squares for the feet. Cut four strips of white paper, each $^{1}/_{2}$″ × 3″, and fold the strips backward and forward to make accordion legs. Cut a strip $^{1}/_{2}$″ × 4″ for the neck and pleat the same way. Make a tail 2″ long.

C. Paper Cutting

1. Bird in a Cage

Begin with a rectangle of paper and cut a $^{1}/_{2}$″ strip for the handle. Cut out the shaded areas and decorate. Paste edges together to make a cylinder. Paste handle in position. Cut out bird shape and decorate. Attach one end of a string to the bird and fasten the other end of the string to the handle.

2. Lantern

Decorate a rectangle of paper. Fold in half, lengthways, with the pattern on the outside. Cut a $^1/_2''$ strip from the short side for a handle. Make $^1/_2''$ cuts along the folded edge to within 1″ of its unfolded edge. Open out the sheet, bring narrow sides together, and paste. Attach handle.

3. Paper Frieze

Fold paper like a fan. Draw a clown (cowboy, Christmas tree, etc.) on the front fold. Cut out shaded areas. Unfold frieze and decorate.

4. Table Mats

Color strips of squared paper with different colors, assigning only two or three strips per child. Arrange the strips on a sheet of construction paper to make a table mat or picture frame.

5. Book Markers

Draw a simple mouse shape. Cut out and decorate. Paste on string for a tail.

Decorate a long strip of paper and cut a fringe at one end.

Use envelopes which have been opened at the narrow end. Cut as shown and decorate.

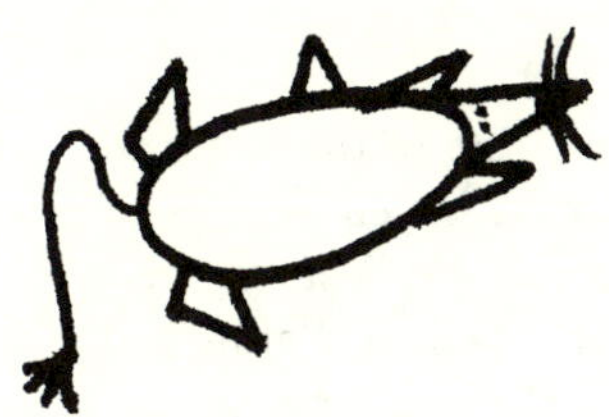

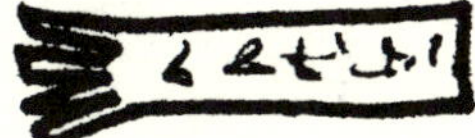

6. Mobile Space Design

Use cardboard, string, paint or crayons, and construction paper. Cut one strip of cardboard 4″ × 24″. Make 4 holes at the top and 8 or 10 holes at the bottom. Glue the ends together to make a circle. Cut out different shapes of paper, and decorate. Make a small hole in each shape and attach a string. Attach the shapes to the holes at the bottom of the circle. Fasten four lengths of string to the holes at the top of the circle to hang up the mobile. These designs may be replaced by animals, birds, etc.

7. Paper Beads

Cut paper into long strips (vary the size of the strips to diversify the size of the beads). Place a pencil or stick at the wide end of the paper strip and roll up. Paste the end of the paper strip and remove the pencil. Paint and varnish the beads if possible. String the beads on thread.

D. Construction Work

1. Eggshell Creatures

Use eggshells, colored sticky tape, and scraps of material, e.g., cotton balls, feathers, etc. Color the shells with food coloring or paint. Use tape to attach shells to pieces of cardboard, or thread yarn through the top of the shells to hang them up.

2. Log Cabin

Use a pint-size carton or cut the top from a quart carton. Paste a piece of paper to the straight strip at the top of the carton, and paste pieces of paper to the slanted sides of the carton. Form strips of paper (the same length as the sides of the carton) into logs by rolling them around a pencil and pasting down their outer edges. Slide the pencil out gently and glue logs to sides of cabin. Decorate small boxes to look like a chimney and paste to one side of the cabin. Make windows and door from construction paper and paste in position. Use paint to color over any white carton which may show through.

3. Boxes

To make a mask, cut holes for eyes, nose, and mouth. Decorate the mask. Yarn may be glued on for hair. Use paper cups for ears.

To make an octopus, thread string through the top of a box and make a loop. Paste on long strips of paper for legs. Decorate the face.

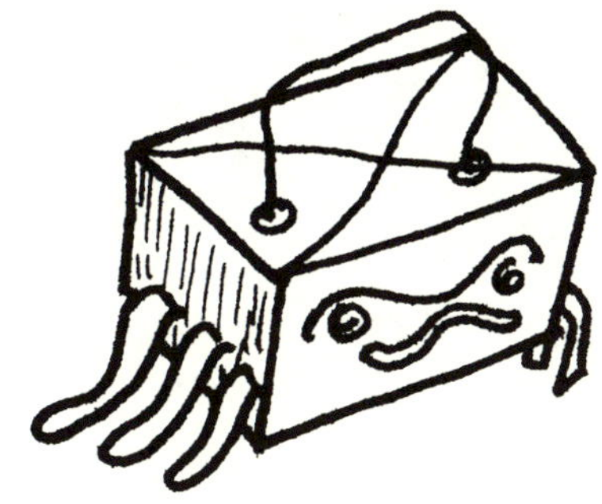

4. Animals Made from Vegetables

Use a potato, etc., for the body, toothpicks or pipe cleaners for legs, yarn for a tail, buttons and pins for eyes. Make clothes with paper shapes.

The head is a small piece of potato attached to the body by a toothpick.

5. Paper Plates

Each child needs $1^1/_2$ plates to make a wall pocket. Paste the edges of the half plate to the whole plate, front sides together. Knot string in holes at the top to hang up.

Cut fins, mouth, and tail from construction paper and paste to the front side of a plate. Paste a second plate over the first one, face to face.

Paste head, tail, and legs to the front of a plate. Paste a second plate on top of the first one, face to face. Decorate. Use toothpicks for legs, feathers or scraps for the tail, and paper for the head.

Cut a plate in half and paste the rounded edges together. Thread string or pipe cleaners through the plates for whiskers. Paste on ear shapes and tail. Decorate. Cut a second plate into sections and paint numbers on the sections. Play throwing the sections at the mouse, with the section nearest the mouse the winner.

Index